ASAP
Implementation at the Speed of Business

Stewart S. Miller

McGraw-Hill
New York San Francisco Washington, D.C. Auckland
Bogotá Caracas Lisbon London Madrid Mexico City
Milan Montreal New Delhi San Juan Singapore
Sydney Tokyo Toronto

Library of Congress Cataloging-in-Publication Data

Miller, Stewart S.
    ASAP : implementation at the speed of business / Stewart S. Miller
        p.   cm.
    Includes index.
    ISBN 0-07-913756-3
    1. AcceleratedSAP. 2. SAP R/3. 3. Business—Computer programs.
4. Client/server computing. 5. Project management—Computer
programs. I. Title.
HF5548.4.A23M55 1998
650′.0285′53769—dc21

98-16490
CIP

McGraw-Hill

A Division of The **McGraw·Hill** *Companies*

1 2 3 4 5 6 7 8 9 0 DOC/DOC 9 0 3 2 1 0 9 8

ISBN 0-07-043413-1

PART OF

ISBN 0-07-913756-3

The sponsoring editor for this book was Judy Brief, the editing supervisor was Ruth Mannino, and the production supervisor was Claire Stanley. It was set in Century Schoolbook by Priscilla Beer of McGraw-Hill's Desktop Composition Unit.

Printed and bound by R. R. Donnelley & Sons Company.

McGraw-Hill books are available at special quantity discounts to use as premiums and sales promotions, or for use in corporate training programs. For more information, please write to the Director of Special Sales, McGraw-Hill, 11 West 19th Street, New York, NY 10011. Or contact your local bookstore.

 This book is printed on recycled, acid-free paper containing a minimum of 50% recycled, de-inked fiber.

ASAP

Dedicated to all the members of my family, whom I love most dearly.

CONTENTS

Contents

Contents

Contents

Contents

Contents

PREFACE

Managing your enterprise is critical to your success regardless of the specific industry. This book is designed to illustrate how the Accelerated-SAP (ASAP) service can implement SAP's R/3 in a matter of months instead of years. The goal is to offer you an unbiased perspective of how an accelerated implementation can be both cost effective and financially advantageous to the future of your business processes.

Implementation is based on three primary factors:

1. Cost
2. Time
3. Return on investment (ROI)

In a typical medium-sized business, cost is paramount. You can't afford to spend an obscene percentage of your annual revenues on a system that may bankrupt your organization. You realize that managing your enterprise is important, but that capability must be within your financial means. Until recently, that power was out of reach of all but *Fortune 500* companies. The introduction of AcceleratedSAP has brought the power to manage your enterprise into your reach. It provides you with a realizable goal at an acceptable cost.

Time is critical. No organization can wait 2 to 4 years to implement an enterprise resource planning (ERP) solution. The effort alone would be outdated by the time you went live. Business objectives change almost on a daily basis. As a successful business, you realize that time waits for no man (or business). As we approach the millenium, it is obvious that, unless we change to meet industry objectives, we will quickly become obsolete. Your ERP solution must be implemented faster, so that you can have the assurance of having a live system in time to meet your business objectives. AcceleratedSAP has reduced an implementation that once took as long as 4 years to approximately 18 months. Depending on the size and complexity of your organization, this time frame may be less, but on average never more than 2 years.

Finally, we cover the actual ROI you will achieve. Your objective is to implement R/3 quickly, go live, and start seeing your investment pay off for your business processes. There are organizations that can help you reach that goal and work with you individually during R/3 implementation and going live. One such organization is Ernst & Young who can assist you in your efforts to improve your business processes and help you maximize that ROI. After covering the primary topics regarding accelerated R/3 implementations, we will discuss how Ernst & Young can help you reach that objective in a timely and effective manner.

In essence, this text gives you a wealth of management and technical information which are key to understanding what ASAP represents to you and your company. Having a firm grasp of tomorrow's technology today will give you the competitive edge, so that you can fully understand exactly what SAP R/3 means to you today, and for your organization in the future. I am very interested in keeping my clients up-to-date with respect to this evolving medium, and I encourage you to contact me by telephone at 1-800-IT-MAVEN or via email at ASAP@ITMaven.com.

—STEWART MILLER

AcceleratedSAP (ASAP) Background

Introduction

SAP has become a cornerstone of modern business operations today. The SAP R/3 product spells success over its competitors and offers an avenue of advancement for any business that chooses it. The issues, however, surrounding enterprise resource planning (ERP) have introduced several aspects that have made all aspects of the IT industry more efficient. However, that efficiency is tempered by the fact that it takes far too long to implement an effective ERP solution. Time to implementation can spell success or failure for many organizations. Since time has become so crucial, SAP has developed a program that implements at "warp" speed.

ASAP: The Beginnings

In order to achieve a successful SAP R/3 implementation, you need to develop a program that can deploy a solution in months instead of years. Industries have hungered for a solution, and SAP realized this need through the development of its program called *AcceleratedSAP* or *ASAP*.

Your business is determined to stay ahead of its competition and ahead of the market. Information is the driving force behind your business, and that data is the catalyst in your business operations for current and future endeavors. The way in which you use that information, as well as how you make it work for you, determines your status in the marketplace. That status will ultimately determine your customer base and your future projects.

You need to make your business ready for a better return on information and a better return on investment (ROI). SAP R/3 allows you to start enhancing your efficiency using a method that is compatible to the way in which your business uses information. ASAP makes that process faster, simpler, and more productive.

SAP permits you to attain faster business results with R/3. AcceleratedSAP allows you to have R/3 working in less time so you can be ready for new business decisions come the year 2000. ASAP allows you to utilize best business practices based on several years of implementation experience. AcceleratedSAP results in a rapid implementation solution created for your enterprise to achieve a quick and observable return on your R/3 investment.

Assistance

A great deal of resources exists to help you within every level of AcceleratedSAP. In addition, ASAP allows you to specifically designate how R/3 fits into your specific business objectives to accurately determine the price and scheduling of your R/3 implementation. AcceleratedSAP gives you the essential ingredients for success. The elements for a successful implementation involve the process, tools, training, and services. SAP's goal is to place the cornerstone within your business processes to form a solid foundation for future R/3 upgrades. The integration between SAP R/3 and an effective business model is illustrated in Fig. 1-1. AcceleratedSAP is the bridge that will take you from where you are today to a higher level of integrated business processes tomorrow. ASAP links together everything you need to successfully implement R/3 quickly, effectively, and accurately.

The ASAP Expressway

AcceleratedSAP produces a process-oriented, direct project plan to specifically yield direction throughout your R/3 implementation.

Figure 1-1
Integration of Business Model and R/3.

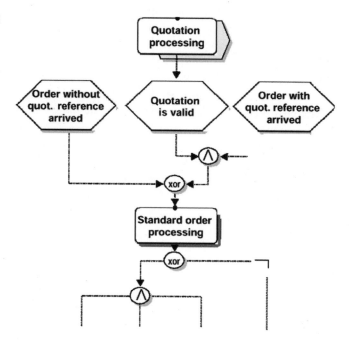

The expressway to implementation is paved with several SAP tools that make an important difference. Your primary task is to communicate with the Implementation Assistant for answers and gain a direction to move you through your implementation program. The following steps provide you with a simple and easy reservoir of information on some very key issues:

1. What needs to be done?
2. Who will achieve it?
3. How long does it take?

ASAP uses the detailed configuration capabilities of R/3's *Business Engineer*. Within this toolbox are tools that are used for modeling, implementation, continuous improvement, as well as documentation. There are also established models and industry templates that will directly act as catalysts to speed your implementation time and provide you with an accurate solution now.

Team Training

SAP offers a pyramid approach that integrates the training process and allows you to create an effective, total training program for faster, superior retained learning throughout your organization.

The fundamental objective is to integrate SAP's support and services network in an effort to provide answers to questions that may occur during your implementation. However, in any implementation, it is not just your installation effort, but also the knowledge that you can get answers after you've gone "live" that really counts. The goal is to provide you with assistance in every phase of your project. Nobody purchases a car without buying a "roadside assistance" plan from the automobile club. Why should your investment have anything less?

TeamSAP

TeamSAP is a major component of your implementation effort. It represents a coordinated network of products, processes, and people who are key to making certain that you acquire a successful SAP solution. Team-SAP enhances AcceleratedSAP and *Business Framework* programs with the goal of adding critical components, solutions expertise, assu.... ject coordination, leadership, and cross-customer knowledge sharing.

We will first examine the *Business Framework* that is SAP's strategic product architecture that permits complementary software partners to constantly convey new solutions into your R/3 implementation.

Then you can add solutions expertise, which is the culmination of the specialized expertise, experience, and training that exists for every TeamSAP member who contributed to the success of your project. Team-SAP makes certain that you have SAP-certified partner resources organized and in a logical, integrated, and comprehensive presentation that supports the knowledge base and experiences with SAP's most effective implementations. You have the resources to utilize both the power and information of TeamSAP to enhance your R/3 implementation time, and reduce costs throughout your effort to allow you to go live and beyond.

ASAP Consultant Specifics

SAP Consultants include SAP's Application Consultants, Remote Consultants, and Technical Consultants. They add a great deal of functionality and technical expertise to your efforts, especially if your business is multinational, because Global Support Managers are available to assist you throughout the specific items that occur within multiphased implementations.

AcceleratedSAP offers certified partners *Powered by AcceleratedSAP*, which permits the use of certain sections of ASAP techniques together with their own implementation practices. Customers who are part of a program with a Powered by AcceleratedSAP partner have a greater chance of speeding up their enterprisewide efforts in addition to complementing continuous efforts when a rapid implementation is required.

AcceleratedSAP Partners involve organizations that are certified as ASAP partners who have nearly three-quarters of their consultants achieve training in AcceleratedSAP and who have totally adopted the ASAP style to their duties. When you select to use an AcceleratedSAP Partner, it is a comfort to know that your partner will utilize the techniques in AcceleratedSAP and link both consistency and speed to your R/3 implementation. Speed, performance, and knowledge are all exemplified within the SAP consultant team. Having a good implementation is only part of the puzzle; the remainder involves acquiring an accurate solution in as little time as possible.

AP: Defined

AP is SAP's extensive, reproducible implementation solution meant refine R/3 projects. ASAP acts as an efficiency expert with respect to time, quality, and productive use of resources in implementations.

ASAP possesses components that make your implementation successful. These components include:

1. *SAP Roadmap:* This is a gradual project structure designed to create refined implementations that incorporate designations regarding the specifics for each activity on the *Roadmap.* You can see the various steps involved in this *Roadmap* in Fig. 1-2.

2. *SAP toolkit:* The ASAP *Implementation Assistant* is the navigation tool for the SAP *Roadmap* that includes all of the specific examples, templates, forms, and checklists. The implementation tools within the R/3 *Business Engineer* (BE) compose the cornerstone of AcceleratedSAP and expedite configuration of R/3 in the most efficient and productive pathway.

3. *SAP consultant training:* SAP offers much more than simple consulting and training. Their service and support products include *Early-Watch,* OSS, concept review, and Going Live check. Each of these tools is used as a quality assurance and quality check. In addition, they also provide active tuning of the R/3 system.

Accelerators

One of the most important mechanisms of the AcceleratedSAP program is the addition of components called *accelerators.* Each of these accelerators is used for all types of implementations. They can either be used together or independently, depending upon your specific needs. In terms of partners, the *Roadmap* can be substituted by their own techniques,

Figure 1-2
AcceleratedSAP
Roadmap (Six Steps).

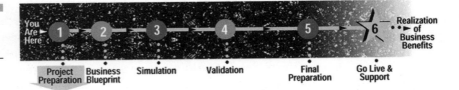

however, they still use the accelerators in order to achieve an effective implementation goal for your organization.

These implementation goals can best be defined specifically to provide you with:

- Much quicker implementation
- Speedier delivery of business results
- Certified quality
- Specific knowledge acquisition during implementation
- Most efficient use of resources
- Communion and utility of results for future implementation phases
- Shortened implementation cost
- Speedier return on investment

Approaching ERP in a New Direction

AcceleratedSAP is wisdom born from time-proven practices and standards that employ the best implementation and business practices from SAP customers. ASAP allows partner consultants to have a uniform approach that allows rapid implementation. The implementation tools of the R/3 *Business Engineer* are the cornerstones of the configuration support present in SAP's R/3.

The new direction SAP America is taking with ASAP started in the United States. However, the project team, called Fox, has offered AcceleratedSAP on a global solution scale. This project had already begun to blossom in the latter portion of 1997, and promises a great deal of potential in the future. At the present time, several countries have begun using the current version of AcceleratedSAP, as well as several of its components. There are numerous AcceleratedSAP projects in Europe, and a European ASAP customers went live in 1997.

Now that we have discussed the past and present directions of ASAP, the future holds even greater potential with more and more businesses coming online with significantly greater implementation times. SAP is dedicating a great deal of resources designed to continually strengthen and broaden AcceleratedSAP. These decisions are the result of both the

United States and Germany working together in combination with the Business Engineering Center in SAP development.

In terms of SAP's R/3 release 4.0, SAP is adapting AcceleratedSAP to assimilate new R/3 functionality. This begs the question of how SAP methodology is altered with respect to its consulting partners. The answer lies in the fact that SAP and its partner consultants are trying to achieve a common goal to provide an accurate R/3 solution that is both quick and inexpensive. The most recent release of SAP R/3 is release 4.0, illustrated in Fig. 1-3. SAP works together with its consulting partners as a whole-team unit to ensure the success of your implementation efforts. This methodology lends itself to the creation of Team-SAP, and illustrates how teamwork can accomplish realistic achievements in a reasonable time frame.

Several SAP partners have begun ASAP training in the United States, while some current AcceleratedSAP implementations are supported by SAP in combination with its consulting partners. Some ASAP implementation criteria are shown in Fig. 1-4. Both partners and those responsible for its implementation utilize ASAP.

Figure 1-3
SAP R/3 Release 4.0.

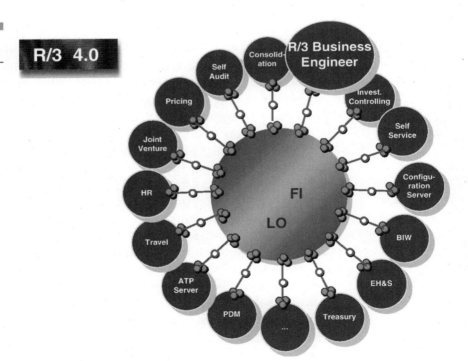

Figure 1-4
AcceleratedSAP
Implementation Criteria. (*Source:*
Aberdeen Group,
June 1997.)

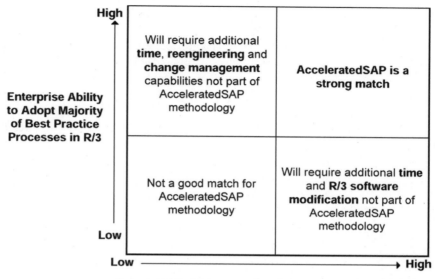

Functionality

AcceleratedSAP is a comprehensive program that has a great deal of functionality that supports both tools and templates. ASAP is effectively implemented in several customer R/3 implementations on both a domestic and global scale.

Compare and Contrast ASAP

It is important to point out how ASAP compares to the R/3 *Business Engineer* and R/3 *Procedure Model*. AcceleratedSAP employs the R/3 *Business Engineer* tools at all pertinent steps throughout the implementation process. ASAP's *Roadmap* is closely related to the R/3 *Procedure Model*. Each effectively handles various concepts of an implementation. The R/3 *Procedure Model* shows a far less specific view at a higher level.

AcceleratedSAP is a complete implementation solution with tools for R/3 service and support provisions that ensure time savings and quality with respect to your implementation.

Essentially, every customer can use AcceleratedSAP because its components are used as accelerators in any kind of implementation. The correct approach will be constructed from the *Roadmap* as part of project planning.

Since the majority of AcceleratedSAP tools and templates can be used in most implementations, ASAP can even be used if you are working on a project that involves different techniques. It is important to note that questionnaires, how-to guides, and standard forms can all be used separately and in combination with the ASAP *Roadmap.*

Most customers try to disassociate AcceleratedSAP with business process reengineering (BPR). However, the fact is that ASAP does not support techniques that involve how to reengineer your business or how to support a given level of change with your company. If a great deal of BPR is needed, you should partner with a consulting company who specializes in your area. In addition, all projects can profit from AcceleratedSAP, including questionnaires, forms, and how-to guides.

Since there is only one version of the AcceleratedSAP *Roadmap* tools and templates, there is less chance of confusion from different implementation efforts. One of the most beneficial features is ICOEs (industry centers of expertise) which handle the development of industry-specific ASAP tools and templates that enhance the overall service.

AcceleratedSAP can also be used in future phases of your implementation project. You will need to watch the next phases of your implementation effort because ASAP results can be used several times to enhance and improve the acceleration since they represent a company-specific starting point for all project methods.

Cost

No extra expense is incurred in using AccleratedSAP because all of the contents of ASAP are part of the services offered by SAP and ASAP partners. Essentially, all tools, templates, and completed deliverables go to customers through their implementors. There are, however, optional services, such as *EarlyWatch,* that are priced separately from ASAP, as shown in Fig. 1-5.

Training

SAP America and SAP in Europe offer three AcceleratedSAP-related training courses, and this is how customers are trained on AcceleratedSAP.

Figure 1-5
Showing How an
SAP *EarlyWatch*
Works.

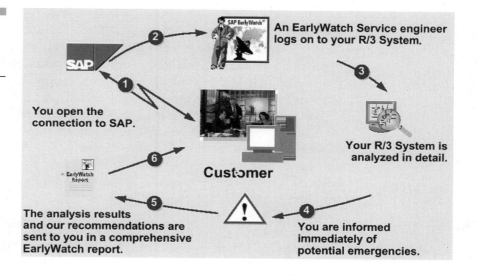

**You open the
connection to SAP.**

**An EarlyWatch Service engineer
logs on to your R/3 System.**

**Your R/3 System is
analyzed in detail.**

Customer

**The analysis results
and our recommendations are
sent to you in a comprehensive
EarlyWatch report.**

**You are informed
immediately of
potential emergencies.**

At this point in the implementation, the SAP implementor designates the specific training for their AcceleratedSAP customers and trains the appropriate staff. ASAP is SAP's total implementation solution to refine R/3 projects. AcceleratedSAP optimizes time, quality, and effective resources in implementations. This complete solution is composed of elements that ensure its success:

1. *Roadmap*
2. Toolkit
3. Service and support
4. Training

The *Roadmap* comprises five elements:

1. Project preparation
2. Business blueprint
3. Realization
4. Final preparation
5. Go live and support

The *Roadmap* also incorporates descriptions in the form of overview information as well as how-to's or best practices.

The toolkit designates all the tools employed in ASAP such as the R/3

Business Engineer and several other software products including Microsoft Project. AcceleratedSAP's *Best Estimator* tool allows you to correctly determine the needed resources, costs, and time frame for the implementation. The AcceleratedSAP *Implementation Assistant* is effectively a how-to guide that assists you through the unique phases of implementation such as the checklists and project plans.

Service and support is an area that needs to be fostered from the first planning stages through completion of implementation and beyond. Services incorporate consulting and training. ASAP also uses the service and support provision for services relating to the SAP environment. *EarlyWatch,* concept reviews, and *GoingLive* checks are all components of the service palette that ensures total quality and allows you to actively refine your R/3 system.

Training strategies for the project team training, in addition to end-user training, are integrated into the plan. Usually, the project team is trained in a combination with standard level 1–3 training classes, as well as onsite training. With respect to end users, the main strategy is a train-the-trainer technique for effective knowledge transfer from the project team.

Rapid Deployment

AcceleratedSAP is becoming a global industry standard for rapid deployment of SAP's R/3. ASAP allows organizations to benefit from reliable implementation best practices founded on the experience of SAP customers. ASAP gives companies around the world one technique for implementing R/3 across global operations. AcceleratedSAP gives customers a much quicker return on investment, as well as significant cost savings that allows you to realize greater operational efficiency now. ASAP is focused on your goals, it supports backward scheduling from your go-live time frame, and makes certain that all functions add value and help you reach your objective.

Teamwork

Teamwork is an essential ingredient in helping to meet your goal. SAP consultants and implementation partners experienced in Accelerated-

SAP objectives are dedicated to your success. SAP professionals work as a tightly knit team with your organization from the initiation of your project through your ultimate go-live date.

Teamwork occurs through automated means such as ASAP's *Implementation Assistant*. This product includes templates, forms, questionnaires, and checklists that provide you with several implementation tools with which to start your project. All of these tools help to organize your systems by evaluating the configuration of core business processes that deal with cycles throughout your departments. This makes certain that you achieve a cross-functional, integrated implementation. Once that implementation is complete, your team tests your system for quality assurance. The ASAP *Roadmap* in Chap. 2 demonstrates the totality and coherence of your project. It designates exactly what must be accomplished throughout each phase.

When your implementation is completed, you can reuse these very same standard procedures to deploy R/3 more widely within your organization. You can accomplish your task by defining and coordinating project team roles for aspects including application design, technical installation, and project management throughout all phases of your implementation. This allows you to make certain that all activities function as one cohesive entity.

AcceleratedSAP Ingredients

The ASAP *Roadmap* gives you a detailed plan for all of your implementation activities that offers you a greater level of detail. The R/3 *Implementation Assistant* is composed of tools that allow you to invent implementation pathways once one already exists that is right for you, resulting in significant time savings. The R/3 *Business Engineer* is a tool that creates a foundation for your system configuration. It has an automated configuration functionality that supports the continuous improvement of your business processes. Service and support are essential ingredients for any consultant working with your implementation partners. This effort allows you to work with customers as one team during your implementation. You can achieve an even greater level of support with *EarlyWatch, GoingLive* checks, and *Online Service and Support* programs to help you on your implementation journey.

The ASAP *Roadmap* Legend

The *Roadmap* takes you from the initial stages of your project to completion. This very specific layout helps you achieve several important goals in order to complete implementation as fast as possible. The first step is project preparation during which you work toward achieving executive commitment. Then, you can form a project team that has the ability to make critical decisions and develop a definitive project plan.

The next step is to bring your plan to fruition through the phase called *Business Blueprint.* Your project team combined with ASAP consultants establish a detailed blueprint of your business on R/3 and provide a copy to your company executives to be approved. At this point you are ready for your simulation. Both your consultants and the project team configure and install four-fifths of your standard R/3 systems just by using the *Business Blueprint* to simulate business transactions with real master data. This procedure refines and confirms the blueprint. That refinement is then validated. Your project team works with SAP consultants to allow the system to grow into a completely integrated solution. Then, the final preparation involves completion of systems testing, training of end users, and coordination of your "go-live" strategy. The point at which you go live and provide support is achieved once you have a productive R/3 environment. This is accomplished by both consultants and project team members who make certain your business environment is completely supported by validating the accuracy of transactions and meeting end users' needs.

Business Engineer

One of the aspects this book deals with is SAP's R/3 *Business Engineer* (BE), a very important configuration tool that allows much quicker and more efficient R/3 implementation of enterprise business solutions. It also allows greater improvement of business processes. R/3 *Business Engineer 4.0* allows you to configure R/3 simply and easily and provides support for your entire R/3 environment. In addition, R/3 *Business Engineer* permits you to implement changes quickly—at any time and at any place—within your existing enterprise system.

R/3 *Business Engineer* Benefits

Version 4.0 contains a very detailed level of configuration for R/3 that permits simple, rapid implementation support for ongoing business growth. It also results in a higher return on investment for R/3 *Flexible* in an open configuration environment.

R/3 *Business Engineer*'s knowledge-based configuration makes implementation simpler through an interactive interface that offers a question-and-answer type configuration process. Its purpose is to provide structure through your R/3 configuration and determine if any problems exist. In addition, it excites the R/3 process chains to determine how configuration decisions influence business processes across the integrated system. It also emulates a live R/3 solution that will operate traditional enterprise modeling with the live R/3 system. It then connects business models and deploys them to make certain that process design integrity and decisions are executed during system configuration. The last step is to ensure there is both consistent and supported R/3 features that have a standard interface which makes R/3 *Business Engineer* accessible to partners, consultants, and customers. It allows you to enhance industry solutions and create corporate rollout templates.

Easy Configuration

The R/3 *Business Engineer* greatly simplifies configuration. For example, it contains 100 distinct business scenarios that aggregate R/3's 1000 business processes into controllable views of the best business practices. Industry templates yield an efficient industry-centered R/3 solution. These solutions are useful for consumer-packaged goods and chemical and steel industries. SAP provides these templates for all of its vertically focussed industries.

Business Engineer is improving constantly. It allows customers to support change and regularly execute system improvements by handling nine-tenths of daily business changes, such as adding or subtracting items from within your corporate structure. These tasks involve business units, production plants, and warehouses. Other tasks include the addition of new staff, promotions, reallocation of work duties, and maintaining authorization profiles for both new and concurrent currencies. These functions may play a critical role with global business clients who have modified legal requirements, including new tax rates or revised employment legislation. In short, you have access to new business process optimization support for current or future implementations of R/3.

Versatility

R/3 *Business Engineer* permits customers to configure several versions of R/3, which allows them to utilize new releases and add new projects into the operating system such as standard APIs and support for major interfaces like COM/DCOM and ActiveX. The goal is to facilitate integration with third-party software, tools, and techniques. There is also a web-browser front-end and HTML-based documentation so that R/3 *Business Engineer* is *not* platform specific. In addition, it provides simpler and easier access.

SAP's *Business Framework* is maintained by the R/3 *Business Engineer,* which handles component-centered implementation that is updated with the delivery of R/3 components.

Reengineering Questions

Although SAP is increasing its profits from one of its popular enterprise software platforms, users believe that implementing SAP software is a prelude to organizational reengineering. Company marketing allows users to make certain that these practices are indicative of a powerful change in management. The corporate business structure that is in place is the cornerstone for current and future planning that guides the organization through the support services migration. In the event that companies are not prepared for such an extensive transition, they will have to pay for very costly SAP consultants and technical support.

The time frame for a very fast SAP implementation is about 2 years, however, it is important to inform your financial officers about the corporate migration costs. SAP realizes the importance that its customers place on technical support. Therefore, they are creating software modules that are simple to install and inexpensive to enhance your organization's ability to handle specific support problems.

SAP is growing rapidly in terms of number of users. When you buy an SAP system, the importance lies in the product you own, indicating that your company realizes the need for extensive, continuous SAP support and consulting.

Consultant Focus

Independent consultants can be very costly, especially when you consider that many of the sessions don't deal directly with technology but on the method of system adoption. For example, how to manage a 24-month migration (a time frame that is more than exemplary for a large corporate implementation) to a completely new computing system that often uses a totally different method for your business, thus requiring that your business be reengineered.

After several sessions, many organizations realize that managing a total system change is even more important than the SAP applications. The most important guideline is the importance of keeping track of your return on investment and business case problems. It is important to note that you may require a special group whose purpose is just to manage change. If you find yourself in a cost overrun, you may wish to discuss your options with your financial officer so you can continue your implementation efforts and put them back on track.

Some large companies warrant special attention from SAP, such as an onsite SAP engineer who can support issues as they come up. In addition, an SAP engineer can act as a liaison between your company and SAP. However, only billion-dollar companies warrant SAP's sending out a highly trained account manager.

SAP is working diligently to take advantage of the support situation by producing an accelerated solution with several preconfigured or easily customized modules. They are creating more vertical business applications, such as bank modules, that are configured to order as opposed to being built to order. This is an effective time-saver that accelerates the R/3 implementation process.

Conclusion

This chapter discusses exactly what AcceleratedSAP (ASAP) does in terms of optimizing time, quality, and efficiency. ASAP can efficiently utilize your business resources and provide you with an effective implementation solution in a shorter period of time. This support structure places a premium on SAP expertise. The entire structure of ASAP is fostered by the fact that all of the experiences of former implementations are gathered into one accelerated solution. ASAP can implement R/3 in a shorter period of time because the implementations are based on SAP's best practices. You will have the power to utilize every aspect of proven solutions to implement R/3 within your organization quickly, efficiently, and most effectively.

The *Roadmap*

Introduction

Your implementation pathway is the expressway to your ASAP solution. Attaining your ASAP solution is analogous to following a good roadmap in your car. That travel destination is your enterprise resource planning solution. A direct pyramid-shaped guide can lead your ERP solution, as depicted in Fig. 2-1. Your guidebook is furnished by the AcceleratedSAP *Roadmap*. This is a map of your entire migration pathway, all items are clearly labeled and provide you with an opportunity to save time and implement quickly and effectively.

At this point, you are only at the beginning of your ASAP journey. The first step you need to take is a careful review of your map and all of its steps. This review will provide you with the ability to achieve an efficient R/3 implementation.

Making a Plan

The first step is project preparation. Your preparation will involve all of your decision makers. Everyone must be in agreement on the various steps in your R/3 implementation project. At this point, you will be able to form your internal and external implementation team. These primary tasks will allow you to start your implementation effort with greater speed and efficiency.

Several layers of preparation must be adhered to when approaching your ASAP solution. Once you have completed all of the preliminary

Figure 2-1
Enterprise Pyramid.

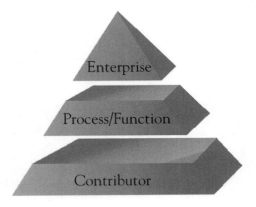

preparation steps described here, you will then be able to go on to your final preparation. At this point, you will need to examine your overall game plan to determine what type of testing and adjustments will be needed in order for you to ensure a successful implementation. This stage is your chance to test all interfaces, train all end users, and migrate your business data to your new R/3 system.

After preparation is complete, then you can design your business blueprint. At this stage, you realize that your company is prepared to embark on an AcceleratedSAP solution. Now, you will need to record your organization's business requirements. The *Business Blueprint* gives you a visual model of your company's future environment once the R/3 installation is complete. This blueprint can help you in your planning process, as illustrated in Fig. 2-2. In addition, it will permit your project team to specifically designate your objectives. These objectives can further be strengthened by the fact that your resources are concentrated on the R/3 processes required to operate your business.

Once your final preparation is done, you have reached the level to go live and support. This is the final step to your implementation effort that will allow you to reach your destination and go live. Knowing your time frame will allow you to set your implementation efforts into motion so you can achieve your ASAP goal in a timely manner. Implementation is tempered by the fact that you may run into problems along the way.

Figure 2-2
Process Planning.

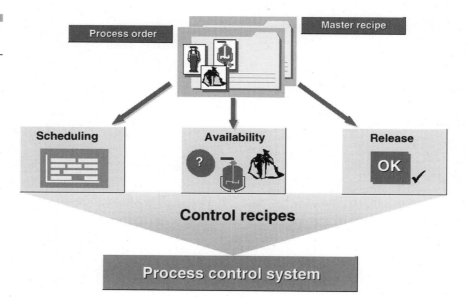

However, the road you take will be eased through SAP's support and services program.

Once your preparation is complete, it is time for realization of all of your hard work. Now you must configure your R/3 system to meet all of your individual business needs. Your Business Blueprint can be used by your team to both configure and fine-tune the specific elements of your implementation. In this plan, you can accurately control all aspects involving your AcceleratedSAP implementation of R/3.

Finally, it is reasonable to conclude that no implementation of R/3 operation is static. You must be prepared to deal with continuous change within your environment. Your support is not over once your operations are functional because you must have the power to get answers to your problems once you have gone live. At any given time, SAP has a large network of professionals to provide global access to R/3 expertise, product support, and maintenance services throughout the entire year, without exception.

Since this is an accelerated solution, you need to have the resources available to meet your changing needs. SAP is constantly creating new services to satisfy your changing needs, answer your questions, and support your implementation. Maintenance service needs are shown in Fig. 2-3.

Figure 2-3
Maintenance Service.

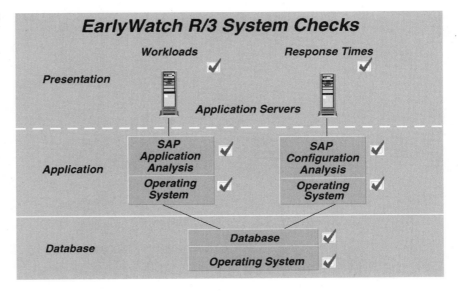

Implementation Assistant

ASAP's *Implementation Assistant* provides several solutions for any component that may be problematic during your implementation effort. The *Implementation Assistant* is simply a storehouse of information that designates what needs to be done, who should do it, and the length of time it should take to complete. It can be consulted at any time to make certain that your project is a success. You will learn how to do specific tasks, complete checklists, review examples, consult questionnaires, and check with technical guidelines.

The *Implementation Assistant* provides details on specific tasks such as designating who should be on a specific project team and determining the project team's duties. It helps you develop the necessary details and guides you through every task in the AcceleratedSAP *Roadmap*.

Following the *Roadmap*

As you progress with your implementation, you need to consider several key factors that will ultimately make you successful. You need to determine the following factors:

1. Cost
2. Time
3. Length of implementation
4. R/3 implementation tools
5. Required resources

Review of these factors is essential to determine how you can best proceed with the planned ASAP steps outlined in the previous section. Specifically, a detailed list of the steps required to guide you through your implementation effort will assist you in achieving your ultimate goal of running R/3 live in your organization.

Phase 1: Project Preparation

You must first collect your resources so you can adequately deal with your entire implementation effort. You can achieve a timely and efficient implementation by planning ahead to make sure your organization is ready for this upgrade. The planning stage can be somewhat simplified through the AcceleratedSAP program.

Full agreement of all of your corporate decision makers who are responsible for this project is needed before you can proceed any further. Once you have total agreement that R/3 will support the majority of your business needs, you will be in a position to make decisions more quickly and efficiently. Garnering acceptance is a key component to accelerating your implementation. The next component is developing a very clear project goal. Your decision-making process will be much more efficient once you determine your primary goals and objectives. Your company can more easily accept change and work together as an effective implementation team composed of people from all areas of your business. At this point you can begin the first phase of your project effort with the confidence that your primary barriers have be removed.

When you effectively eliminate problems at the beginning of your effort, change will occur much more quickly. Your TeamSAP consultants will work together with your organization to effectively determine your needs and requirements.

The ASAP *Project Estimator* is a tool that leads your team through several predefined questions. It facilitates interviews with your organization's senior executives, as well as key operating managers, in terms of their respective objectives. Since these objectives are tempered by the actual speed of your deployment, they become the objectives of your AcceleratedSAP solution.

TeamSAP consultants will assess each of these responses and determine the overall project scope and resources needed. These needs include three basic elements:

1. Time

2. Cost

3. Personnel

This is the jumping-off point that allows you to prepare your internal team members through introductory training to create R/3 awareness. You will find that product awareness allows you to tailor your expectations to meet product development. Level 1 training allows you to analyze SAP's architecture for service and support, the cornerstone of your implementation, and SAP terminology. The R/3 program is organized around essential business processes that cross application modules as well as emulate your organization's business processes.

The team you assemble can utilize realistic business process flows, scenarios, and models to permit both quick and cost-effective execution of business tasks. Standard service inspections will allow you to keep business processes flowing smoothly as you move down the ASAP roadmap that leads to your ultimate implementation. This journey is fortified by the quality of your business processes. That quality is further realized through use of an SAP quality assurance professional who performs inspections on a regular basis.

This very detailed quality assurance check and independent audit ensures that your implementation efforts have been worthwhile and are proceeding according to schedule. You have the confidence that your implementation is supported by your top-level executives, therefore, you can be certain you are ready for your team to develop the details of the project plan, as well as all of the key benefits that will assist both top-level management and all personnel.

At this point, you can enumerate all of the issues relevant to goals, budgets, and timing. Subsequently, you can acquire the required level of approval for your R/3 implementation plan from the decision makers within your organization. You can then instruct your team to complete all of its preparation duties and then proceed with the next phase of your implementation effort.

Phase 2: The *Business Blueprint*

The *Business Blueprint* allows you to record and designate your R/3 implementation. At this point, you will need to answer several questionnaires within such events as executive sessions, group discussions, and individual interviews. The answers you provide will assist Team-SAP consultants in determining your core business strategy. This information permits them to specify your future business processes and requirements.

AcceleratedSAP balances the power of the *Business Engineer*. The *Business Engineer* (BE) provides a total toolkit of specific business processes to accelerate your activities. This acceleration not only works in the present but also in the future to keep R/3 operating as the cornerstone of change as your business needs grow. A blueprint created for the methodology you use now can meet your growing needs, and is designed to keep track of your needs as your market changes.

Throughout the *Business Blueprint* phase, TeamSAP professionals refine R/3 to meet your industry-specific business processes. As you use both the questionnaires and the models from the *Business Engineer,* your project team will determine your business processes to depict the future of your business. Industry templates also work as an accelerator to facilitate your implementation process by designating industry best practices for your business. The end result of this effort is a total blueprint of your business. Your business plan will form the foundation for your ultimately successful R/3 implementation.

ASAP can be an integral part of any project regardless of its scale. It does not concentrate on projects that need to be reengineered or require operational enhancements. However, TeamSAP professionals will assist you in developing new approaches for your business processes. They will help you to create a basis by which you can achieve continuous improvement for your R/3 implementation. These phases essentially define the blueprint for the remainder of your implementation in addition to that of future upgrades.

In order to concentrate on the blueprint that is being created for your specific industry focus, your project team members will initiate Level 2 training on R/3 integrated business systems. Furthermore, an invaluable element of basic training exists across application modules, in addition to that of learning key success factors necessary in implementing total business solutions. Level 2 training will walk you through a detailed education level of R/3 business process skills. Your project team will be able to construct and maintain R/3 to meet your individual business processes.

ASAP *Business Process Inquiries* often helps to determine your focus areas. You may find it useful to determine how your customers are linked with your sales cycle, pricing, and discounts. In fact, you can tailor your individual setup to detect the most commonly used techniques to determine cost factors by product, customer type, and geographical location. Then you can set factors that detail sales processing within your organization, as well as the level of centralization involved in determining individual aspects associated with it. Finally, you may wish to look at the methods your company uses for reporting sales figures with respect to specific customers, regions, and districts.

Essentially, this example helps you to determine how to best use your *Business Blueprint* to specifically configure all of the details of your own R/3 system. You can use this information to create an environment that answers your growing organizational needs—both as an organization today and in the future.

You can use your established *Business Blueprint* to initiate a two-level process to configuring your R/3 system. The first level involves your TeamSAP professional who will efficiently configure your standard system. The next level is where your project team refines the system to satisfy all of your business and process requirements.

In terms of the previous sales example, imagine that most of the orders for your business are through the Internet. Your TeamSAP professional will configure your standard system. This is the basis of most of your transactions. Your standard system will be made up of four-fifths of your daily business transactions. Due to the fact that your original configuration is rooted in the blueprint that your team has created, your standard system will provide you with a realistic view of how your business transactions will operate in R/3. It is possible for you to continue to gain speed as the AcceleratedSAP process constructs every element of your implementation for the most efficiency in terms of resource utilization.

Parallel activities will be completed together and initiated earlier in the process, effectively reducing your time constraints significantly. Next, you need to focus on the full configuration that incorporates the remaining one-fifth of your business transactions. Your project team will now be able to configure the exception transactions, such as sales orders, that come in via fax or telephone. Your TeamSAP professional will segment your business processes into cycles of associated business areas. The cycles act as project landmarks and permit you to test distinct sections of the business process. The end result is an instantaneous report providing specific feedback. It is at this point that detailed learning by example enables you to comprehend the specifics about your R/3 system.

While you configure your system's exceptions, it is important to check your *Implementation Assistant* for specific tips and examples. Your organization will profit from the extensive consultant experience within each industry that has made R/3 live on a global scale. The *Implementation Assistant* has an extensive testing guide within it to assist your group and configure associated business processes. These time-savers offer increased configuration efficiency, as well as the most direct path. An automatic travel log will designate your pathway to implementation.

Phase 3: Realization

At the realization phase, you can proceed with balancing your *Business Engineer* functionality with its *Implementation Guide* (IMG). You can then utilize your blueprint and objectives and link them to the IMG. The result is a clearly laid out guide that explains what must be configured for each process. At this point, you can utilize the guidelines, steps, and configuration data for every element of R/3 functionality. In addition, IMG permits you to record your implementation pathway to R/3. It also allows you to establish a detailed implementation log that records each step along your roadmap or pathway. It designates each and every change or addition you make to your R/3 system. Your IMG travel log accesses the most current configuration status at any time frame in your pathway. This action will greatly simplify reporting to top-level management and keep communication and support at a highly accelerated level.

The next step is to enhance your skills to Level 3 training. At Level 3, the training gets even more fast-paced because you are closing in on your realization. By utilizing advanced training, your project team can gain the expertise they need to manage your R/3 system. This detailed training incorporates advanced topic workshops to create expertise specific to your organization's individual requirements. Furthermore, your project team will have access to industry workshops, as well as self-directed reference and training for continuing education.

The purpose is to capture the future and incorporate all associated enhancements that will be incorporated into your overall R/3 implementation plan. The system your team creates during the realization phase acts as the platform for continuing business modifications. These processes and tools are used constantly to refine business changes, expansions, and system improvements during and after your implementation.

It is important to create corporate guidelines for a simple deployment for all associate areas within your organization when changes, upgrades, and improvements are required. Knowledge transfer allows you to control your project and make certain that its team is in control of the implementation of R/3 now and its operation in the future. You will become very self-sufficient when your TeamSAP professionals transfer R/3 system knowledge to your project team. Then your R/3 standard system can become fully configured and move on to the next phase.

Phase 4: Final Preparation

The final preparation phase takes your system through a very detailed level of testing. At the same time, it takes your end users through a very detailed level of training. It is at this stage that you can refine your R/3

Figure 2-4
Pathway to Performance Management and Implementing a Strategy.

system prior to your "Go Live" stage. You have the power to execute any needed modifications in order to prepare both your system and your business for production initialization. As you prepare to Go Live, it is important to execute final system tests, as well as end-user training. Figure 2-4 illustrates the pathway to performance management, as well as guiding you through your strategy implementation. The next stage is to migrate business data to your new system. Then you must test and tune your system for optimum performance.

Your testing time is minimized due to the fact that you have been testing your system throughout your implementation process. At the final preparation, you will need to execute volume and stress tests. Each of these tests is essential for optimizing performance of your system. Integration tests are also important so that you can emulate live conditions. These conditions will test your conversion and interface applications for both accuracy and usability. In addition, you will test your system to be certain that your end users will accept their new system for a seamless transition to Go Live.

Preventative maintenance is an excellent check that allows you to make certain you achieve optimal performance of your R/3 system. The R/3 *GoingLive* Check permits SAP professionals to log on to your R/3 system via a remote connection that allows them to analyze the configuration of each of your individual systems, resulting in important recommendations that allow you to optimize your system. Education is a key component to the success of your R/3 implementation as it allows your end users to become more familiar with the system. Your goal is to promote a level of familiarity with your new R/3 system.

One method that is used to gain acceptance is called the *train the trainer* method since users will be trained by experienced coworkers within your organization. Your end users will then be prepared to utilize the skills they learned to operate and optimize R/3 for their daily business tasks. Training specific to each person's job is important so that each end user will know exactly how to use the R/3 system for his or her daily tasks. Then, you must be prepared to Go Live as your project team prepares a production initialization method. Your straightforward data conversion plan will ensure that all of the data from your old systems is transferred correctly into your R/3 integrated information system.

Your preparation to Go Live is analogous to preparing for your end users' questions as they begin to use their new R/3 system. The point at which you Go Live is an important transition that must foster the general feeling that every user and manager is going to be supported. Each worker will need to know whom to call for any questions or reports about system performance.

The *Help Desk* is key to protecting your internal system and providing end users with the answers they need to successfully perform their daily tasks. Ultimately, your project team will create the first audit procedures, as well as a project team support structure as part of the final stage of preparation. Once that final preparation is completed, you must proceed with the fifth phase of your project which involves your system actually going live with support.

Phase 5: Go Live and Support

The actual point at which your organization is Going Live is more than simply flipping a switch, as you have seen in all of the preparatory steps detailed in this chapter. Since you have carefully detailed all of your objectives, you have been able to create a rapid form of implementing R/3 that allows your company to realize significant business benefits that have taken place as soon as possible.

During this final phase of your project, it is important to create procedures and measurements to provide details on all of the benefits of your R/3 investment at regular intervals. As your business travels take you further along the ASAP *Roadmap,* you will begin to feel comfortable with the convenience of key elements including:

1. R/3 expertise
2. Product support
3. Preventative maintenance

Support and services allow you to keep R/3 working perfectly along with SAP support and services that help you make certain that your system will continue to run efficiently and effectively. Since your business is always working on new areas and projects, it is important to note that support does not conclude once you have gone live. SAP assists you during each and every phase of your R/3 project. An expansive network of consultants is available whenever you need them. They effectively yield global access to R/3 support and maintenance services all the time. These support services can provide assistance via a remote connection or through your local SAP office.

The Online Service System (OSS) is a centralized communications network that exists between you, your SAP partners, and SAP itself. OSS enables you to electronically transmit your problems or questions to SAP via a remote connection. In addition, you can automatically monitor their progress toward an ultimate solution. The OSS (shown in Fig. 2-5) permits you to access a library of notes detailing specific event solutions that have been achieved by other SAP customers. Remote Consulting

Figure 2-5
Online Service System.

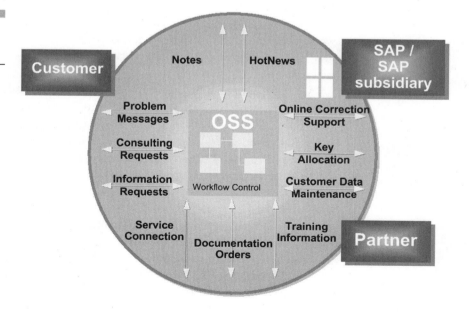

Services allows SAP professionals to log onto your R/3 system through a direct remote connection (e.g., video conferencing). Then you have the ability to transmit your Remote Consultant requests and questions from technical assistance to process- or application-specific support.

Once you do Go Live, *EarlyWatch* gives you a proactive system diagnosis. SAP can diagnose possible problems and resolve them at an early stage so you can be certain you achieve optimal system availability and performance. SAP's support and services are created to help your organization, realizing that every company is an individual. Furthermore, as your requirements grow, SAP helps you continue with your roadmap to gain an even more successful solution. Utilizing both speed and skill allows you to gain a competitive edge when your R/3 system is live. Knowing that ASAP helps you implement a working solution quickly and efficiently, permits you to use your business resources more effectively at a greater profit. When you have your R/3 system working at its full potential, your company can realize a far greater return on its information investment.

SAP Modules Ease Implementation

SAP produces both modules and versions for its ERP solutions to cater to their client/server software. SAP has created sales and implementation tools to make R/3 suite-applicable to midsized companies. SAP has two new tools to help midsized companies with its CBS (Certified Business Solutions) program that involves more front-end planning for R/3 implementations.

SAP salespeople who function under AcceleratedSAP come to new accounts at midsized companies and make projections with SAP's *Estimator* tool. This tool allows SAP to evaluate both your business and equipment needs. The objective is to provide a practical idea of your project's cost in terms of both time and money.

SAP's *Implementation Assistant* desktop application acts as a guide to take you through the six-step process above. It permits you to have a closely configured system with the *Business Engineer* configuration tool.

In addition, SAP offers a new development environment that permits your organization to integrate third-party components into the pre-cast R/3 enterprise system much simpler. ABAP *Objects* is a component of SAP's CIM software *Business Framework* method. IT builds on the backbone of SAP's ABAP programming language and object programming technology. Furthermore, this development environment allows both individual and team development tools as well as a virtual machine to produce cross-platform application portability. Its functionality also includes both publish & subscribe and event-trigger mechanisms to support business application needs. ABAP *Objects* is part of R/3 4.0, due in the second quarter of 1999.

Conclusion

The ASAP solution is composed of several elements to provide you with both a fast and effective R/3 implementation. The ASAP *Roadmap* acts as a guide that prepares you for your accelerated implementation. In this chapter you have learned the basic five stages, including the project preparation, *Business Blueprint*, realization, final preparation, and finally how to Go Live and maintain support.

When you employ a straightforward set of conditions, you can implement your ERP solution quickly and cost-effectively. Your goal is to find a way of improving your business processes with the least cost and quickest time. This *Roadmap* "guides" you to an effective solution for your ERP needs.

SAP Tools

Introduction

SAP introduces new tools based on their best business practices to help speed R/3 implementations. AcceleratedSAP is a program that takes advantage of every successful implementation, and the tools can assist in reducing implementation time by not making you reinvent the wheel. Instead of trying to tackle an implementation from scratch, preestablished tools can take a great deal of the guesswork out of the process and help you refine your time frame to gain the most from your installation efforts.

Unicenter Management Tools

Computer Associates offers a version of its Unicenter TNG systems management software created to support SAP R/3 applications throughout distributed UNIX, Windows, NT, OS/2, AS/400, and mainframe-dispersed operating environments. In the past, each R/3 implementation needed its own management console. Unicenter TNG provides one individual point of control that has been integrated with the CCMS management applications SAP includes with R/3. This permits Unicenter TNG to schedule tasks throughout several R/3 systems, as well as non-R/3 systems.

The demand for both manufacturing and resource planning applications is high. SAP works diligently to code application-specific products created for ERP users.

Efficient Interfaces

An efficient tool that assists many organizations is the SAP R/3 *Interface Adviser,* which yields both efficiency and quality in defining and implementing distributed business processes. Nearly all R/3 implementation projects involve design, implementation, and maintenance of permanent interfaces that exist between the R/3 system and any non-SAP systems. This often happens in a phased R/3 system implementation that takes place piecemeal—application by application or by replacing old systems with an R/3 system at individual branch points of an organization.

You may also be required to integrate current business processes into your R/3 system by connecting satellite systems. The *Interface Adviser* pro-

vides centralized information so that you can de
manent interfaces between SAP R/3 components :
When dealing with R/3 systems, it is very imp

38

1. The point at which existing business process
with non-SAP systems, and if that implemer
requirements of the system or processes.

2. The specific subprocesses also needed for system integration and process organization.

3. The subprocesses that could be combined into one component.

4. BAPIs or other solutions needed for the interface.

5. If a program already exists in the standard system for yielding the interface with data.

6. APIs in the standard system that can import data into the SAP R/3 system.

7. Basis technology that can be utilized if no standard solutions are possible.

8. Determine whether the interface can be set up by utilizing certified products from third-party suppliers.

9. Determine your advantages.

10. Reduce time for defining and implementing cross-system business processes.

11. Reduce cost for defining and implementing cross-system business processes.

12. Avoid interface designs that lead to problems with performance, data consistency, and handling.

SAP R/3 *Interface Adviser* Content

The SAP R/3 *Interface Adviser* guides you through the specific stages of your R/3 implementation project. It helps you in the initial design stage by allowing you to compare your requirements with the process distribution plan that is available in *Interface Adviser.* You receive detailed explanations of the encapsulation of subprocesses within your specified systems. You must also review several functional constraints of your plan that can ultimately result from processes that do not become completely integrated in R/3.

In the end, *Interface Adviser* will provide recommendations that tell you how to proceed with your implementation effort, such as the initial profile of your cross-system process flow, number of application objects to be exchanged, and the technology that makes it easier to estimate needed resources and project duration.

The detailed design stage sets up specific Business Objects that include the material master and vendor. These components as well as the techniques that can be used must be exchanged between systems. When dealing with each technique, you will receive object-related notes that deal with the functions that are proper for importing objects, as well as the application exits that are proper for exporting an object.

Feasibility checklists assist you in choosing specific interface methods that can be used in your system environment. During the implementation phase, you can use the proper basis technology to implement the actual import and export of objects. In order to achieve this task, you can refer to the sample programs for the individual application objects. General descriptions of the interface methods can be used, including BAPI, Remote Function Call, batch input, IDoc, CPI-C, and program exits, to greatly simplify implementation of the interface. An example of the type of information included in an electronic batch record is shown in Fig. 3-1.

Figure 3-1
Information Included in an Electronic Batch Record.

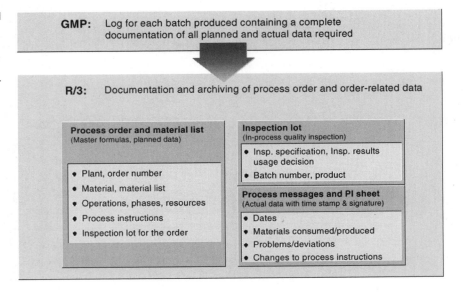

The SAP R/3 Interface Service provides a great deal of support for both procedure and implementation consulting and answers questions that involve process distribution methodologies and their associated interfaces.

You may also find SAP consulting beneficial if you need to determine alternative procedures to determine the practicality of several interface solutions. Both technology and service R/3 software is rooted in a client/server architecture. R/3 is created to be an open system used on various operating systems.

In addition to the software, SAP provides you with a complete range of services throughout the R/3 product life cycle as illustrated in Fig. 3-2. These services include:

1. Preventive system checks
2. Professional consulting for both organizational and technical issues that involve:
   A. Project planning
   B. System implementation
   C. Qualified staff training
   D. 24-hour per day, 7-day per week customer support
3. SAP's quality management system for software development satisfies the international ISO 9001 standards.

Figure 3-2
SAP R/3 Services and Support in the Product Life Cycle.

Implementation Tools

Implementation tools and services enable rapid implementation of SAP R/3. They add a great deal of expertise and complement ASAP. The tools work to refine your implementation through SAP's *Business Engineering Workbench* (BEW)—the cornerstone that initiates an implementation with best practices. BEW provides the power to effect changes within the SAP R/3 storehouse. You can also work with professional service firms comprised of the major consulting firms, as well as other global consulting organizations.

ASAP is positioned exceedingly well to balance the capabilities of BEW, via business and industry knowledge, not an accelerated implementation to meet your individual needs.

Deloitte & Touche Consulting Group/ICS (ICS) was the first SAP implementation partner who brought BEW functionality and the business and industry expertise of their consulting organization.

ICS now yields industry metamodels designated as "IndustryPrints" which build on the BEW's functionality to refine an SAP R/3 implementation. IndustryPrints provide a long-term functionality that adds value by both increasing the initial benefits of SAP R/3 for an enterprise and decreasing both the cost and effort of maintaining the systems over time.

Going Live in Record Time

SAP customers have very specific goals and objectives that must be met in order for them to achieve a successful client-server enterprise software implementation. Success is achieved through the fastest possible implementation that both reduces costs and relies on consultants for configuration settings. The purpose of AcceleratedSAP is to offer your company the best possible avenue for R/3 implementation to provide you with attainable benefits.

SAP R/3 can meet your implementation resource functionality by offering you several preconfigured tools and templates under the ASAP implementation. Your objectives with respect to implementation results from SAP and their partners should yield realizable benefits to your basic business strategy. These tools provide you with the best practices from previous successful, functional SAP R/3 system implementations. This complex system achieves success through its tools and your selected consulting organization whose primary responsibility is to assist your implementation team with R/3's complexities. These consultants utilize both their SAP knowledge and business experience to accelerate your implementation.

Business Engineering Workbench

SAP's work in meeting customer imperatives is met using the *Business Engineering Workbench*. This tool created by SAP provides a configuration initiative to your organization by including several hundred best practices and processes that can both be acquired and used for your SAP R/3 implementation. The short-term benefits involve refined implementations with respect to both design and configuration.

BEW permits R/3 customers to modify processes in the SAP R/3 system on a continuing basis. This functionality makes BEW more accessible to your staff and it reduces the need to have third-party consultants both during the creation and configuration periods. Having these capabilities integrated into the BEW will permit you to concentrate on the business engineering duties that truly add value to your organization.

Finding Solutions

Implementation consultants consider that both tools and initiatives are important components in meeting your specific implementation requirements. These needs often focus on specific industry solutions. The industry tools and techniques utilize the resources of your consulting firm, and are available through general industry knowledge and the cooperative efforts between these agencies, SAP's Industry Centers of Expertise (ICOEs), and proprietary industry templates. A great deal of this information comes from implementation consultants, as depicted in Fig. 3-3.

Deloitte & Touche Consulting Group/ICS provides applied industry expertise for R/3 implementations. ICS is creating a model-based industry technique that balances the best-practice functionalities of BEW, as well as establishing these best practices into workable industry environments. IndustryPrints by ICS offers the first practical implementation

Figure 3-3
R/3 Implementation
Consultants 1997.

of a model-based tool. IndustryPrints uses BEW's functionality to assist your R/3, by lowering the cost, time, and complexity. However, it is important to note that these factors are achieved while accelerating the benefits of your investment.

Industry Knowledge

SAP tools within the AcceleratedSAP process help you implement R/3 in a timely manner. However, the ability to find the necessary industry knowledge to use these tools effectively for your specific environment is a question that some SAP customers ask. During some of the very early SAP R/3 implementations, it was believed that industry knowledge was something that came from internal project team members' knowledge of their specific industry. This knowledge had to be tempered with both strategic business and industry issues and would effectively describe documented processes that demonstrate your organization's industry requirements and best practices.

Specific elements of the R/3 implementation process are crucial to your success. However, actually applying this industry knowledge often comes from outside professional service organizations that meet your reengineering and business process requirements for R/3 current functionality. They have the ability to personalize the solution to meet your needs. Today, industry knowledge and best practices must be brought together with industry tools to allow consulting organizations to supplement their skills and allow their team and yours to work together toward a common goal.

BEW and Consultants

The most important skills to look for in an implementation provider should reflect three important elements critical to your success:

1. SAP R/3 product and tool expertise
2. Application of SAP R/3 product expertise to your specific reengineering requirements
3. Modification of your management skills.

SAP's BEW alters the information you receive from your consulting agency. BEW accesses and supports one centralized, integrated set of information for your business. This singular set of data concentrates on operating and maintaining your R/3 system. This operation reflects objects, processes, functions, data, configuration, and personalized information that is interconnected and recorded in the R/3 *Repository*. One set of data guarantees data integrity and permits you to utilize several tools, methodologies, and implementation strategies. BEW is very useful when you need to integrate your work with that of your consultant.

BEW is the only SAP R/3 tool that permits you to save changes within the R/3 *Repository* from one version to another. This functionality makes BEW critical for any company that will be depending on SAP R/3 in the future and upgrading the application software and adding new modules as their business grows. Consultants will find that these capabilities make BEW beneficial for customers implementing SAP R/3 in current and future revisions.

BEW Functionality

BEW allows access to *Business Blueprint* models. It offers configure-to-order techniques that use R/3 functionality to meet your specific business requirements. The first stage begins with determining your individual market conditions and business practices. This information is compared to processes in the R/3 *Reference Model* tool, and results in a best-processes output model.

BEW permits you to allot resources so that you can automate domains where SAP is not yet able to provide adequate functionality, as opposed to areas where it can achieve definable results. The majority of executives within your organization will want their implementation to be the starting model that examines your business and works with it as it grows.

Consultants can provide expertise, techniques, templates, and specific tools to enhance your implementation speed and match your business requirements to SAP R/3's functionality. These objectives were created to ensure that SAP R/3 functionality meets your needs. BEW allows both consulting partners and your project team to develop services to match SAP R/3 functionality with your business process requirements in the most time-efficient method possible.

Tool Evaluation

Consultants may feel the need to evaluate their current tools and techniques with respect to the functionality of BEW. Consultants add significant value from applications that involve business, industry, and change management expertise reflected in BEW's R/3 *Repository* access.

As a software organization, SAP promotes using best practices as a jumping-off point for developing efficient core-business strategies. Software development is at the heart of core-competency, while practical business skills should be the responsibility of consultants whose core competency reflects diversity in best business practices.

Business Tool Offerings

BEW offers a graphical view of your business plan and provides the crucial access to the SAP R/3 *Repository*. However, the look and feel is a tool created by technical people for technical people. SAP's implementation partners often act as the interpreter and guide for enterprise management looking to attain business benefits from enigmatic implementation solutions.

BEW is a significant enhancement to the R/3 software. SAP's implementation partners can use this enhancement, translate it from technology to business, and add value for process models that provide their customers accelerated implementations. Linking BEW with your consultant's business expertise and capabilities allows SAP R/3 consultants to implement your system in a shorter time frame.

It is important to note the extent to which your unique enterprise is driven by the industry standards and best practices for its day-to-day business operations. This is illustrated by the ability of your business to maintain exclusive processes that allow you to retain a competitive advantage. R/3 software allows your business to meet its challenges through several industry-focused ASAP tools that help you accelerate your SAP R/3 implementation.

Unique processes can help you acquire a competitive advantage in your market segment. Most organizations acquire a competitive advantage from the majority of their business processes. The most obvious advantage comes from the consistent time business process delivery that benefits your company.

The architecture of your business processes comprise your advantage and preserve your lead in the market. SAP R/3 enterprise software offers you a very effective tool that allows you to enhance your business performance and improve your business processes through utilizing best-practice tools added by implementation partner services. These elements work together to provide industry expertise that offers the capabilities and best practices within SAP R/3 to produce strategic benefits for your organization.

Accelerated Benefits

Accelerated benefits come from the distinct strengths that SAP's implementation partners offer in your implementation. Larger implementation partners supplement SAP's software with a great deal of business knowledge. BEW permits supplementary business skills within significant and additive industry expertise.

In order to achieve the best industry expertise application, along with SAP's BEW, you need to use consulting companies that have individual industry expertise. As a result, they can successfully utilize their expertise in terms of industry frameworks that can initiate an SAP R/3 implementation.

Applying Industry Expertise

In order to add industry expertise to your SAP R/3 implementation, several options allow you the most benefit from AcceleratedSAP, including industry-specific:

1. Expertise
2. Best practices
3. Preconfigured templates
4. Industry Centers of Expertise (ICOEs)

Standard industry expertise is achieved in an SAP R/3 effort via your consultant's experience that is applied to your implementation team. This industry knowledge is a crucial element for creating your SAP R/3 framework of your optimal business practices. Standard industry expertise is the origin of your implementation effort, however, it doesn't have the power to integrate a business framework into your scenario to seize knowledge or reuse learning from former SAP R/3 efforts for other implementations in your specific industry.

Industry best practices are often part of the techniques and competency centers of the various consulting organizations. Best practices are compiled by consulting organizations from their business practices and SAP expertise. These elements are combined to provide a deeper understanding of both current and emerging industry process standards and improvements.

The industry best-practice approach enhances standard industry expertise by linking both the best attained resources that your consulting organization can provide in a given industry segment. You can consult with a competency center to view a demonstration of the association between SAP R/3 capabilities and industry expertise. You can then compare that against specific objectives, goals, and benefits of SAP R/3.

Industry templates build on the idea of industry best practices by providing a foundation for an SAP R/3 implementation. AcceleratedSAP templates are preconfigured SAP R/3 solutions designed specifically for individual industries that provide best practices in standard industry terms for your particular industry.

It is not entirely accurate to say that there is one industry template for everyone—no one size fits all. However, having predefined processes can illustrate core business processes that are often used within your industry. This will provide you with the foundation for a substantial and productive origin. Industry templates can be tweaked to reflect general industry trends, as well as your own individual needs.

Industry Centers of Expertise (ICOEs) are established by SAP as a central point for industry expertise for SAP's implementation partners. ICOEs represent vertical resources and support for increasingly active user groups. ICOEs often illustrate core processes that are integral components of your industry.

ICOEs give you an invaluable resource and can benefit both you as an SAP R/3 customer and your consulting team. This resource tool allows users within ICOEs to continue to increase as SAP approaches vertical alignment of customer support. ICOEs are, however, the first form of assistance for you as a user. They are not meant to be a complete solution.

Templates: Foundation to Functionality

Templates dynamically connect industry foundations to SAP R/3's functionality. SAP and Deloitte & Touche Consulting Group/ICS (ICS) created model-based solutions for SAP R/3 implementations that enhanced the connection between business engineering and SAP's software functionality. While SAP created BEW, ICS created model-driven industry templates that connect to SAP R/3 via third-party tools with the goal of adding the crucial component of industry expertise into today's accelerated implementation.

BEW offered an SAP platform for ICS to build a dynamically integrated business model that would initiate an implementation via the integration of industry expertise. ICS has worked simultaneously to accelerate R/3 implementations. This effort has permitted Deloitte & Touche to develop an initiative that adapts to and improves on SAP's BEW. This led to the ICS consulting product IndustryPrint.

IndustryPrint Defined

IndustryPrint is a Deloitte & Touche Consulting Group/ICS blueprint of industry best practices. This blueprint offers potent lessons from implementations that were saved and utilized for the next one. The blueprint then connects to SAP R/3 via the SAP *Reference Model*. IndustryPrint offers a detailed foundation for an SAP R/3 implementation, as well as for Going Live. Each IndustryPrint depicts the best practices that Deloitte & Touche consultants have designated in a given vertical industry. They take these best practices and then accelerate them so they can produce even more effective implementations.

Each IndustryPrint is composed of a repository of preconfigured solutions that deals with crucial industry issues that often reduce cost and time in your R/3 implementations. The CS issues repository is then linked to the industry models and templates.

IndustryPrint was first given to industries that involve process, consumer-intensive businesses, high technology, and utilities. IndustryPrints is now used for SAP's emerging markets such as aerospace and defense, financial services, automotive, and healthcare.

The IndustryPrint procedure begins with identifying industry issues, and then converting them into very specific business goals that match the individual requirements of a given ICS client. This is achieved through the ICS proprietary methodology designated as FastTrack 4SAP. This method is connected to SAP's *Procedure Model*, which is essentially a planning component of the BEW. FastTrack 4SAP establishes the path for the client's SAP implementation and acts as the blueprint for coordinating continuing efforts.

Industry and process models are connected via the ICS industry foundation that is attached to both the SAP R/3 *Reference Model* and *Business Navigator*. ICS allows you to use a modeling tool called LiveModel for R/3 from IntelliCorp. This tool is designed to assist in accelerating your design stage. IndustryPrints combined with LiveModel is a successful platform for maintaining value-added services.

The *Business Navigator* converts the design requirements into SAP's Implementation Guide so it can begin to build the SAP R/3 foundation. ICS uses a universal portable interface (UPI). UPI is a proprietary tool that permits ICS consultants to create data interfaces and generate interoperability between SAP R/3 and current third-party applications.

IndustryPrint Benefits

IndustryPrint offers you significant benefits as it takes care of the three major factors involved in a successful implementation:

1. Reducing cost
2. Reducing time to Go Live
3. Reducing complexity

Reducing both the cost and time to Go Live are difficulties that are intertwined with your SAP R/3 implementation. Each IndustryPrint offers an initiative for quickly moving toward productive work. You can acquire a realistic model where you can resolve design issues with respect to your needs and wants verses your objectives and goals. You can obtain benefits with this model that permit your project team to concentrate their resources on the business processes that compare and those that don't.

This working model is also beneficial in that it can recall the modifications executed by the team. It can then convert these modifications to SAP R/3 via tools that access the SAP R/3 *Repository*, as well as the BEW. This functionality permits the implementation team to greatly lessen the amount of time spent on both creation and reconfiguration by reducing exhausting table-setting work.

Reducing complexity is an elementary problem also handled by IndustryPrints. The degree of difficulty usually increases when teams with good intentions attempt to handle a business solution with business managers who employ technology terms. IndustryPrint offers a superior method for attaining a common form of communication for complex problems. IndustryPrint development teams authoritatively work to meet customer concerns, so that clients achieve the "right" answers based on a common, usable form of communication.

An added benefit involves the development of a centralized data repository. ICS consultants have the ability to provide a "living document" that contains object-oriented links. This allows you to have one more point of control within your own business implementation, and indicates that speed does not necessarily have to degrade quality.

IndustryPrint: Set Apart

IndustryPrint lays the foundation for industry templates that originate from the best-practices approach of BEW. However, IndustryPrint is set apart from other techniques. Industry templates provide an accelerated origin that enables you to effectively avoid any type of whimsical modeling. You can then start your implementation with the best information possible. ICS IndustryPrint utilizes this benefit and yields a greater connection directly to the SAP R/3 *Reference Model* with BEW.

IndustryPrint supplements and builds on BEW. IndustryPrint's objective is to use models and tools that enhance and increase the BEW's functionality along with ICS consultant business expertise. Instead of accepting the R/3 *Reference Model* as the only application of your business processes, you can use an alternate modeling tool to illustrate your individual business requirements. IndustryPrint is utilized to reduce time, effort, and risk involved in an SAP R/3 implementation in this type of business scenario.

IndustryPrint Obstacles

SAP's BEW and ICS' IndustryPrint enhance the SAP implementation marketplace. There are two main obstacles that ICS must overcome in order to accelerate the benefits of SAP R/3. The first involves how successful ICS' IndustryPrint and BEW are when connected. The test lies in its ability to be an effective SAP R/3 configure-to-order tool. When you don't use BEW as a new R/3 customer, IndustryPrint will turn into just another industry template as opposed to a dynamic industry foundation. IndustryPrint is distinct in that it links with the SAP R/3 *Reference Model*, as well as with ICS consultants having the ability to bring those links to life.

Deloitte & Touche Consulting Group and ICS must have a future offering to create a centralized service that meets growing needs. The IndustryPrint philosophy was created by senior management at ICS and Deloitte & Touche. This cooperative effort permitted each organization to offer specific SAP R/3 skills in the conglomerate. ICS offered very detailed product knowledge, while SAP offered R/3 accelerated implementation expertise. Deloitte & Touche also has a great deal of global management consulting, reengineering, and industry knowledge, which assists your implementation and gives you significant leverage. IndustryPrint is the result of the combined capabilities of both companies.

SAP's BEW helped precipitate the acceptance of AcceleratedSAP implementations by providing an attractive alternative to a crucial service that is executed for the most part by third-party consultants. BEW has the power to meet business process requirements with existing R/3 functionality. It can then quickly determine where customization of the R/3 system is needed. ASAP becomes an even more attractive prospect when you consider the fact that it is enhanced by BEW's ability to maintain modifications to the R/3 *Repository* that varies from version to version. This is an important requirement for enterprises planning a multiyear or multirelease implementation. Many implementation

Figure 3-4
Multilayer Client/
Server.

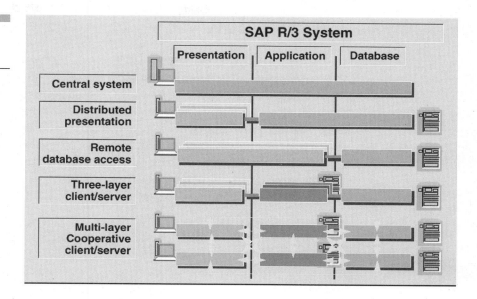

environments are rooted in a multilayer client-server environment, as shown in Fig. 3-4.

BEW also has the ability to automate a certain degree of SAP R/3's design and configuration, which was previously accomplished through standard consulting measures. BEW neither substitutes for SAP's R/3 software nor replaces business expertise, industry, and change management or best practices that third-party consultants offer you.

SAP continues to be the best resource to provide the most efficient R/3 implementation that allows you to actually realize your business benefits in an acceptable time frame.

Deloitte & Touche Consulting Group/ICS is at the cusp of developing more efficient implementation methodologies that utilize the benefits of both ASAP and BEW, along with the business and industry expertise of an international consulting organization. IndustryPrint builds on BEW's functionality with dynamic and automated business processes and then combines industry best-practice models that are connected to BEW.

This depicts formidable teams that lay the foundation for Accelerated-SAP implementation offerings for you as an R/3 customer. Upper management will find that evaluating IndustryPrint with BEW will offer them an efficient enterprise prior to, during, and after their accelerated implementation efforts.

Conclusion

In this chapter, we have dealt with the tools you need to accelerate your R/3 implementation. Some of the tools listed in this chapter include the *Implementation Assistant*, a tool that provides answers and guides you through the *Roadmap* described in Chap. 2. We have taken a step-by-step look at all of the tools that assist your efforts, such as modeling, implementation, continuous improvement, and documentation. These models, combined with customized templates for your business, will efficiently speed your implementation and provide you with a competitive advantage in your business processes.

CHAPTER 4

SAP Project
Team Training

Introduction

One of the most integral parts of your implementation effort is to have your project team totally prepared for the implementation journey that SAP has mapped out for you. One particularly important area is training for services that focus on R/3 products and all associated topics. Once your project team is prepared to handle your implementation, they will then be ready to deal with all of the support issues that will become pertinent once your operation goes live—and with ASAP that time frame has been significantly reduced.

Training Services

SAP publishes Training Services for R/3 at regular intervals, including numerous sets of valuable reference CDs. Information can be obtained easily by system administrators, as well as other people who must know more about R/3. Some of the concepts deal with R/3 implementation, system management, database administration, and migration.

International Demonstration and Education System (IDES)

IDES is a demo of the whole R/3 system. It is initiated by data that is taken from a sample corporation. IDES is sent to customers who request it, but it is an excellent platform that illustrates SAP's R/3.

Workshops has an interactive classroom format that provides a forum for discussions about important topics around the R/3 system. Some of the concepts that are excellent models include OSS, network management, and Going Live. Customer interests are obtained during the registration process, becoming the main element of discussion during the workshop.

Training is the cornerstone of all certification for both customers and partners. SAP offers over 150 courses divided into three distinct areas. These courses deal with R/3 profiles to detailed client-server technology sessions. Some of the other courses deal with the 1000+ preconfigured business processes within the R/3 system that handle cross-functional approaches to R/3 configuration.

AcceleratedSAP in Less Than 6 Months

ASAP is successful because of close teamwork between your staff and SAP professionals. These professionals are referred to as TeamSAP. This group empowers you with a global network of SAP expertise in combination with Partner Expertise to achieve the most potent R/3 implementation.

SAP has received some very positive feedback from their initial ASAP implementations. Specifically, Cultor Food Science Inc., and Intersolv Inc., were two companies that had successfully gone live in less than 6 months, and they were on time and on budget. These real-life examples illustrate that the ASAP techniques and applications can generate a rapid return on customer investment. AcceleratedSAP ties together reliable accelerators that integrate tools, templates, and best-implementation techniques that experienced R/3 consultants have found to simplify and refine an R/3 implementation. SAP is striving to provide more efficient R/3 implementations. As a result, TeamSAP ties together the expertise of SAP and those of its partners in the best of implementation practices for each R/3 customer.

TeamSAP is composed of about 3000 consultants and about 20,000 partner consultants. Interaction takes place prior to purchasing your R/3 solution during the period when SAP consultants designate specific experts from a pool of TeamSAP resources. TeamSAP develops the most effective implementation team to meet your individual requirements. You are guided through the entire process that deals with your implementation from the origin through the support of your live implementation. Both SAP's consultant team and your own works as a tightly coupled entity with members who have the ability to evaluate, create, and install the best solutions for your specific business operations.

ASAP proved its success with Cultor Food Science and Intersolv, two of the first SAP customers to Go Live while adhering to a tightly coupled cost- and time-savings schedule realized through the combined power of AcceleratedSAP and TeamSAP. This type of teamwork is common among SAP consultants who work with numerous partners. They are able to make important decisions to achieve powerful business solutions for each customer. These facts were examined and used to obtain quick and well-planned solutions. AcceleratedSAP is accredited by SAP's partner organizations that finish AcceleratedSAP training. This project team training helps you utilize this industry standard for SAP implementations. SAP is dedicated to accelerating R/3 implementations and giving you the power to achieve a faster, more significant return on your information investment.

ASAP Results

The industry as a whole is impressed with AcceleratedSAP implementation techniques. These techniques allow faster implementations and have made R/3 a favorable option to incorporate in a variety of industry-specific organizations. This is readily seen with Hewlett-Packard Rapid/3 accelerated implementation approach for R/3. As a result, AcceleratedSAP may allow Hewlett-Packard to implement R/3 with greater speed, resulting in a higher-quality end product at a reduced cost.

AcceleratedSAP is constantly growing in terms of its ability to disprove the common perception that R/3 takes too long to implement. Intersolv was in need of a quickly implemented solution to manage their various transactions involved in serving the needs of their installed base of more than 25,000 customer sites. The AcceleratedSAP implementation program enabled them to Go Live with R/3's financial accounting, controlling, assets management, production planning, and sales/distribution modules in only 5 months.

Their Windows NT-based platform works well with SAP's direct consulting expertise to yield a cost-effective pathway to quickly implementing R/3 to support their continued growth.

The AcceleratedSAP program is a crucial element for any IT organization that deals with the important business requirements of transferring your systems from your old parent company's IT system in just a 6-month implementation. The goal is to completely restructure your international business operations and implement R/3 throughout your operating stations worldwide through the AcceleratedSAP program.

The AcceleratedSAP philosophy and accelerators are elemental to ASAP's flexibility. SAP consultants utilize techniques and tools to satisfy your individual implementation needs along with your specific business needs and internal resources. The technique gives you several choices for proven accelerators that SAP has observed during your implementation process to enable your rapid implementation.

TeamSAP works together with you to determine the specific accelerators that are proper for your R/3 implementation. This allows you to utilize as much or as little as you want. TeamSAP can adapt your R/3 implementation to individual business, industry, and timing requirements.

AcceleratedSAP implementations start with SAP's customer-centric *Estimator Kit*. This kit allows TeamSAP to work with customers early on, and allows you to appraise their business functions as well as the appropriate consulting expertise and implementation needs. The goal is to produce a detailed evaluation of your overall implementation cost, effort, and time. TeamSAP begins implementation when your process requirements are completed using ASAP techniques and accelerators that involve tools, templates, consecutive checkpoints, and best practices created after use by many of SAP's customers.

Crucial to all quick implementations is the AcceleratedSAP *Roadmap* created to improve the proficiency of implementations via a flow of five stages, detailed in Chap. 2, that take you from the initial project preparation to finally Going Live with your rapid R/3 implementation. There are also several other important implementation tools that involve the *Business Engineer* and with its business-process reference models and configuration guide that acts as a level of support for your initial implementation configuration and the processes of continuous business engineering.

Partner Training

AcceleratedSAP Partner Training SAP offers an AcceleratedSAP training program for partners who advocate rapid R/3 implementations and who have a standard rapid R/3 implementation philosophy. This training program is used by smaller regional partners, as well as larger implementation partner organizations who have completed ASAP training classes. Partner consultants trained by AcceleratedSAP instructors are able to produce an effective, rapid implementation practice for your specific needs. SAP provides many ASAP training classes that promote the accelerated program and allow for training to allow customers to achieve faster results based on their SAP-acquired expertise.

The SAP Professional Services Group is a professional team of consultants who achieve an effective, accelerated deployment of SAP software.

SAP's Professional Services Group works with and promotes its partners as important elements to achieve successful implementations. Professional Services consultants also provide application consulting and project management to guarantee their efforts.

SAP has a sizable presence in the client-server enterprise application software because they provide total solutions for organizations regardless of size or industry sector. SAP is developing new technologies and ways to implement them quickly and effectively. That implementation experience is built on a solid foundation of business experience that allows them to accelerate the process with their ASAP program. ASAP allows SAP to offer scalable solutions to improve your business based on the best business practices they offer on a continuing basis. SAP products allow users to respond quickly and precisely to fluctuating market conditions in an effort to help your business attain its competitive industry advantage.

Easier Integration

SAP offers plans to provide a more effective supply chain management to all of its R/3 customers. This supply chain is called SCOPE (supply chain optimization, planning, and execution). This technique incorporates supply-chain planning interfaces that permit third-party interoperability with the R/3 enterprise software.

SCOPE is SAP's *Advanced Planner Optimizer* (APO), a tool that integrates planning, optimization, decisions, and execution capabilities. APO also examines product and resource accessibility and allocation and then automates planning, scheduling, and forecasting.

SCOPE incorporates collaborative forecasting, vendor managing inventory, and live cache capabilities. Specifically, the live cache capabilities allows you to process large volumes of information at a rapid pace that was not possible in previous applications of this technology.

Making It Happen

This technology can assist your ERP solution through constant, dedicated teamwork. One of the methods in which this is accomplished is through TeamSAP, which allows you to increase the speed of your efforts and makes your R/3 implementation easier through superior logistics, processes, and people.

The *Business Framework* is the means by which SAP provides its solid R/3 system to vertical markets in individual prepackaged sets. There are six distinct components to this SAP offering, including:

1. *Consolidation module.* Collects data from all areas of the R/3 system to optimize group reporting.

2. *Self-audit.* Incorporates auditing functions and default configurations including auditing procedures.

3. *Joint venture accounting.* Permits numerous organizations to combine money and human resources for projects that are at high risk, including large capital investment and long payback periods.

4. *Investment control.* Handles corporate consent of the capital investment process.

5. *Treasury.* Supports money-market funds, securities, and loans.

6. *Sales configuration engine.* Allows users to plan sales proposals and reuse master data in R/3 so that product models can be used offline by your organization's sales division.

Public Sector Solutions

This can best be illustrated by SAP's Public Sector Solution that supports the needs of governments, universities, and nonprofit organizations.

The SAP Public Sector is an enterprisewide solution based on the R/3 business application software. In order to assist U.S. public sector customers, SAP has a subsidiary called SAP America Public Sector Inc. This division balances SAP's global public sector expertise and offers planning, administrative, and information management solutions for government, education, and nonprofit organizations in the United States. SAP industry experts will team up with customers and partners to offer dedicated consulting, implementation, and training services for public sector customers. The development of this organization empowers SAP to take a commanding role in offering government and public sector solutions.

There are more than 300 public sector institutions in Europe, Latin America, the Asia-Pacific region, Australia, and Canada that utilize SAP software. SAP has implemented its solution at several important public sector customer sites. The R/3 solution assists public sector organizations. The SAP Public Sector Solution relies heavily on SAP's industry expertise and the technology that permits public sector organizations to take advantage of highly integrated working relationships and have the power to make more informed decisions. This organization allows SAP to devote a great deal of its resources to support customers and increase their presence within the public sector market.

SAP America Public Sector

SAP America Public Sector Inc., supports federal, state, and local governments; public authorities; and educational and nonprofit organizations. These organizations want a rigorous environment that allows them to grow since they must meet an increasing demand for social services as they manage the shortage of personnel and financial resources. In order to support these various and difficult needs, public sector managers and management must utilize the services and support available from SAP America Public Sector Inc.

SAP Public Sector functions under SAP America to meets the requirements of the U.S. public sector market. SAP America Public Sector Inc., incorporates the proper groundwork for public sector sales, presales, contract management, and proposal management functions.

Refining Processes

Enhancing both the workflow and productivity of government, educational, and nonprofit organizations is a necessary step in determining how to change outdated processes that no longer satisfy the needs of today's evolving society. In order to achieve this goal, several public sector organizations are trying to determine the best business practices available to them that have proven successful for the private sector. SAP Public Sector modifies these best business practices to assist public sector organizations in creating much more effective long-term planning and updating programs that allow them to more rapidly achieve their goals and satisfy their needs and wants.

Just as in the private sector, public sector organizations require both planning and control tools that use stable, secure information management environments. However, the most important ingredient is flexibility to satisfy changing requirements in missions, priorities, organizational structures, and business practices.

Year 2000 Problem

Many organizations are struggling with their year 2000 compliance issue. It is often difficult to divert the efforts normally reserved for your regular projects to the year 2000 problem. Implementing an ERP solution can drain your resources significantly, therefore, it is imperative that you deal with this problem through the most expedient means possible. SAP offers year 2000-compliant software, but the real trick is to make certain your systems can handle the four-digit data it produces. In order to become year 2000 compliant, you need to start thinking in terms of four digits. Every date computation that you input into your computer system, and every date within your existing computer records, must be translated from two to four digits in order for you to truly become year 2000 compliant. Unfortunately, the only option for coping with the year 2000 problem is a full migration of all of your computer systems to this new standard.

In an effort to solve your own year 2000 problem, you need to make real-time information accessible so that your R/3 system will provide you with the tools you need to support new methods of performing business processes and distributing information throughout your organization.

There is a robust solution that produces results for public sector organizations regardless of size. The SAP Public Sector Solution will specifically meet the varied functional and technological R/3 needs required by public sector organizations. In addition to more than 1000 standard business processes inside the R/3 integrated system, the SAP Public Sector Solution offers industry-specific enhancements, expertise, dedicated consulting, implementation, and project training services for public sector customers.

R/3 has permitted organizations to leverage their need for service against their staff's ability to use and distribute the information they need to provide service. R/3 has provided a common database warehouse for the purpose of integrating your information decision-making processes. The need for less manual intervention in daily inventory, purchasing, and financial processes allows workers to spend less time managing data and unimportant duties and more time in providing direct services.

These programs are designed to reduce implementation time and cost for Public Sector users. SAP is assisting in the reduction of public sector implementation times and costs with programs like TeamSAP. Working with TeamSAP allows public sector organizations to work together with SAP professionals and partners to utilize rapid implementation accelerators for AcceleratedSAP to enable organizations to realize their total SAP Public Sector Solution quickly and effectively.

Using ASAP

Many organizations are currently using the AcceleratedSAP technique to implement various R/3 applications in more than one corporate division (for example, finance departments). Information systems managers are finding the prospect of an R/3 three-tier architecture with the power to simultaneously process online and batch transactions advantageous. Managers can plan for the future and use workflow-driven Internet and Intranet applications.

As an administrator, you would find that you have a significant advantage in accessing and managing your information. You also gain the power to execute business transactions with greater flexibility and control than your larger competition has had.

R/3 functionality in the public sector includes budget management to assist you in planning and controlling income and expenditure flows by managing budget formulation and execution, monitoring funds administration with active funds availability checks, and gaining project or program revenue at any time within the budget cycle. Financial accounting creates the groundwork for business decisions by providing an integrated technique for managing your corporate operations.

Materials management shortens the time and costs that are elemental in purchasing. It employs exact inventory management and warehouse management to reduce procurement and warehousing costs, improve warehouse control, and incorporates settlement processes in budget management. Your procurement cycle and inventory management use R/3 integration to make certain that a business transaction can be entered only once to correctly update all affected fields. An example of external procurement is depicted in Fig. 4-1. Human resources management offers a precise account of planning and management for personnel-related topics, including administration, payroll, automated travel expense accounting, full-time equivalents (FTEs), and available funds. Maintaining control of all links in managerial accounting processes is achieved through advanced planning and controlling mechanisms

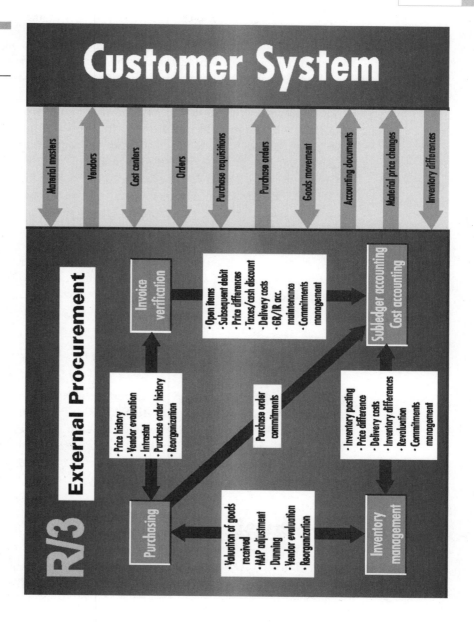

Figure 4-1
External
Procurement.

composed of a methodical cost and activity accounting functionality. In addition, it uses business methods that include activity-based costing (ABC) and project controlling.

Treasury management handles effective cash management in public sector agencies and institutions. It also assists in attaining profitable financial budgeting and liquidity management besides facilitating payment transactions with electronic banking. Capital spending management and project system offers the functionality to track and direct your total process flow by connecting the planning and coordination of investments to bring your projects to completion.

Real estate and maintenance management provides the ability to manage real estate and maintain it through the link between commercial and technical applications. One of the points stressed in the previous section was that year 2000 compliance is an important issue, but it is a feature that has always been standard in R/3 business applications.

The R/3 flexibility of modules permits your company to personalize its software based on best practices so that your system will satisfy your individual corporate needs. Internet and Intranet enablement permits real-time global processing of transactions, including payment requests or fund requests. Business workflow integrates the rules-based consent for both routing and integrated electronic mail system that supports each of the business applications in an open computing environment.

Public Sector Center of Expertise

SAP's Public Sector Center of Expertise (PSCOE) offers the resources and expertise to supplement the SAP Public Sector Solution. PSCOE offers an environment that allows SAP team members to work together with global public sector leaders to establish detailed and innovative ERP solutions quickly and efficiently.

Conclusion

This chapter has discussed SAP's three-level methodology that integrates the training process and gives you the ability to create a training program that fosters faster learning throughout your entire organization. Training strategies for project team training in combination with end-user training assist you in an accelerated R/3 implementation. The goal is to transfer knowledge to your project team so that they can learn through standard training classes as well as onsite training. Furthermore, end users gain knowledge from the project team and put that training into practical use for your ERP solution requirements.

Support and Services

Introduction

Your ability to meet corporate client-server needs is a major factor for an easier implementation. SAP's business software suites reflect the needs of client-server environments and simplify your implementation. SAP has what is called *SAPsalespeople,* a new tool that is part of the Certified Business Solutions program for midsized companies that currently have what is called the *Estimator* tool. This software tool evaluates your business and equipment needs and assists your users in determining the extent of your implementation project. In addition, it also starts the *Implementation Assistant,* a program created to guide customers through a six-step planning process.

SAP is targeting midsized companies with its Certified Business Solutions program which involves new front-end planning for R/3 implementations. *SAPsalespeople* functions under AcceleratedSAP projects that benefit new accounts at midsized companies who are equipped with the *Estimator* tool. This new tool allows SAP to evaluate a business and its equipment needs. It also provides you with a realistic estimate of your project's cost, time, and energy.

The *Implementation Assistant* tool reviews the six phases of the project, including the following:

1. Project preparation
2. *Business Blueprint*
3. Simulation
4. Project validation
5. Final preparation
6. Going live and future support of your project

Each of these aspects is very closely controlled and configured with SAP's *BusinessEngineer* configuration tool, as shown in Fig. 5-1.

Achieving a Smooth Implementation

Many midsized businesses have not considered SAP's R/3 a feasible alternative. The common perception was that it was far too expensive and difficult to implement. However, SAP's rapid implementation pro-

Figure 5-1
BusinessEngineer.

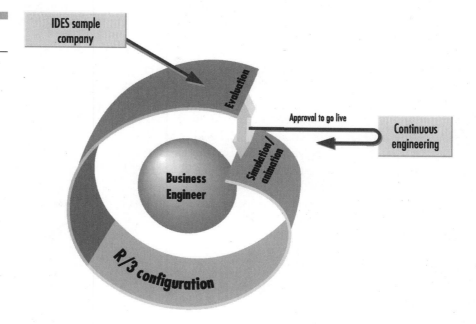

gram, AcceleratedSAP, is designed to bring customers live with the R/3 ERP suite often in less than 6 months without a great deal of business process engineering or external consultants.

For midsized businesses R/3 is often considered somewhat negatively because it is commonly associated with lengthy, expensive implementations. SAP has been known to command the higher end of the market. However, it has yet to get a commanding lead with respect to midsized ERP solutions.

Midsized companies are a prime focus for ASAP programs, as SAP can be viewed in an entirely new light in terms of both software and consulting. It is the essential one-stop shop for all solutions. The ASAP program creates tools, templates, implementation methodologies, and a professional team of SAP consultants for any organization that wishes to implement R/3 without reengineering in a very short time frame. SAP is highly focused on furnishing a high-level of customer success because they wish to be involved with every implementation.

While SAP doesn't wish to compete with smaller consulting partners, they offer ASAP training in combination with them instead. ASAP represents a new avenue of opportunity for SAP that allows them to become involved in an entirely new market segment. Not only are they known for developing large-scale corporate R/3 implementations, but they also have the power to get involved with small- and midsized companies as well.

The ASAP program is a clear, definite movement in the direction of addressing midsized organizations. The only drawback is that SAP still doesn't have APIs that would interface in the third-party market arena. The end result is to permit customers to more easily alter business policies and customize applications.

SAP's goal is to be able to have APIs as open as anyone else's. SAP has also published specifications for nearly 100 business application programming interfaces available at their Web site on the Internet. It is important to point out that the BAPIs are Microsoft COM/DCOM-compliant and support OMG standards. In addition, additional BAPIs are being produced.

R/3 Service and Support

The R/3 system will give you an excellent return on your information investment. However, it is important that your R/3 system be configured to your specific organization's needs to run correctly. This serves to maintain your cost level at a reduced level. In order to achieve your accelerated implementation objectives, SAP's R/3 service and support provide you with a necessary level of assistance that incorporates:

1. Check and monitoring services
2. Consulting
3. Training
4. Active information management.

The basic features required involve a global SAP service and support structure that provides you with international help 24 hours per day, 7 days a week. In addition, you need remote and local services specifically designed for your individual needs during the life of your R/3 system. R/3 system adjustment and expertise transfer are improved by utilizing services provided by SAP's partners. Finally, an Online Service System (OSS) provides both fast and effective solutions for R/3 problems via direct online access to SAP and its partners.

Service and support are the basis for providing you with qualified assistance that allows you to invest in the ongoing growth of SAP's global service and support infrastructure. In order to satisfy all of your requirements, SAP uses your feedback and incorporates it into their research and development optimization process.

R/3 support is available as part of your R/3 license and ensures that you acquire all future R/3 software upgrades. R/3 support includes R/3 system maintenance. Maintenance deals with the correction of defects, access to an Online Service System, and R/3 product information. R/3 service involves add-on services that allow you to support the R/3 system during important implementation stages and to enhance its use. These services are tightly coupled with all of the R/3 project stages. These stages are specifically designed to satisfy your corporate needs to ensure that you have an optimized R/3 system for your company. SAP's purpose in R/3 service and support is to provide key elements that yield both service and support for your R/3 implementation.

R/3 service and support allows you to access SAP R/3 service and support at any location where SAP R/3 systems are being used. SAP's global organization, as well as the ongoing integration of their partners, makes certain that they achieve global availability. When your customer's messages are sent through OSS, they are initially processed by your SAP subsidiary. These messages are transmitted to the SAP Regional Support Center or to SAP's corporate headquarters.

SAP's R/3 service and support is rooted in different requirements you will have throughout the product life cycle as shown in Fig. 5-2. During each stage of your R/3 project, you can access services and support at any given time. The primary objective is to make certain that your R/3 system works at its best, hence the reason why preventative maintenance is often the best cure. Active information management is an important aspect that is pertinent to both your needs and those of your project partners. This information is accessible and updated often via online sources, including the World Wide Web. SAP institutes the modern technology and disseminates information at various levels for different target groups.

SAP considers the quality of our service to be crucial, and, as a result, places a great deal of importance in the developmental efforts and knowledge expertise of our employees and partners. In order to make certain that a continuous high level of service and support is available, performance is checked regularly, updated, and certified. SAP's quality management system is certified at meeting the international ISO 9001 standards that deal with product development, consulting, and R/3 service and support. SAP R/3 offers service and support that features real business-world expectations and requirements tempered with several years of experience with the production of R/3 in several customer projects.

Figure 5-2
R/3 Service and Support in the Product Life Cycle.

Installation	Implementation	GoingLive	Production
Check & Monitoring Services			
SAP R/3 Concept Review	SAP R/3 Concept Review	SAP GoingLive Check	SAP EarlyWatch
Training Services			
Training Workshops	Training Workshops	Training Workshops	Training Workshops
R/3 Knowledge Products	R/3 Knowledge Products	R/3 Knowlege Products	R/3 Knowledge Products
Consulting Services			
On-Site Consulting	On-Site Consulting	On-Site Consulting	Special Conversion
Remote Consulting	Remote Consulting	Remote Consulting	Remote Consulting

Services

Support

HelpDesk, Regional Support Center, Online Service System, Online Correction Support, Development Enhancements, Information Management

At times, unexpected system events can be avoided through project experience. OSS yields information on how to prevent R/3 system errors. This is found by checking and monitoring services to determine possible problems in your individual R/3 installation. SAP works to provide you with system optimization recommendations. Service and support are designed to enable you to satisfy your individual needs because all customers' needs are not the same. This permits you to link the standard support you receive with R/3, as well as with several individualized services. This detailed service offering allows you to choose the service you require, at the time you need it, and at the level you need. You use only the R/3 services that you actually need in each R/3 life-cycle stage, and the specific services are implemented as required.

Quality of Service

Your R/3 services, by either SAP or its partners, are checked and enhanced periodically to make certain you receive high-quality service. These services are certified to the quality standards of ISO 9001. There are also certification programs that SAP offers for its partners and consultants. Conditions can be predesigned to meet certification with customers. Your specific needs for service quality are crucial in the determination of your quality standards of service. You—and your organizational business processes—are the cornerstone of your R/3 service and support. SAP's objective is to make services available to you at any given time so that you can optimize both the performance and availability of your R/3 system. The foundation of this is our global service and support network that is constantly available.

Service and Support Network

SAP R/3 service and support is available globally, and was created as a service and support network that provides a comparable level of quality to make certain that country-specific requirements are satisfied. Integrated processes and standardized service groundwork create the foundation for satisfying these requirements.

SAP subsidiaries, SAP's Regional Service, Support Centers, SAP Corporate Headquarters, and SAP Partners design the R/3 service and support groundwork. SAP subsidiaries and their associated *Help Desks* are the local contact points for customers. During regular working hours, these *Help Desks* respond to all inquiries that deal with service and support in the language of the individual country. They can then forward these inquiries to the proper local partner or the nearest Regional Support Center when needed. These subsidiaries also provide local services—either remotely or onsite—that include both training and consulting. In addition, they also execute the initial processing of all support inquiries. Most inquiries are input through the Online Service System which provides all the benefits of automatic dispatching.

Global Service and Support

SAP Partners offer add-ons that assist your support scheme with the proper organization of SAP's services for escalation management that runs the gamut of SAP and partner service and support. This service vigorously monitors the processes involved and allows quick response to any inquiries received from subsidiaries. SAP's worldwide service and support organization is composed of: SAP subsidiaries, Regional Service Centers, Regional Support Centers, SAP headquarters (local, regional, and global), and SAP Partners Escalation Management.

Supporting the Product Life Cycle

SAP's R/3 service and support have been configured to the specific stages of the R/3 product life cycle to satisfy the needs of your R/3 system implementation. During the period when the R/3 system is installed at your site, it is examined so that the technical environment satisfies the requirements for an efficiently performing system.

Once the installation stage starts, your system is configured to satisfy your organization's individual needs for daily business processes. During the *GoLive* stage, your system is made ready for productive operation in a total client-server environment. This involves system analyses, at which time your hardware needs and other technical conditions of your installation are examined. When these comprehensive tests are finished, your configured system can *GoLive* and be used in your daily business operations.

R/3 support is provided during all stages of the R/3 project, and it is supplemented by the R/3 services you need for your existing project status.

SAP's experience has indicated that R/3 projects can be optimized by employing specific services at each project stage. In order to provide an integrated solution for all R/3 projects, SAP has linked these services into R/3 Service Packages. The requirement for training courses and consulting services can change drastically for any given project, depending on the company and the characteristics of the R/3 project. These services can be bought at any time to satisfy your needs.

R/3 support deals with several key issues, including:

- SAP *Help Desk*
- Regional Support Centers
- Online Service System (OSS)
- Online changes
- R/3 service uses
- Check and monitoring services
- Training services
- Consulting services

Availability

SAP support provides assistance and information when you are working with the R/3 system. R/3 support provides you with simple-to-use tools for self-service, an advanced messaging and information system, and professional support from the SAP *Help Desk*. R/3 support provides functional improvements and updates to the R/3 system, 24-hours-per-day, 7-days-per-week help with software problems, program version and improvement data, and access to our Online Service System. R/3 support works with all details of R/3 software maintenance.

Your R/3 support software maintenance incorporates R/3 software improvement functionality in addition to ongoing changes in the software to new database and operating system versions. Emphasis is placed on eliminating errors, however, functional enhancements are also created and posted through software maintenance channels.

Correcting System Errors

A crucial element of your R/3 maintenance support is the correction of system errors. SAP offers detailed support from their local *Help Desks*, and Regional Support Centers. There is a second level of customer support which allows you to avert and eliminate problems at any location and at any time.

Your local *Help Desk* is your contact point for all information regarding your R/3 system. Any inquiries you submit are sent to R/3 experts. It doesn't matter whether you use OSS or contact SAP by telephone. It is also possible for you to indicate the seriousness of your problem by designating a priority. Then, SAP professionals respond immediately—if not sooner—as determined by the priority of your problem.

SAP provides support beyond standard working hours. Your questions are sent directly to the next Regional Support Center to make certain you have the ability to receive help all the time.

Online Service System

The Online Service System (OSS) is the foundation for SAP's service and manages customer problems. It is the technological connection between customers, consulting partners, and SAP. It offers access to important information about known problems and assists you in resolving them yourself or with the assistance of the SAP support team. You have free access to OSS wherever you are and at any time.

OSS features elements that help you to avert system difficulties before they occur. Should these problems actually occur in your R/3 system, OSS gives you fast, effective solutions. If you link remotely to the OSS, you have direct access to SAP's Notes database. In this database, you can look for solutions to system problems via a guided keyword search or by inputting an error message.

If you are not able to locate a solution, you can send a message to SAP's support staff. This message is part of an advanced workflow process that then forwards it to the proper system specialist. There is also a "HotNews" capability that highlights the critical news from the Notes database. SAP's Notes database offers solutions for all known system problems.

When you have developed and transmitted a problem message in OSS, the system automatically analyzes your message and then examines the database for notes that tell you how to solve your specific problem in as little time as possible. There are numerous message types within the OSS to assist you with your difficulties.

If you do not know who to contact about your specific problem within SAP, you can rest assured that your message will be sent to one of SAP's Regional Support Centers. If you need Remote Consulting, you can input a consulting request. OSS records data regarding both your company and R/3 system, and that data allows SAP support personnel to respond to your questions more effectively.

When you periodically monitor and maintain the data that deals with your company in the OSS, you can hasten the support processes and achieve the best answers for your needs more quickly and efficiently. It is also important to inform SAP on how your R/3 project is doing, so that you will have the power to mark project events in the OSS. This will assist your service and support staff on particular services that can be employed in your operating environment to improve the functionality of your R/3 project.

There are several important complimentary services that are offered by SAP including:

1. *EarlyWatch*

2. Remote consulting

Each of these services is supported by a remote connection. OSS offers the link between your R/3 system and SAP, which allows you to utilize your complete SAP service provisions.

OSS also allows you to access some very general SAP information. This is a record of all training courses provided by SAP, as well as their availability. There is an initiative to computerize this process more broadly so that you can register for SAP courses via OSS. This would give you the ability to order SAP documentation or brochures via OSS.

Hot Packages

Hot Packages consist of a series of corrections to the R/3 software provided by OSS and SAP Notes. These corrections can be downloaded and imported into your R/3 system through a simple interface. If you introduce errors by entering code manually, the changes can be removed. Any Hot Packages that deal with your maintenance level are integrated into the next maintenance level. Essentially, your system will not have modifications that vary from the standard system. It is important for you to periodically import Hot Packages into your R/3 system.

Conflict Resolution Transports

Conflict Resolution Transports (CRTs) are software patches that resolve conflicts between Hot Packages and any of SAP's industry-specific components. CRTs are also available through the OSS. To have fast, simple support, some of the central OSS functions, including Notes search and inputting customer messages, are available through SAPNet, illustrated in Fig. 5-3. This solution provides the simplicity of an Internet browser and access to multimedia documentation such as screencams that illustrate specific areas of R/3 functionality.

Customer Competence Centers utilize specific OSS functions or group messages to offer first-level support to the R/3 users within their company. OSS Access allows you to use OSS, as well as its functionality, however, you need a remote link to SAP.

Data Security

SAP uses several methods to make certain that data is protected, including protected access through a password system that secures your

Figure 5-3
SAPNet Infrastructure.

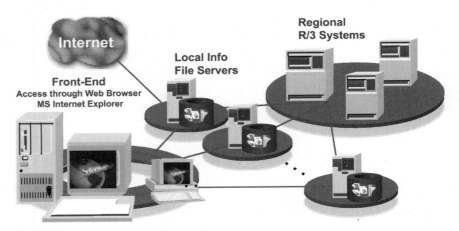

Figure 5-3
SAPNet Infrastructure.

computer accounts. Data transfer occurs only in one direction—from you to SAP. Data cannot be transferred until you open the connection. Therefore, only you can configure the remote connection that allows data to be transferred to SAP for just R/3.

Active information management is an elementary aspect that makes certain you receive quick, constant information as it is posted in online media.

In order to protect your data, you must work toward integration of your R/3 clients, partners, and prospects into SAP's information flow: you must make certain that you obtain regular and reliable upgrades that are pertinent to your corporate needs, you must also have access to information regardless of time or location, you should be able to utilize a graphical user interface (GUI) for simple search and retrieval of information, and you should be able to both store and maintain information in one centralized location so you can avoid redundancy. Finally, you need to have an ongoing review of your information to make certain that it is current.

SAPNet

SAPNet is SAP's online information and communications service that provides a centralized, congruous set of reliable information and communications services. It affords a simple, easy medium for your users on a global scale. It was created for SAP's clients to be a Web-based service created on an R/3 system using the R/3 information database.

Information outlines for the standard public SAP's information offering on the Web provides potential customers with a wide range of information regarding SAP's background, products, services, strategies, and developments.

Some of the information for potential customers must incorporate detailed, current information, presentations, brochures, and demonstrations from all areas of SAP strategy, technology, products, R/3 service, and support that can be read online or downloaded.

SAP provides information on two globally available Web servers both with the same information. These servers are located in Philadelphia, Pennsylvania, and Waldorf, Germany. SAP provides customers and partners with extensive information in addition to that which is available through the public SAP Web Home Page. This data is more detailed since the daily updates make certain that the data is always up to date. Customers and partners have the ability to access the information through the World Wide Web or the Online Service System.

Information Database

In order to satisfy the tasks of modern information transfer, SAP created the R/3 Information Database which acts as a master system for all SAP information objects. It can also be utilized for your own particular company data. SAP information objects are designated as information units (that is, presentations) that can be recalled individually or combined. The R/3 Information Database foundation was created to improve the benefits provided by the R/3 system with respect to its administration of information objects.

The Information Database works with the Internet. Its features include a central source for all information types without redundancy through the storage of individual objects. These objects can be combined as needed to form information units. It also offers global information access through replication along with up-to-date and reliable data through a simple graphical user interface that has definable information views.

The R/3 Information Database is the perfect supplement to an open Internet or Web server that can be totally integrated into corporate Intranets. This permits a level of ongoing access to online information through the Web. In addition, the R/3 Information Database can be used locally to update information onsite through replication.

If you have questions for R/3 support, you can send an information request in the OSS or you can always contact your local SAP Help Desk. R/3 support is part of your agreement with SAP because SAP warrants ongoing software maintenance. R/3 support comes as part of your R/3 system purchase and is complemented by several R/3 services that are divided into the following main divisions:

1. Check and monitoring services
2. Training services
3. Consulting services

Check and monitoring services are achieved through preventative analysis. These services make certain you attain optimal performance for your R/3 system throughout all project phases. These services are:

1. SAP R/3 Concept Review Service
2. SAP *GoingLive* Check
3. SAP *EarlyWatch* Service (shown in Fig. 5-4).

SAP R/3 Concept Review Service is available during the installation and implementation phases of your R/3 project. At this time, there are

Figure 5-4
Excerpts of the *Early-Watch* Service Report.

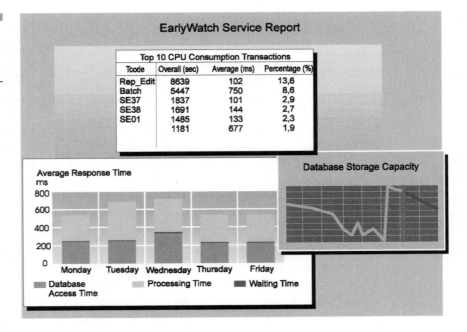

many decisions and settings that must be made that alter the performance, scalability, and administration of your system. The SAP R/3 Concept Review Service's goal is to identify possible problems early in your process and then take the proper steps to avoid them.

The SAP R/3 Concept Review Service has goals that make sure you have optimized use, greater R/3 functionality, minimized risk, and the highest level of cost-effectiveness.

The SAP R/3 Concept Check is a computer tool created as a result of several years of consulting and development experience in various industry-specific sectors. This check should can be executed regularly throughout the installation and implementation process of your R/3 implementation project.

It is beneficial to ask questions at each stage of your project as they occur. Implementing the tool checklists allows you to analyze the project and implementation work yourself or utilize the help of your SAP consultant. This checklist concentrates on project organization, as well as the configuration of the R/3 applications. The checklists are created dynamically so that, as each question is answered, the following questions are successively restricted. In this way, you need only answer questions that are pertinent to your system configuration. This is best illustrated through project organization, system infrastructure, client conception, workbench organizer, file size threshold, and determination of processes that can cause critical bottlenecks and analysis of critical functions.

Once you have completed each checklist, you will receive a report that provides valuable recommendations with respect to optimizing your configuration, as well as important information that enables you to execute stress tests and *EarlyWatch* sessions. This report also provides you with critical data sets and values that indicate when to contact SAP to schedule a review. These recommendations will allow you take advantage of the full potential of your R/3 functionality and, as a result, optimize your business processes. This check will concentrate primarily on performance issues of the specific applications and basic system settings.

Once you have developed all checklists, you can create a global report that provides you with a synopsis of the critical attributes of your core functions.

The checklists of the SAP R/3 Concept Check are constantly being updated. The most recent analysis concentrates on performance-critical factors and parameters that are very hard to modify in the future. The SAP R/3 Concept Check tool is available in English, German, and Japanese.

SAP R/3 Concept Review Service Phases

The first phase involves the *Concept Review*. This is when you can sort important theoretical questions via the upon with your project leader in advance. These questions that are handled in the first step of *Concept Review* are employed to analyze problem areas that are identified by the SAP R/3 Concept Check tool in further detail. This analysis creates the groundwork for solutions that are given to you over the telephone once consultation with the back office, consultants, and developers is complete.

The second step in *Concept Review* deals with your particular corporate needs. The questions handled in this review include those that could not be solved in the first step of *Concept Review*. Your preparatory work deals with recalling the report created using the SAP R/3 *Concept Check* tool, as well as the questions and answers from the first step of *Concept Review*. The third step in *Concept Review* deals with all-day video conferences, as well as onsite consultant calls. During the second step of *Concept Review*, you may formulate an alternative concept quickly or schedule a new consulting project by reworking either parts of or your entire concept.

Whenever you need to deal with the constant modification of your mission-critical applications, you can't afford delays, indecision, or mistakes from poor service. The level of competition from both domestic and international sources can not permit it. SAP service is a crucial element that has fostered a great degree of their client's success. SAP provides high-level customer service and support that most assuredly increases the return on your technology investment. The SAP service and support network integrates the expertise of over 3000 SAP consultants and support personnel with a tightly integrated network of over 20,000 certified partner consultants.

The combination of consultants and their professional expertise is available to satisfy your needs at any given time. SAP R/3 service and support is the end product of experiences from 25 years of giving global business software solutions to multinational corporations. SAP R/3 service and support meets industry-specific requirements all over the world. At the same time, it maintains high-quality standards. There is, and continues to be, extensive efforts to improve service delivery and deliver valuable new services to meet your growing needs.

Expert advice and assistance are key to remote consulting. Remote consulting permits you to obtain expert advice from SAP consultants, while at the same time reducing your unproductive costs by more than one-tenth with respect to onsite consulting that includes travel and expenses.

The SAP *Help Desk* is your first point of access to SAP service and support, including the more than 25 regional *Help Desks. Help Desk* employees have a high degree of product knowledge, as well as a high level of proficiency in their areas of expertise on many specific modules. If a technical problem cannot be resolved by the *Help Desk*, it is sent to the first-level customer support (FLCS). The main objective of the FLCS is to solve customer problems.

Each member of the FLCS is an expert in a specific module for your own needs. If these specialists believe the problem is the result of software flaw, they analyze the problem and send it to the development department responsible for the second-level customer support (SLCS).

SAP consultants answer inquiries on implementation and configuration of the R/3 system that cannot be answered by the SAP consulting staff. These people are available either onsite or through remote consulting. As a result, SAP makes expert service and support advice available to satisfy your needs at any given time.

Conclusion

In this chapter we have discussed SAP's support and service network and how it provides answers to questions that may arise both during your implementation and after you've gone live. These services are designed to assist your implementation and offer you a comprehensive service. In addition, we see the various ways services have assisted other organizations in the past and how they can assist you today in your accelerated implementation efforts.

SAP Consultants

Introduction

Implementations need a certain amount of guidance in order to reach completion. However, with so many consultants entering the market, it is often difficult and sometimes impossible to determine which consultants offer a viable solution and which can hurt your efforts. This is why many medium-sized consulting organizations are working feverishly to register with SAP's consultant certification program.

The Consultant Certification Program

SAP's Consultant Certification Program is part of SAP's current effort to remedy the generally held conception that R/3 implementations are complex and often incur risk and time delays.

AcceleratedSAP reduces the time to implement for organizations in the $200 million to $2.5 billion range by enhancing onsite SAP support and producing a consistent implementation technique that incorporates both cost and schedule estimates. SAP is training consulting partners in this technique and producing a definable certification plan that refines the implementation process to minimize implementation delays.

Efficient and Inexpensive Consulting

TeamSAP is an innovation in consulting that works in combination with ASAP technology transfer. It allows freelance R/3 consultants to charge several hundred dollars each day for their expertise.

SAP utilizes staff at a technical level to remove the implementation burden from the major consulting and accounting firms so that they can focus on the type of change management desired. The end result allows more experts in R/3 who are integrally involved with this project to earn a fair rate for their efforts.

Certified Business Solutions Program

SAP offers a quick implementation solution, called the Certified Business Solutions (CBS) program, for businesses under $200 million. Upper-level management in organizations with revenues under $200 million who need to implement R/3 quickly, cost effectively, and use minimal internal resources turn to SAP's Certified Business Solutions program. This program is designed to satisfy the business needs of these organizations by providing a centralized location for rapid R/3 implementation solutions.

Meeting Challenges

SAP is working toward meeting the goals of smaller companies by creating programs and services designed to quicken the implementation process. The core of that effort rests in AcceleratedSAP. The biggest challenge to satisfy these needs involves implementation time.

SAP's R/3 was designed for larger businesses with high revenues. However, the trend in recent years has favored small- to medium-sized businesses that require the resources of R/3 in order to survive. That need has been tempered by the fact that smaller businesses haven't had the internal resources necessary to manage all of the components of an SAP solution. However, these enterprises often have the same operational and business complexities of their larger counterparts. The problem is that they lack the internal resources to manage several suppliers. This methodology was utilized for R/3 solutions in larger enterprises.

The Certified Business Solutions program provides a low-risk, centralized shopping solution to meet specific enterprise requirements. It provides smaller businesses with SAP solutions expertise that encompass:

- Deployment services
- Hardware procurement
- Project financing
- Dealings with one SAP-certified supplier

Higher Return on Investment

CBS customers are realizing their R/3 solution in a matter of only a few months. However, the benefit demonstrates significant business returns for an investment of less than $1 million. These results are consistent among CBS customers who implement R/3 solutions and experience project costs of only several hundred thousand dollars.

The number of CBS customers is growing significantly in North America, many of which have successfully completed their R/3 deployments.

The CBS program is a rapidly implemented R/3 technology infrastructure deployed by using very little internal resources. The goal is to meet business demands in a timely manner.

The CBS program provides a tightly integrated R/3 solution that can be implemented in only a few months via a centralized, local contact point. CBS is distinct from other SAP implementation options since it was created with the goal of working with businesses with under $200 million in revenue. It provides a total R/3 solution for hardware, software, and services from an SAP-certified local provider. CBS needs only minimal customer involvement throughout the implementation because this program provides the implementation staff.

Providers

The CBS provider involves a certified SAP distributor for businesses with lower revenue. In this program, each provider is the sole CBS program partner in an SAP-specified area. CBS providers are in North America and globally in areas such as Australia.

The majority of CBS providers involve new companies who have a great deal of SAP experience. Several of the techniques involve using companies who have worked for SAP directly as one of their bigger implementation partners for an extended period of time. These companies also receive under $200 million in revenue, therefore, they live on the daily business environment operations of their CBS customers.

There is a congruous interface between the CBS provider and the needed resources that involve an SAP solution. CBS providers utilize various solutions for a typical R/3 deployment, therefore, managers can concentrate on operating their business as opposed to running the information infrastructure implementation.

CBS providers must be knowledgeable in their business environments as it is their business to become experts in the business requirements of smaller enterprises and to satisfy these requirements through tools, techniques, and staff skill sets. These providers must use the correct SAP solution for each customer's operating needs.

The CBS program affords your business the opportunity to utilize SAP solutions that, under normal circumstances, would not be available to you. It provides you with a total level of information infrastructure solutions support.

The CBS program is essentially a partnership for an SAP-enabled business solution. CBS customers and providers recognize the need for a high level of both business and SAP expertise. This requirement is a critical component in the recruiting, training, and staffing strategies for CBS providers. It allows providers to offer CBS customers the right technology infrastructure such as attractive outsourcing options to satisfy specific business and operating requirements. Ernst & Young often acts as a consultant for many accelerated implementations. The outsourcing options they offer are listed in Fig. 6-1.

Recommendations

The CBS program provides a very efficient, rapid, and low-cost SAP solution for smaller enterprises—an option once seen as available only for large businesses. Small organizations will see the CBS program as a method of achieving both enhanced internal efficiency and customer satisfaction based on SAP's integrated processes that only very large organizations are seeing. This program is the best program for smaller enterprise decision makers as they determine they have the same need for advanced management tools that their larger counterparts have had for several years.

Meeting Corporate Client-Server Needs

SAP produces modules and modular versions of their business software suites to satisfy the needs of client-server environments and ease R/3

Figure 6-1
Outsourcing Options
Offered by Ernst &
Young.

Key Differences Between Outsourcing Options

Comparative Benefits	Traditional Outsourcing	E&Y SAP Transformational Outsourcing
Continual application of leading practices.	NO	YES
Continual package-enabled reengineering of business processes.	NO	YES
Continual "mining" of application software functionality to support competitive demands and maximize software maintenance investment.	NO	YES
Continual training of business personnel to maximize their efficiencies.	NO	YES
Continual training of your infrastructure support environment to maximize your IT investment.	NO	YES
Flexible infrastructure support options that support on-site, off-site, local, and remote support options.	NO	YES
Continual "joint venture" options that can support domestic and global operations.	NO	YES

implementation. SAP offers what they call *SAPsalespeople*. This tool is a component of the Integrated Certified Business Solutions software program. It is utilized at midsized companies who use project management solutions, such as SAP's *Estimator* software tool, to evaluate an organization's business and equipment requirements to help users realize what will be involved in their R/3 implementation.

SAP uses these modules and versions to personalize their client-server software for specific corporate needs. SAP's sales and implementation tools make R/3 available to midsized companies. SAP's tools help mid-sized companies work in conjunction with CBS to facilitate more upfront planning for individual R/3 implementations.

SAPsalespeople is part of the AcceleratedSAP project that works with new accounts at midsized companies that have the *Estimator* tool. This tool allows SAP consultants to examine both your business and equipment needs. They can then attempt to give you a reasonable idea of your project's cost in terms of both time and money.

Reducing Implementation Time

SAP is basically a one-product company due to R/3's success and SAP's ability to be first in the UNIX- and Windows-based client-server business operating system environments. R/3 was one of the first well-established products to gain distinction through several large implementations around the world. It is useful to review R/3's system environment (see Fig. 6-2). The only impediment to R/3 was the length of time it took to implement into a company. AcceleratedSAP has the benefit of eliminating the perception of lengthy implementation times by utilizing best practices from past implementations and close attention by SAP consultants.

Figure 6-2
R/3 System Environment.

Most large systems integrators and consulting firms have an R/3 section with many smaller companies. R/3 offers several functionalities, including flexibility and quick integration. R/3 allows your users to set up close-knit automatic links that exist between core financial human resources, manufacturing modules, and customized add-on features. This integration assists many domestic and international companies in the ability to replace several core software products with R/3, with the result that they often don't have to reengineer their businesses around it.

SAP has often experienced difficulty in terms of the complexity of R/3 implementation times. The standard is usually anywhere from 6 months to 1 year to get started, while an all-module corporatewide implementation could take as long as 3 to 4 years. This has been a significant problem for small- to medium-sized companies, a need that fostered the creation of ASAP. This fast implementation version of R/3 is achieved primarily because it is delivered in a preconfigured package to cut down on implementation time.

Another problem involved the fact that R/3 has a highly centralized architecture. This difficulty is going to be alleviated by breaking down R/3 into components, so that its various modules could be installed, maintained, and updated individually. This is a desirable approach but could create concerns among users who are very dedicated to using the platform as is.

Value-Added Services

Finding the right consultant to help you implement SAP R/3 can require that you plan your effort in detail. Implementing SAP's R/3 necessitates outside professional services for both implementation support, as well as installed support. SAP R/3 implementation is a valued professional service that provides support to your growing infrastructure. Implementation support services involve key services such as:

1. Planning

2. Design

3. Implementation

An installed support base incorporates services that are created specifically to maintain or upgrade a live R/3 system within an organization. One of the major reasons why ASAP is a success is the fact that support, combined with a well-defined template, saves a significant amount of time during implementation.

The most value-added services in SAP's R/3 include professional services involving both implementation and support structures such as

1. Utilizing SAP knowledge
2. Integrating process reengineering
3. Instituting organizational modifications
4. Creating SAP R/3 custom applications
5. Complementing IT skills
6. Yielding both training and documentation
7. Upgrading and enhancing SAP's R/3 capabilities
8. Outsourcing SAP R/3 management
9. Auditing SAP R/3 installed performance
10. Initiating project management groups

ASAP Partner Certification

The AcceleratedSAP partner certification program provides consultants to work according to the same standard for rapid R/3 implementations. AcceleratedSAP partner certification programs give you a workable standard for R/3 rapid implementations. AcceleratedSAP Partner and Powered By AcceleratedSAP are elementary components of SAP's Team-SAP program, and it is used specifically to certify consulting firms that have expertise in SAP's AcceleratedSAP implementation technique.

SAP has a growing number of certified AcceleratedSAP partners who have the ability to identify other potential certified partners. These people will help make certain you receive a much quicker and cost-effective implementation with the ultimate goal of getting you a much faster and more significant return on your information investment.

TeamSAP is the meat behind SAP. Its partners and customers construct a team that makes the initial planning cycle through implementation and beyond your growth cycles to provide you with a lasting solution that never goes stale and is as flexible and personalized as day one. Partners are extended members of TeamSAP so long as they are certified in any of SAP's partner certification programs.

TeamSAP was created to produce a highly dedicated project team for your specific needs. The entire point of ASAP is that although you are an individual, you are working from all of the proven methodologies obtained from past experience. You don't want to reinvent procedures and methodologies that have already been done, do you? Even though you are working from preconfigured tasks and templates, you have the benefit of a consultant. No tool or implementation methodology can compete with an independent consultant guiding your company throughout its implementation. This is why you are an individual working with a "real" person who is there for your needs, wants, and objectives.

Consultant partners have previously proven themselves an excellent byproduct of TeamSAP certification programs. This program is indicative of the fact that SAP's partners realize the value of AcceleratedSAP and believe in it as the most productive industry standard for rapid implementations.

Ingredients for Success

AcceleratedSAP puts together experienced consultants and proven accelerators. These accelerators help consultants by incorporating tools and templates to integrate the best practices to ease and refine implementations. ASAP was created for long-term success by giving you a proven, flexible platform that will allow your company to grow in the future and embrace new business strategies while SAP works with you in every capacity.

Companies that are certified as ASAP partners need to have about three-quarters of their consultants trained in the appropriate AcceleratedSAP technique. In addition, they must adhere to SAP's ASAP standards. This certification allows consulting partners to attain immediate credibility in the market.

Any customer can use SAP certified partners with the confidence that he or she will utilize the techniques in AcceleratedSAP with the goal of achieving both consistency and speed to your R/3 implementations. This allows you to make certain you have a successful relationship.

Once you select an implementation partner, your confidence rests in his or her SAP certification as a consulting firm that has successfully satisfied the requirements for quick and cost-effective R/3 installations.

By early 1998, SAP will have more than 50 partner organizations certified as ASAP partners, and they are striving to satisfy the growing demand for more certification classes. SAP's original AcceleratedSAP partner certification efforts concentrate on existing partner programs. The certification process incorporates AcceleratedSAP implementation training classes, management courses, and continuous quality control programs.

The AcceleratedSAP program gives you an implementation foundation and techniques to steadily thrive to meet your implementation needs much faster.

Powered By AcceleratedSAP partners, certified as Powered By AcceleratedSAP, utilizes components of the ASAP methodology together with each consultant's own implementation best practices. This program gives partners a better chance to accelerate enterprisewide efforts and subsidize continuing efforts wherever there is a need for a rapid rollout in a certain area, business unit, or project. This program is especially useful for partners who work with the shortened implementation time required for a crucial year 2000 migrations.

Big Consulting Firms

SAP selected three consulting firms to start its Powered By AcceleratedSAP certification efforts: Ernst & Young, Deloitte & Touche Consulting Group/ICS, and Price Waterhouse LLP. At the present time, there are more than 10 consulting firms dedicated to starting the Powered By AcceleratedSAP certification process.

Certification necessitates that a specific AcceleratedSAP philosophy be part of each consultant's implementation practices. Several additional AcceleratedSAP ideas are optional with respect to each consultant's experience and implementation objectives.

These consulting agencies are excited about being a part of TeamSAP and achieving certification as a Powered By AcceleratedSAP partner. Employing the ASAP philosophy together with Deloitte & Touche's Fast Track program provides customers with the best practices and standards for successful R/3 implementations that are completed on time and within budget. The certification process is an important approach in the enterprise application market that SAP has achieved.

Both AcceleratedSAP and Powered By AcceleratedSAP certification programs are important hurdles in the enterprise application industry's movement toward achieving successful implementations in a standard, timely, and cost-effective manner. This program allows SAP to demonstrate its dedication toward long-term customer success.

Partnering for the Internet

SAP, Sun Microsystems, and Microsoft are key players helping SAP to link its R/3 client-server platform to the Internet. Linking Sun's CTI (computer telephony integration) and Java development language with R/3 Cooperative make it possible to build a variety of industry-specific applications.

R/3 implementations allow customers to order materials from a manufacturer and check the status of orders through the Internet. These applications will connect Java Internet ordering applications with R/3 and yield CTI links to a manufacturer's customer service representatives.

SAP consultants are partnering with Microsoft and standards organizations to create R/3 implementations that are conducive to conducting business over the Internet once you Go Live. One standard involves BAPI (business API) that enhances R/3 Internet capabilities with respect to:

1. Business-to-business
2. Consumer-to-business
3. Corporate intranets

SAP's R/3 Internet capabilities will be built in several Microsoft products such as the Microsoft Internet Information Server, Merchant Server, and Internet Explorer browser. SAP is maintaining an open system so that it is still accessible through other browsers including Netscape Communications Corporation's Navigator.

SAP users are finding a wealth of new opportunities available to them between R/3 and the World Wide Web. R/3 and the Internet represent a future that is far more obtainable with a rapid implementation solution such as ASAP.

R/3's Future

SAP partners with Microsoft, Sun, and others, as previously mentioned, but these partnerships will provide R/3 with new avenues of opportunities and give consultants new ways to implement R/3 business processes.

These business processes are best demonstrated through interactive order entry from Internet product catalogs, real-time order status tracking, electronic commerce for business-to-business transactions, and call center applications that utilize the Internet as a front end.

Conclusion

This chapter has discussed the benefits from SAP's application consultants, remote consultants, and technical consultants. It details how their expertise and experience can directly benefit and speed your implementation. If you are responsible for a multinational business, you can benefit from global support managers who guide you through a multiphased implementation tailor-made for your corporate needs and business processes.

TeamSAP

Introduction

The purpose of the SAP partners program is to increase the speed of your deployment. SAP America Inc., offers partner certification programs to assist customers in increasing the speed of implementation for SAP products. AcceleratedSAP practices partner and Powered By AcceleratedSAP are components of SAP's TeamSAP objectives created specifically to certify national and local consulting firms that have conquered SAP's AcceleratedSAP implementation methodology. TeamSAP's objectives translate into specific deliverables for you, as illustrated in Fig. 7-1.

Figure 7-1
TeamSAP
Deliverables.

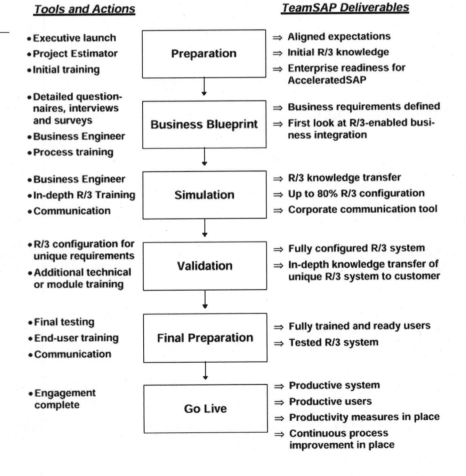

The Six Steps of AcceleratedSAP for R/3

Tools and Actions		_TeamSAP Deliverables_
• Executive launch • Project Estimator • Initial training	**Preparation**	⇒ Aligned expectations ⇒ Initial R/3 knowledge ⇒ Enterprise readiness for AcceleratedSAP
• Detailed questionnaires, interviews and surveys • Business Engineer • Process training	**Business Blueprint**	⇒ Business requirements defined ⇒ First look at R/3-enabled business integration
• Business Engineer • In-depth R/3 Training • Communication	**Simulation**	⇒ R/3 knowledge transfer ⇒ Up to 80% R/3 configuration ⇒ Corporate communication tool
• R/3 configuration for unique requirements • Additional technical or module training	**Validation**	⇒ Fully configured R/3 system ⇒ In-depth knowledge transfer of unique R/3 system to customer
• Final testing • End-user training • Communication	**Final Preparation**	⇒ Fully trained and ready users ⇒ Tested R/3 system
• Engagement complete	**Go Live**	⇒ Productive system ⇒ Productive users ⇒ Productivity measures in place ⇒ Continuous process improvement in place

Teamwork

AcceleratedSAP is SAP's rapid implementation program that combines experienced consultants with SAP's implementation methodology to ease and refine deployment of SAP software. The combination of AcceleratedSAP and TeamSAP are shown in Fig. 7-2. Companies that are certified as an AcceleratedSAP partner need to have more than three-quarters of their consultants complete the appropriate training in AcceleratedSAP and have adopted the AcceleratedSAP technique.

The Powered By AcceleratedSAP program suggests that companies employ specific AcceleratedSAP techniques together with their own best practices. Three companies were selected by SAP to initiate its Powered By AcceleratedSAP certification efforts:

1. Ernst & Young LLP
2. Deloitte & Touche Consulting Group/ICS
3. Price Waterhouse LLP

Customer Success

R/3 customers need to know they will achieve rapid, realizable results from their SAP investment. SAP provides both business and technology

Figure 7-2
AcceleratedSAP and
TeamSAP.

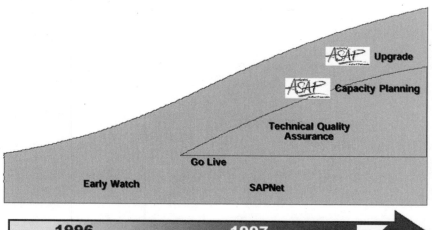

leadership throughout the sales cycle. This expertise is initiated from the start of your project right through implementation and later with continuous business upgrades that make certain the right suppliers are components of the right solution. This effort provides fast results and a substantial return on information investment. One of the primary elements of attaining customer success is to satisfy customer requirements through an extensive team that builds on a distributed management capability supplemented by effective technique, dedicated strategy, expertise, and substantial staff resources.

TeamSAP

TeamSAP signifies both responsibility and dedication to your needs and serves to further instill SAP's definition in its ability to ensure your success. TeamSAP is the linked network of products, processes, and people required to ensure you receive a successful SAP implementation. TeamSAP's components, shown in Fig. 7-3, reflect the tools that fulfill your implementation objectives. TeamSAP provides SAP with an overview of the entire process for the cycle of every customer's usage of R/3 over the long term.

The TeamSAP concept is indicative of a dedication to project management from SAP professional services that offer the means whereby superior expertise is transferred to your organization. It also illustrates an enhanced commitment to expand the R/3 solution set via partnership programs.

Each SAP partner is crucial to achieving success. Every individual plays an important part in your overall R/3 implementation. TeamSAP will make certain you work with an SAP-certified partner who has sufficient resources that are organized and provided as a rational, integrated, total offering. This combination, balancing SAP's experience as well as best practices from several implementations, ties together the exper-

Figure 7-3
TeamSAP Components.

tise that SAP has in the continuous management of R/3 business processes.

Customer Demand

The TeamSAP program has grown due to the customer demand for increased accountability, accelerated benefits, and increased SAP involvement in all areas of the R/3 life cycle. SAP works with small/regional companies to global organizations. However, it is clear that each R/3 implementation is facilitated by a dedicated team who can provide clear, definable perceptions. You know exactly where you stand in your relationship with SAP or your consultant. Your organization's upper management knows that, in selecting SAP or its extended supply-chain management solution, you can have confidence in the expertise offered you for success.

TeamSAP allows SAP to guarantee its customer's success. SAP places a greater involvement in the implementation process by making certain it can obtain real results in a market where the software needs functionality and the power to acquire business results in a reasonably short time frame. The objective is to meet the quickly changing market demands, as well as new technology conditions that illustrate the commitment of SAP's partners. TeamSAP certifies and works with all partners by placing importance on quick business results for customers. Furthermore, every partner certified by SAP has the capability of being a part of TeamSAP.

TeamSAP Programs

TeamSAP programs utilize the *Business Framework* and Accelerated-SAP but produce results with their solutions expertise. Computers can automate many tasks, but you really need a well-oiled team to conduct project coordination, leadership, and cross-customer expertise. Solutions expertise offers both a proficient team and leadership, based on developing the best implementation and producing an ongoing level of business process improvement. TeamSAP utilizes the success of any technology transition to your advantage. They reduce your time to implement and offer an accelerated solution with effective staff training and leadership.

TeamSAP is customer-centric, therefore, it offers you significant benefits that incorporate components to reduce your overall risk while enhancing cost and schedule controls. TeamSAP offers a more detailed business solution whose components can be integrated quickly and easily. Their goal is to provide you with accelerated business results by using new tools and accelerated implementation techniques that focus on component integration and achieving quality assurance. The benefit is through direct SAP contact providing an accelerated R/3 solution.

The goal is to concentrate on customer results through TeamSAP. It is important to note that company growth is fostered by increased reliance on partners and obtaining significant results for your organization.

Fostering Change

You may find yourself in a position where change may offer you a significant operating advantage over your competition. Most organizations are looking for a cost-effective standardized approach with a tailor-made R/3 deployment or upgrade path. Often best practices can take implementations that work and use that knowledge to speed up deployment and offer a more cost-effective solution. The best method of accomplishing a quicker deployment is by using an implementation approach that focuses on business results as opposed to reengineering your organization—a long and costly endeavor. Speed is dependent upon increased participation by SAP, procurement and deployment of R/3, and R/3-specific solution needs.

These needs translate into cost-effective SAP solutions that involve R/3 and supplemental software products that allow you to satisfy your various business requirements. It provides you with a more detailed level of quality assurance for your R/3 *Business Framework* of several SAP and partner-software components. You gain that important element of speed that allows you to reengineer business processes. At the same time, you achieve quick, operational business enhancements from technological investments.

As you begin to realize your implementation goal and changing needs, you will find that TeamSAP assistance is a tremendous asset, allowing you to enhance your supply-chain options as specified by your specific ERP system. These quickly changing business requirements necessitate implementation and ongoing support options that are pliable and can be rapidly deployed. TeamSAP essentially provides the infrastructure you need to support your new functionality.

TeamSAP offers several significant changes in the way in which SAP and its partners work together with its respective customers. These changes emphasize a greater level of attention placed on your implementation by SAP consultants. This reflects the fact that your R/3 implementation provides SAP with the ability to coordinate partners and gain control over the timing elements needed in your business. It permits you to use certification programs available for your partners so that you can employ implementation techniques and best practices into your business. The result is a rather large increase in SAP resources dedicated to knowledge transfer that allows you to enhance the dedication of every TeamSAP member. You profit through better techniques and tools that support accelerated implementations, upgrades, and continuous business modifications, while you improve the level of available supplementary products available to you from certified software and technology partners. This allows you to make certain you achieve a comprehensive solution to meet your specific requirements.

TeamSAP Defined

TeamSAP is the coordinated network of products, processes, and people who are important ingredients in a rapid solution. They provide rapid and cost-effective R/3 solutions together with enhanced solution sets. They employ third-party products and stress quality assurance in their work. TeamSAP provides a higher level of integration, coordination, and certification. These ingredients form crucial elements that offer faster business results for your organization.

Business Framework

The *Business Framework* is SAP's strategic product foundation that supports the inner workings of an implementation. The inner structure involves R/3 business components, integration techniques, and open interfaces that permit R/3 and associated software to work together. Third-party software and hardware products are certified by SAP in this structure. Certification programs for TeamSAP partners are important elements of the *Business Framework* that incorporates joint develop-ment partners, certified interface partners, and technology partners.

AcceleratedSAP Solutions

AcceleratedSAP partners, Powered By AcceleratedSAP, and Certified Business Solutions link techniques, tools, templates, and best practices to refine implementations. SAP service and support tools within the AcceleratedSAP program include SAP *EarlyWatch,* Concept Reviews, *Go Live* Checks, Hot Line and education, and upgrade support. These AcceleratedSAP programs are different from former implementation strategies in that they are the first implementation solutions to be cre-ated and directly supported by SAP. These TeamSAP solutions are com-posed of the services illustrated in Fig. 7-4. They offer an early SAP estimate of resource requirements of time, cost, and customer staff input. These ASAP programs need partners to confide in shared SAP-standard project strategies that yield accelerated solutions that can be used by all implementation partners that satisfy and perpetuate SAP certification standards.

ASAP can standardize R/3 implementations in various businesses, regions, countries, or continents and results in providing the best possi-

Figure 7-4
AcceleratedSAP and TeamSAP Services.

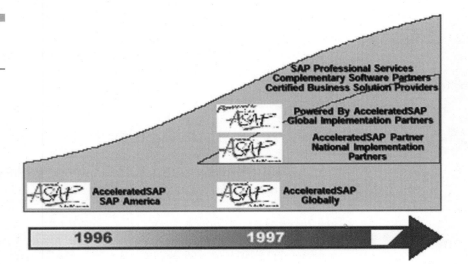

ble foundation to rapidly balance the future of R/3 upgrades with fewer custom software alterations.

SAP remains dedicated to the *Business Engineer,* which is the foundation for business modeling and the R/3 configuration tool that provides a standard AcceleratedSAP methodology founded on best practice process models.

Certification Programs

Quick R/3 implementation certification programs for TeamSAP incorporate items for AcceleratedSAP Partner certification. This certification indicates that the partner will utilize the AcceleratedSAP program with clients, train managers and consultants in the program, and allow an SAP quality assurance team to audit the progress of your project.

Powered By AcceleratedSAP offers a quick implementation certification provided to the biggest implementation partners. International logo partners, listed in Fig. 7-5, permits you to utilize SAP's best practices in AcceleratedSAP and match them to their own offerings. This ensures that you acquire an accelerated methodology. Certified Business Solutions offer programs for R/3 customers whose annual revenues are under $200 million. It yields a bundled R/3 solution that can be rapidly implemented through a local centralized contact point.

Figure 7-5
International Logo
and Implementation
Partners.

International Logo Partners

- **Andersen Consulting**
- **CAP GEMINI**
- **Coopers & Lybrand**
- **CSC Ploenzke**
- **Digital Equipment**
- **EDS**
- **Ernst & Young**

- **Hewlett-Packard / PSO**
- **IBM**
- **ICS Deloitte**
- **KPMG**
- **ORIGIN**
- **Price Waterhouse**
- **SNI**

National Logo Partners

National Implementation Partners

TeamSAP Architecture

AcceleratedSAP programs are growing to support customers' ongoing change efforts as SAP enhances its accelerators throughout an R/3 project life cycle. The root tool for AcceleratedSAP programs is a project guide or what is commonly called the ASAP *Roadmap*, a tool that both partners and customers can adhere to ensuring a standardized, quick R/3 implementation. AcceleratedSAP *Roadmaps* are beneficial when implementing business and technology modifications that regularly occur in operating environments. Such environments may need successive R/3 site deployments, R/3 upgrades, or several simultaneous installations.

TeamSAP uses the *Roadmaps* with its customers to make certain of R/3 consistency and predictability on a continuing basis. Solutions expertise is seen from TeamSAP which ties together the *Business Framework* and AcceleratedSAP programs. These programs are crucial as they integrate the TeamSAP resource that employs them to achieve and maintain rapid, successful SAP results from dedicated professionals interested in your organization. Solutions expertise depicts the combination of specialized experience combined with training that each Team-SAP member furnishes to make certain you succeed.

How Does TeamSAP Work?

You receive the expertise of TeamSAP and can utilize SAP resources as much as you need from TeamSAP. They will provide a great deal of assistance for much broader business objectives. TeamSAP will make certain that customers have SAP certified partner resources offered in a sensible, integrated, and total package.

SAP

SAP is the vehicle for TeamSAP. SAP utilizes account managers to work specifically on your SAP solution. SAP offers services that provide you with a solution, and then coordinates TeamSAP's capabilities for customers via its global support managers, local professional services managers, and account executives.

SAP has made a significant commitment to enhancing its professional services organization and resources to supplant this level of growth. SAP's abilities incorporate Platinum Consulting. This level of consulting is a quickly deployed team made up from SAP's most experienced applications consultants and troubleshooters. *EarlyWatch* offers a proactive system diagnostics program that identifies and resolves potential difficulties early in your implementation to make certain you receive the best level of system availability and performance. In addition, SAPNet is the online competency center established to facilitate these services along with partner and customer knowledge transfer.

The direction in which SAP is moving is for TeamSAP to provide service to customers and gain a comprehensive level of TeamSAP resources that permit fast technology upgrades or change-outs to access enhanced functionality together with existing SAP systems.

Partner Expertise

Implementation partners offer a great deal of solutions expertise and techniques to TeamSAP for your benefit. These people bring your implementation project to realization and utilize SAP benefits to your advantage. In addition, TeamSAP takes a supportive position with SAP in the capacity of the project facilitator.

TeamSAP implementation partners involve Global Logo Partners—global service providers that have a great deal of R/3 experience to add to your enterprise's implementation. Global Logo Partners now also have the power to provide SAP-certified AcceleratedSAP and Powered By AcceleratedSAP to you. There are also national partners for R/3 national implementation partners. These people are certified as AcceleratedSAP partners and offer a variety of solutions expertise in specific industries in addition to certified AcceleratedSAP techniques.

Certified Business Solutions (CBS) Partners were established for businesses with less than $200 million in revenue. The CBS program certifies a partner as a value-added reseller (VAR) and can provide a comprehensive SAP solution, most notably in the area of accelerated implementations with ASAP, illustrated in Fig. 7-6. They provide services to smaller business operations with a limited amount of resources.

Besides supplementing the resources required to support the increasing R/3 market, these implementation partners provide a great deal of value to both you as a customer and TeamSAP through an

Figure 7-6
Accelerated Implementations.

ongoing level of both business and industry expertise. Implementation partners have the ability to adequately manage business transformation and transfer that learning to TeamSAP enabled through rapid implementation technology.

Supplementary Solutions

SAP has increased its available resources in an effort to support AcceleratedSAP and, as a result, offers certification for a larger number of supplementary solutions. There are two types of complementary software partners:

1. *Joint development partner.* These partners have entered into a contract for a specific area of work that reflect research from both SAP and the partner. This effort is initiated to integrate third-party products with R/3's functionality.

2. *Certified interface partner.* This type of certification illustrates SAP's confirmation that the partner's software works cooperatively with a particular version of R/3 via a certified interface. It also operates on identifiable customer requirements.

SAP has significantly increased the availability of its support resources and education services for all complementary software program (CSP) partners. CSP certification also lets you know that the CSP partner will have access to SAP resources on an ongoing basis to sustain the integration specifications that satisfy your requirements.

SAP's technology and hardware partners have a great deal of experience in mutual certification and coordination with SAP's services. Certification is linked to a particular R/3, RDBMS, OS, and hardware release combinations. As these programs don't change, technology partners provide the foundation that makes them important components of TeamSAP.

In order for the TeamSAP program to be successful, a definite strategy is needed which specifies the level of SAP involvement that would involve increased participation. SAP must offer a standard direction to its partners in terms of early involvement of SAP professional services account managers in every phase of a project. This involvement must also illustrate how account managers work with and supplement partner efforts efficiently and without extraneous efforts.

Global logo partners must overcome difficulties with the way in which SAP's standards and controls integrate into TeamSAP because it may be an obstacle to their own successful business models. However, the basic factors of AcceleratedSAP indicate rapid results, continuous improvement, and resource integration. All of these elements combine to meet the requirements of the majority of experienced managers within global partners who are dedicated to the success of your businesses. These partners are part of various aspects of your business operations. In addition, these partners will see your resources available through TeamSAP as a method of continuing to make certain that you achieve success on your ERP projects in a timely manner.

TeamSAP Coordination

TeamSAP has significantly fostered advancement in speeding your R/3 implementation. It was established to meet the specific vendor coordination requirements, technology integration, cost, and scheduling controls for implementations. The majority of implementation phases are available to customers and partners; however, SAP's commitment to coordinating your strategy and making your implementation proceed smoothly, cost effectively, and quickly allows you to get someone interested in your business activities.

TeamSAP also provides the means for SAP to create a nurturing environment that utilizes the knowledge they achieved from early R/3 implementations in an effort to create a strategy that provides more predictable results. SAP shares its technological framework and expertise with its partner and customer network to facilitate your efforts. SAP provides you with more detailed information by achieving your project objectives of reducing cost, time, and the level of your reengineering.

The creation of TeamSAP illustrates a significant movement with regard to how companies deal with business changes fostered by enterprise technologies. The idea of reengineering is now being replaced by smaller business changes permitted by rapid technology improvements. The ideals of TeamSAP maintain this philosophy of business change as a continuous level of improvement. This should offer significant customer benefits looking for quick and continuous R/3 results in a shorter time frame.

TeamSAP Challenges

As an R/3 customer, you need to know you can get quick, substantial results from your SAP investment. SAP will provide you with business and technology administration support, including your initial sales and project implementation. As you proceed with your implementation, TeamSAP must satisfy your business challenges. They must ensure that you deal with the best suppliers to achieve quick results and a decent return on your information investment. Satisfying your requirements involves a great deal of team building in combination with a distributed management capability. These factors must be supplemented by effective techniques, an efficient strategy for knowledge transfer, and staff expertise and resources.

Commitment

SAP is dedicated to TeamSAP, as this program defines both the responsibility and pledge that you need to define SAP's place in making certain you succeed. TeamSAP is a logistics framework for a network of products, processes, and people needed in order to make certain your R/3 implementation proceeds as soon as possible. TeamSAP treats SAP as the guidance counselor and acts with you full-circle from implementation until after your project is completed.

Teamwork Growth

TeamSAP acts as the conduit through which SAP facilitates the implementation process by working to make certain you receive results in your software functionality and gain the ability to quickly achieve desired business results. This corresponds to quickly changing needs as new technology requirements make SAP's partner contributions an even more important asset to speeding your implementation.

TeamSAP certifies and works with all partners to stress the fact that achieving fast business results for customers is essential and that every partner certified by SAP is a critical component of the TeamSAP program.

The growth of the TeamSAP program results in a significant customer demand for enhanced accountability, accelerated results, and increased SAP involvement in all areas of each customer's R/3 implementation. SAP's customers and prospects are mainly seen from both small, regional companies as well as multinational organizations. You will become increasingly practical with respect to the results you expect to see from a working relationship between SAP and its partners. Selecting SAP and an associated extended supply-chain management solution is a major business decision, and each requires that you receive immediate knowledge transfer to make certain your project is successful.

TeamSAP takes two SAP programs further. The first is SAP's *Business Framework* which links crucial components and solution expertise to the rapid results achieved from AcceleratedSAP to make certain you leverage project coordination, leadership, and direct knowledge-sharing. Solutions expertise offers both people and guidance from all stages—presales, implementation—through the ongoing business improvement process. TeamSAP understands that the success of your transition is a direct result of dedicated people who are well trained and effectively led. All of these elements work because they show a personal interest in you and your business processes.

The concurrent network of products, processes, and people from SAP and partners produces fast, integrated, and guaranteed solutions in a short time frame. TeamSAP concentrates on you, the customer, but the most important benefits you receive are reduced risk via improved cost and schedule control, a more detailed business solution through integrated components, accelerated business results as a result of using new tools and accelerated implementation techniques, ongoing dedication to component integration, quality assurance, and direct access to SAP for guidance to achieve the most productive R/3 solution.

SAP is increasingly concentrating on customer results that result from TeamSAP. This move is helping customers realize the benefits of an accelerated solution. It demonstrates that SAP is growing and can offer an even higher level of mutually beneficial relationship with partners. This relationship helps you acquire real results.

As you receive the benefits of TeamSAP, you can choose to use as much of the TeamSAP services as you feel you need for your larger business goal. TeamSAP makes certain that you have SAP-certified partner resources organized and provided in a logical, integrated, and complete package.

SAP guides TeamSAP either directly or indirectly. SAP account managers play a significant role in every aspect of your SAP solution. The SAP professional services organization will instruct, coordinate, and leverage the scope of TeamSAP functionality for customers via its global support managers, local professional services managers, and account executives.

SAP demonstrates its dedication to the growth of its professional services organization and resources to support an expanding role in your accelerated implementation. They offer the resources to incorporate services such as Platinum Consulting. This type of consulting can be quickly deployed by one person or by a team. These people utilize SAP's most experienced applications, consultants, and troubleshooters to achieve this task.

EarlyWatch offers a proactive system diagnostics program that identifies and solves possible problems early in your implementation process. This allows you to make certain you receive the best possible system availability and performance. SAPNet is another critical component that helps you with an online competency center created to promote SAP, partner, and direct knowledge transfer.

TeamSAP's short-term direction will provide you with a technology crew who can yield a full complement of TeamSAP resources that allow you to receive rapid technology upgrades or change-outs. This allows you to access new functionality with existing SAP systems.

Implementation partners offer you an enhanced level of solutions expertise and techniques. This information can be used by TeamSAP and your staff. They will usually lead your project and utilize SAP as the key to guiding your overall effort. SAP supports you as the project leader and counselor.

Implementation partners on TeamSAP incorporate three main areas:

1. Global logo partners offer big, global service providers that offer you the most extensive R/3 experience through implementations at Global 1000 enterprises. Global logo partners have the power to provide you with SAP-certified AcceleratedSAP and Powered By AcceleratedSAP to customers.

2. National partners offer several R/3 national implementation partners that are certified as AcceleratedSAP partners. These partners provide you with a combination of solutions expertise in distinct industries, as well as certified AcceleratedSAP methodology.

3. Certified Business Solutions (CBS) partners were created for businesses with less than $200 million in revenues. The CBS program certifies a partner as a VAR who has the ability to bring a comprehensive SAP solution that includes an accelerated methodology to smaller business operations with limited resources.

Besides sustaining the resource pools required to support the growing R/3 market, these implementation partners offer a great deal of value for you. This is especially seen through TeamSAP and continuously refined business and industry expertise. TeamSAP provides you with the power to successfully manage a technology-enabled business transformation and offer that expertise back to TeamSAP, which can continue to enhance the TeamSAP program.

Conclusions

SAP has significantly increased the resources it has to support the AcceleratedSAP program to provide certification for a more diverse array of complementary solutions. There are two primary types of complementary software partners:

1. Joint development partner whose partners have a signed contract that details the extent of work on research and development needs by both SAP and its partners for the purpose of integrating a third-party product with R/3's functionality.

2. Certified interface partner where this certification depicts SAP confirmation so that the partner's software works together with R/3 for a particular version of R/3 through a certified interface as well as for an identified type of customer requirement.

SAP has greatly increased its availability of support resources and education services for all complementary software program partners. CSP certification lets you know that the CSP partner has access to SAP resources on an ongoing basis to sustain the integration points of your implementation.

SAP's technology and hardware partners also have a long background for mutual certification and coordination with SAP. Certification is linked to specific R/3, RDBMS, OS, and hardware release combinations. These programs will not shift; however, technology partners offer the foundation that makes them critical components of TeamSAP.

The evolution of TeamSAP illustrates a more diverse movement in terms of how companies approach business changes permitted by enterprise technology. The static model of reengineering that accompanies your implementation is steadily being replaced by business changes permitted by continuous technology improvements. The basic principle behind TeamSAP support adheres to the idea of continuous business change as opposed to an initial static incident. This should offer you significant benefits by receiving rapid and continuous results with TeamSAP and your AcceleratedSAP program.

Personal attention can assist you in using the preconfigured processes outlined in ASAP. You can utilize the benefits that SAP and its partners offer to speed your implementation and achieve a well-defined model that allows you to implement R/3 as quickly as possible. ASAP is a model that takes the best business practices observed from SAP's experience. However, the personal touch of TeamSAP takes those processes one step further by implementing them precisely so you can see realizable returns on your information investment.

TeamSAP consists of a network of products, processes, and people who are exceedingly important in helping you achieve a quick, successful implementation. TeamSAP builds on SAP's AcceleratedSAP and *Business Framework* programs by adding important components and solutions expertise to accelerate your project coordination, leadership, and knowledge-sharing. This cycle of expertise is depicted in Fig. 7-7.

Finally, this chapter discusses how TeamSAP consultants can evaluate all responses and develop a high-level estimate of your project scope and resource requirements such as time, cost, and people.

Figure 7-7
TeamSAP Cycle.

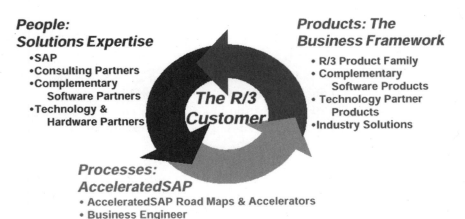

People:
Solutions Expertise
- •SAP
- •Consulting Partners
- •Complementary
  Software Partners
- •Technology &
  Hardware Partners

The R/3 Customer

Products: The
Business Framework
- • R/3 Product Family
- • Complementary
  Software Products
- • Technology Partner
  Products
- •Industry Solutions

Processes:
AcceleratedSAP
- • AcceleratedSAP Road Maps & Accelerators
- • Business Engineer
- • Support, Services & Education

CHAPTER 8

Business Framework

Accelerated *Business Framework*

SAP offers a very detailed *Business Framework* that has an integrated, open, component-based product architecture that comprises SAP R/3 enterprise applications, as well as third-party products and technologies. *Business Framework* offers you a much simpler method for upgrading and maintaining systems. It provides you with increased interoperability between R/3, legacy systems, customer-centric customizations, third-party solutions, and an enhanced platform that permits continued growth for your business.

SAP is responsible for your entire technology stack with *Business Framework*. That responsibility includes SAP and any software partner solutions that supplement its product. The end result is a greatly reduced cost of ownership for R/3 business implementations.

SAP's philosophy for enterprise computing involves making R/3 into a unit of integrated components that can be upgraded individually. This philosophy is highly dependent on upgrading your software, a problem that has been prevalent in networked software systems. You can make this process easier and reduce your time-to-market by enhancing your business upgrade solutions.

The motivation behind the *Business Framework* involves new, independent components, as well as methods of interfacing and integration.

Componentization

SAP is striving to have its R/2 system available as a multicomponent system with new financial components, an independent *Human Resources* component, a *Business Information Warehouse* component, and *Logistics* components. The continued development of new components results in more effective business solutions. Several of these components allow you to take advantage of new functionality far more easily and without the need to upgrade your entire computing system.

Integration

SAP has significantly enhanced the application-link-enabling (ALE) distributed integration scenarios in its most current release (4.0) of R/3.

ALE scenarios ensure the integration of various components at the business-process level by yielding essential matches. Due to the increased number of ALE scenarios, you have a higher degree of flexibility for the distributed deployment of your R/2 system.

Extended Supply Chain

SAP's objective for supply-chain optimization, planning, and execution (SCOPE) ties together the power of your R/3 ERP implementation along with new SAP *Advanced Planner and Optimizer* (APO) products, third-party specialized products, and detailed business intelligence capabilities, including SAP *Business Information Warehouse*. SAP SCOPE enhances the *Business Framework* by offering extra business application programming interfaces (BAPIs), as well as an APO solution as a component. In addition, it also integrates technologies including *LiveCache* (a memory-resident, data-object processing capability).

Technology

New technology is constantly being developed for the business client that yields client-component-enabling technology for executing *ActiveX Controls* and *JavaBeans* applets at the presentation layer. This allows you to obtain a higher degree of personalization for your end-user interface and seamless DCOM integration with BAPIs under *Business Framework*. This permits DCOM component-level integration between BAPIs, as well as the full complement of Microsoft development and run-time technologies. This incorporates the Microsoft Transaction Server. Open-standards compliance is achieved through BAPI access from CORBA-compliant object request brokers (ORBs).

Rapid promotion of advanced technology, including memory-resident object storage, is achieved through technology independence provided by *Business Framework*.

BAPI Availability

There has been a significant increase in the number of BAPIs, resulting from creating components from the core R/2 system. BAPIs are available for almost all application areas. BAPIs can be accessed from leading development environments, such as Microsoft Visual Basic, Microsoft Visual J++, and IBM Visual Age. BAPIs work with pure Java applications. There is also support afforded for both synchronous and asynchronous BAPIs.

Business Framework is a good model for producing flexible, component-based enterprise business solutions. There is a much easier upgrade strategy that allows *Business Framework* customers to install new R/3 applications, called *Business Components*, without the need to upgrade their complete R/2 system. The result is that you realize benefits very quickly and start using your new functionality, balancing current implementations and reducing business disruption.

The objective of *Business Framework* is to curtail R/3 costs via simpler maintenance. One of the benefits that your project team can achieve is to quickly implement your Internet application components together with new business components without upgrading your entire R/3 system. SAP is essentially opening up R/3 under the *Business Framework* to give you the ability to distribute your applications without relinquishing the high-level integration provided by R/3. Overall, SAP is offering many new functionalities that allow you to migrate to new release levels at a much quicker rate. The result keeps your support costs down while allowing you to acquire greater functionality at an accelerated pace. Your project training costs are kept to a minimum since you don't have to perform extensive upgrades to your systems every few months.

Componentization Strategy

R/3 componentization strategy provides a road map so you can add components to your core applications in three primary functionality areas:

1. Financial
2. Logistics
3. Human resources

R/3 Release 4.0 makes *Human Resources* accessible as an independent business component with its own release cycle that can be closely linked to the R/3 core via BAPIs and new ALE scenarios. SAP is working toward implementing components in the financial and logistics elements with the creation of new BAPIs and ALE scenarios.

Agile Application Backbone

Business Framework offers an integrated, open, component-based product architecture that supports R/3 enterprise applications and third-party products and technologies. *Business Framework* produces key benefits to customers such as the power to:

- Shorten the time needed to deploy and enhance business processes
- Reconfigure live R/2 systems quickly
- Deploy new components on distinct release cycles
- Extend R/2 systems using component development tools
- Integrate complementary software via *Business Framework* technology

R/3 applications were integrated only via access to a common database before the introduction of the *Business Framework* strategy. At this point in time, separate applications are incorporated as business components that can operate on their own dedicated databases. They can be transmitted to other areas. In order to make certain that there is a close integration among all components, *Business Framework* incorporates several SAP and third-party product integrations, interfaces, and communication technologies for combining distributed business components and custom applications throughout wide area networks (WAN) and the Internet. These technologies support application link enabling, which is an integration technology that makes up distribution models, distribution scenarios, and tools to provide semantic synchronization of business components. ALE tells you the specific business meaning of a given message and tells you what to do with it, whom to inform about it, and when to do something.

Business objects and BAPIs provide open and stable access to business components afforded through business objects, as well as their BAPIs. Business objects depict stable, real-world units (for example, customers or invoices). These real-world units change more slowly than the implementation foundation technologies seen in software. Business objects form the most suitable means to structure the interfaces to business components and have an interface that is both business-oriented and stable for the future.

R/3 *Business Engineer*

R/3 *Business Engineer* is a knowledge-based configuration tool that is employed for the initial and continuing configuration of components in your *Business Framework*. *Business Engineer* concentrates on the business process perspective of distributed components.

The SAP *Business Workflow* in *Business Framework* provides active process control for SAP and non-SAP components. SAP *Business Workflow* allows you to improve R/3 and corresponding software with new or changed business processes without altering the source code. SAP *Business Workflow* is a major driver behind semantic synchronization of the various business components. This level of synchronization is best accomplished through process control management (see Fig. 8-1).

Business Information Warehouse is used for enterprises who wish to implement distributed applications. *Business Information Warehouse* gives the business manager a centralized perspective of the entire operation. This permits detailed analysis and decision making across all of your installed components.

SAP and the Internet

SAP is producing Internet components for the R/2 system, together with a set of APIs that designate business rules for R/3. These new modules

Figure 8-1
Process Control Management.

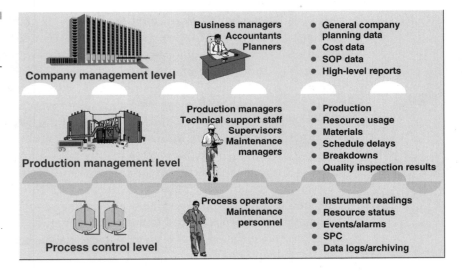

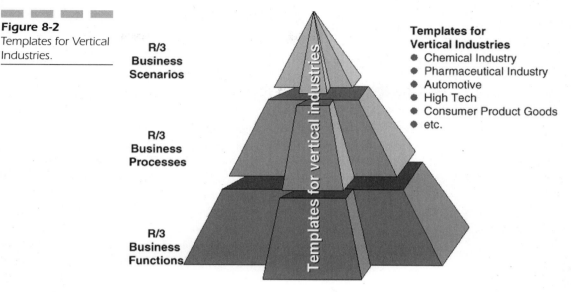

Figure 8-2
Templates for Vertical Industries.

R/3 Business Scenarios

R/3 Business Processes

R/3 Business Functions

Templates for vertical industries

Templates for Vertical Industries
- Chemical Industry
- Pharmaceutical Industry
- Automotive
- High Tech
- Consumer Product Goods
- etc.

were created to modify R/3 for specific vertical industries. The introduction of predefined tables, as well as some sector-specific templates, for organizations to adopt is a great help, as seen in Fig. 8-2. The foundation for this modularized R/3 technique is the SAP *Business Framework*.

Business Framework incorporates modules defined as multiindustry components. These modules possess functions that deal with everything from *Human Resources* to finance. Each module can operate on its own database, therefore, permitting it to function as an independent system while it remains integrated with other R/3 modules.

Inside the *Business Framework*

SAP's *Business Framework* includes the following modules:

1. Multiindustry modules where each module operates on an independent database and possesses functions that deal with everything from *Human Resources* to finance.

2. Industry-specific modules that add vertical-industry functionality, such as oil production management.

3. Internet modules that make R/3 available on the Internet or on an Intranet using an Internet Transaction Server.

4. Complementary modules are written by organizations for R/3 that follow new business APIs.

SAP Technology

SAP created messaging technologies that permit users to maintain cohesive integration when the applications are built on a component-based model. The SAP Middleware Application Link Enabling Workgroup Software technology executes company technology replication tasks that ensures that data created on different databases is synchronized.

Many organizations depend on SAP messaging technology that is used within enterprise client-server applications to synchronize data in global organizations. You can use SAP's technology, designated as ALE, along with separate installations of the SAP R/3 suite to do what only replication could previously achieve. In addition, you need to make certain that data created on separate databases are in agreement.

Client-server messaging technologies that are both proprietary and based on standards are increasingly serving as a means to sustain the integration of enterprise applications as they emigrate into a component-based model. In fact, implementing ALE can occur quite easily, even though the general feeling is that ALE is difficult to implement. ALE can meet with a great deal of success in your organization.

Business Framework for Specific Industries

SAP has created a comprehensive plan to modularize and ease their extensive suite of client-server business applications, for example, production of Internet-specific components for the R/2 system together with a set of APIs that outline business rules for R/3.

SAP is moving to reengineer itself so it can respond to customer concerns regarding issues of open architecture issue and cost. The direction in which SAP is headed is toward a component architecture, based on its R/3 client-server system. The cornerstone of this movement is SAP's *Business Framework* that was first introduced at its Sapphire '96 conference in Philadelphia. The *Business Framework* architecture is comprised of business components, integration technologies, as well as busi-

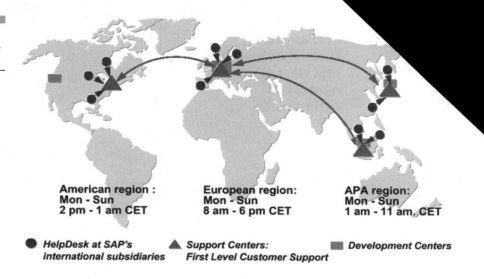

Figure 8.-3
SAP Service and Support Infrastructure.

American region :
Mon - Sun
2 pm - 1 am CET

European region:
Mon - Sun
8 am - 6 pm CET

APA region:
Mon - Sun
1 am - 11 am CET

● *HelpDesk at SAP's
international subsidiaries*

▲ *Support Centers:
First Level Customer Support*

■ *Development Centers*

ness APIs. *Business Framework* is supported by the SAP service and support infrastructure as seen in Fig. 8-3.

Consultants at SAP and its alliance partners work with customers inside *Business Framework* by employing SAP's *Business Engineering Workbench* (BEW), as well as crucial AcceleratedSAP (ASAP) implementation techniques.

The ASAP framework is tailored toward midsized organizations with revenues between $200 million and $2.5 billion. These organization utilize a roadmap that outlines several tools and templates elemental to an implementation process. The SAP *Roadmap* can refine your process to a maximum time of about 9 months for certain midsized organizations.

BAPI Compliance

SAP, together with the Open Applications Group Inc., is working to accelerate specifications and embrace enterprise application integration standards. SAP, in an effort to support open application standards, is working with TSI International Software Ltd., to make all pertinent business APIs compliant with the Open Applications Group Integration Specification (OAGIS). This is indicative that all pertinent BAPIs are prioritized by your requirements. In addition, they may also be provided as OAGIS business object documents (BODs).

123

n Applications Group supported SAP's BAPI in an effort to
eroperability. SAP needed to send pertinent BAPI specifica-
group's member submission process. The group then exam-
he submissions to be included in its specifications. The Open
s Group realized that input from SAP BAPIs represents a
effort.

a charter member of the Open Applications Group, which is
o open application interoperability. The BAPI methodology
organization to have an even greater level of functionality to
integrate SAP applications into their environment.

SAP allows all pertinent BAPIs to be compliant with OAGIS. SAP has
contributed a great deal to the Open Applications Group specification
process and has led in the application interface development. This working relationship between SAP and the group balances significant
resources that assist you in accomplishing a superior method for integrating your enterprise applications. SAP enhanced its partnership with
TSI Software to offer compliance with Open Applications Group specifications. TSI Software utilizes its Mercator for R/3 software to develop a
mapper for the OAGIS BODs and the BAPIs.

TSI Software is a partner in the SAP Complementary Software Program. Mercator for R/3 was the first application-link-enabling (ALE)
translator certified by SAP. Mercator for R/3 is successfully employed
across several SAP customer sites, and works to decrease time and cost
factors involved in creating R/3 interfaces with legacy and third-party
applications.

Mercator for R/3 is a powerful product that utilizes the SAP *Business
Framework* strategy. Therefore, the partnership with TSI Software is
the means by which SAP can develop increased value for its customers
and provide BAPIs that are compliant with Open Applications Group
specifications.

The Open Applications Group Inc., is the leading enterprise application software vendor whose responsibility it is to promote the interoperability of enterprise applications through the creation of integration
specifications and marketing the development and implementation of
software in compliance with the specifications.

The Open Applications Group's specification offers a great deal of the
functionality required for your ERP integration processes, including primary financial, *Human Resources,* manufacturing, and logistics applications. The corporate membership of the OAG is comprised of several
large enterprise application vendors, including American Software Inc.,
CGI Systems Inc., CODA Inc., Computer Associates International Inc.,

IBM Manufacturing Solutions, J.D. Edwards & Co., Marcam Corp., NEC C&C Systems Group, Oracle Corp., PeopleSoft Inc., QAD Inc., SAP AG, Siemens Nixdorf Informationssysteme AG, Texas Instruments Inc., and TSW International Inc.

TSI International Software Ltd., offers software for business application integration that ties together computer applications. TSI Software's main product is Mercator which is a crucial element for your business application integration solutions, including the transformation of electronic commerce data to and from applications, integration of Web applications with back-office systems, and integration of enterprise applications. This includes linking R/3 with legacy and third-party applications. TSI Software's products are used globally by companies integrating their internal applications or executing business electronically.

Delivering *Business Framework*

SAP is making delivery of its *Business Framework* easier through an integrated, open, component-based product architecture that includes SAP R/3 enterprise applications, as well as third-party products and methods. *Business Framework* offers you a much simpler system upgrade and maintenance schedule. You benefit by increased interoperability between R/3, legacy systems, customer-specific, third-party solutions, and a much more pliable platform that allows ongoing modifications.

SAP provides employee self-service Intranet application components. These components enhance SAP's complementary software programs by permitting BAPIs to be used with Java and IBM's VisualAge or the Java Development Environment. SAP and Microsoft have cooperated on Windows DNA, COM+, as well as the *Business Framework* for Internet and business applications.

R/2 System Componentization

The creation of components in the core part of R/3 is part of the continuous struggle to provide customers with component compliance combined with the efficiency of close integration and the components of the core application components in the R/3.

R/3 has the power of close integration throughout its core application areas, including financials, logistics, and *Human Resources*. These elements lend to operational efficiencies with a higher return on your information investment.

The growth of the Internet as well as the continuous increase of business change allows you to gain significantly increased compliance as you maintain the benefits of close integration. The *Business Framework* component strategy can effectively meet your business requirements.

In R/3 Release 4.0, the methodology for creating components increased with the addition of fresh business components, including *Human Resources,* financials, logistics components, and the *Business Information Warehouse*. More current R/3 releases demonstrate more complete financial and logistics applications provided as business components.

Business Framework techniques allow you to have networked application components with independent release cycles. At the same time, you maintain the usual level of close integration of SAP software. This permits you to upgrade application components one section at a time, and you can also utilize enhanced application functionality (that is, supply-chain or Internet access) far easier without interfering with your existing R/3 environment. In addition, you can also simplify the integration burden of adding custom or third-party applications to your R/3 solution.

When R/3 was first released, you always had the option of using R/3 applications either on an independent basis or as a totally integrated solution. After that, you could successfully upgrade a large-scale, fully integrated enterprise application. However, that upgrade can provide you with a significant task for both you and your in-house staff, mainly because of staff retraining and data migrations that must occur simultaneously across many functional areas. However, the labor in upgrading a single functional area is much easier for your staff to manage.

SAP's core componentization strategy permits you to adopt a far easier approach that deals with items independently. This results in making certain you have easy access to the most recent advances in both features and technology.

The componentization of the R/2 system is illustrated through the method of integration that involves sharing a common database, loosely coupled networking, and closely coupled networking. *Business Framework* in addition to its interface and integration technologies make both loosely coupled and closely coupled networking feasible.

Before *Business Framework* there was the standard form of integration. R/3 Releases 1.x and 2.x integrated core applications via access to the same database. In terms of integrated systems, simultaneous upgrades of all application areas was needed to migrate to a new R/3 release. When dealing with standalone applications, R/3 core applications *Financial* and *Human Resources* may be employed as standalone applications and then integrated with other R/3 applications that can be used in distributed and customized environments.

Versions

Business Framework Release 3.x offers loosely coupled networking. The advance of *Business Framework* in Release 3.x saw the addition of using a loosely coupled integration option for your core software. You can use this to support geographically dispersed or remote sites.

In *Business Framework* Release 4.x there is a closely coupled *Human Resources*. R/3 Release 4.0 depicted SAP's growth to the new functionality of closely coupled core applications. This refers to the introduction of *Human Resources* as a Business Component. It is employed on an individual footing as it has its own database. In addition, *Human Resources* can sustain its close integration with the other core applications due to the delivery of pertinent application-link-enabling distribution scenarios between *Human Resources, Financials*, and *Logistics*.

In *Business Framework*'s next advanced release, closely coupled *Financials* and *Logistics* will be noticeable. In the next release, *Financials* and *Logistics* are provided as closely coupled Business Components. When these components are used on an individual, separate basis on separate databases in a network configuration, then all business processes will be closely integrated. This will grow even further into a family of closely integrated, but separate Business Components that are easily upgraded and where each has its own release cycle.

Conclusion

This chapter examines the *Business Framework* as SAP's product architecture. This open architecture permits complementary software partners to constantly offer new solutions to your R/3 implementation. This important level of solutions expertise is fortified by the combination of product expertise, experience, and training.

Project Preparation

Introduction

AcceleratedSAP implementation projects include Texoprint B.V., which is a company in the eastern Netherlands (Boekelo). They finish textiles (printing) and have nearly 250 employees. The implementation at this company took only about 6 months, and their implementation partner was Coopers & Lybrand. It is important to note the implementation performance exhibited in each specific company and industry. This performance data is shown in Fig. 9-1.

The next AcceleratedSAP pilot was at Sekisui S-Lec, based in Roermond in the southern Netherlands. Sekisui S-Lec creates interlayer film and is part of the Sekisui Group (a Japanese company). The ASAP implementation at Sekisui S-Lec also took approximately 6 months, and their implementation partner was C/TAC (a Dutch consultancy partner with a great deal of SAP expertise).

Reviewing these AcceleratedSAP implementations allows you to see some live examples of how specific companies prepared their projects and excelled with the ASAP program. Since you are already aware of some of the advantages of the ASAP program, you can review the ASAP accelerators and the benefits that each company and implementation partner possess. In reviewing these specific examples, you can tailor your own ASAP implementation and achieve greater success in your company.

Figure 9-1
Implementation Performance.

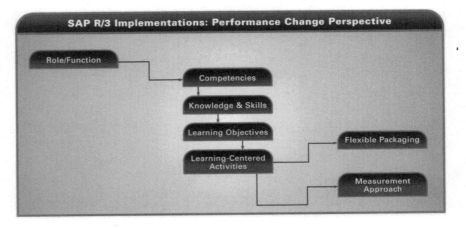

Planning Your Project

Sekisui S-Lec is part of the Sekisui Group, a collection of companies that has sales of nearly $36 billion and more than 200 companies. One company is Sekisui Chemical Co. Ltd., a division of S-Lec interlayer film. Sekisui S-Lec B.V. is part of this division and has production facilities in Japan, Mexico, and The Netherlands. Sekisui S-Lec has approximately 50 employees, and their plant capacity is 6000 tons of PVB film per year. In order to see better the types of capacity available, see the chart in Fig. 9-2. They produce PVB film by extrusion for the laminated glass industry. Their specific segments include: automotive (windshields) and architecture (offices). They create the film in various thicknesses, widths, and lengths. However, they concentrate on customer satisfaction by producing quality products.

SAP R/3 is an excellent means for refining your business processes and enhancing your long-term strategy. It is designed to fit your business, so you can manage your enterprise effectively. Sekisui Alveo (part of Sekisui Chemical Co. Ltd.) went live with SAP R/3 and has already

Figure 9-2
Capacity Available
Chart.

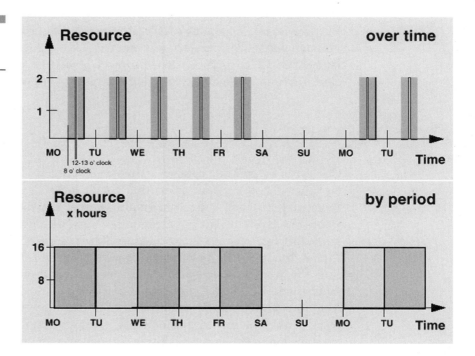

produced significant benefits in the areas of financial savings and customer service.

The implementation partner at Sekisui S-Lec B.V. is the C/TAC consultancy agency which concentrates entirely on SAP support. Their SAP expertise is apparent from the number of partnerships they have. For example, C/TAC is the technical partner, SAP system reseller, R/3 consulting partner and migration partner. C/TAC provides complete solutions in three areas:

- ABAP/4
- Technical
- Functional consultancy

These complete solutions are evidenced in AcceleratedSAP Implementations, SAP Operational Services, Migrations, SAP Technical Academy (S/TAC), SAP @ WEB, and as an R/3 Solution Provider. C/TAC is a partner that can support software, hardware, and implementation for maintenance purposes. In terms of SAP Internet applications, you gain a strategic advantage in having both their knowledge and experience which will make your AcceleratedSAP implementation project a success.

Sekisui S-Lec implemented specific SAP R/3 modules including: FI (Financial Accounting), CO (Controlling), MM (Material Management), SD (Sales and Distribution), PP (Production Planning), and QM (Quality Management). This project was named *Access* (AcceleratedSAP at Sekisui S-Lec). The organizational project structure was established by a steering committee and six project groups at a rate of one per module.

Cabletron Project Preparation

Cabletron is another company that completed its SAP implementation on time. It had been assumed that SAP's R/3 rollouts at Cabletron Systems would exceed budgetary requirements, but that thinking changed. Cabletron Systems Inc., is a computer networking systems and services manufacturer located in Rochester, New Hampshire. They determined that it was possible to implement within 12 months and made certain that the work was completed both on time and on budget. The implementation of SAP R/3 supports over 1000 global users on Windows NT company process application servers and a management Oracle database. This implementation included the installation of a total set of R/3 logistics modules, as well as three finance and accounting modules.

Small Company Installation

SAP is growing through the addition of a tier of resellers. These people will assist SAP in gaining a stronger presence for implementations involving smaller organizations. SAP has always been known for their work with large organizations who have a great deal of revenue, however, their new strategy, in combination with ASAP, allows them to pursue a market segment that needs R/3 to compete in a growing business environment.

These resellers will work together with consultants and implementors to promote installations of the SAP R/3 client-server application environment in organizations with sales of $200 million and less.

SAP feels that their reseller program concentrates on convincing users that they need not be a part of a multinational conglomerate just so they can take advantage of the R/3 system for their corporate ERP needs.

Some smaller organizations are just now becoming aware of the fact that they can utilize an R/3 implementation at their company. They wonder if it is really necessary to utilize a comprehensive resource such as R/3 for a smaller organization. It seems that smaller companies are growing at a phenomenal rate, making the introduction of SAP's R/3 an important step in the success of larger business processes and projects.

Preparing for an R/3 project requires several initiatives that focus on simplifying the process of implementing R/3, as well as marketing it to smaller companies. These tasks incorporate new business-modeling tools that facilitate the AcceleratedSAP program.

Third-Party Vendors

Several third-party vendors are embracing the SAP R/3 platform in various methods. Primavera Systems Inc. (Bala Cynwyd, Pennsylvania) developed an interface between its P3 Project Planner and the R/3 Project System, while JetForm Corp. (Ottawa, Canada) has created the JetForm Self Service Access Center for R/3. In addition, AutoTester Inc., produced Version 1.2 of AutoTester client-server testing software for R/3.

Oracle and Informix are also working hard to bridge the gap to R/3. Oracle offers a toolkit that allows developers to extract R/3 data and direct it into an Oracle7 database. Informix Software created a business unit to enhance the integration of SAP's R/3 application suite with Informix's Online Dynamic Server.

Financial Component Planning

SAP's financial components add a great deal more to a very complete financial solution. SAP offers five business components for financials including:

- Consolidation
- Treasury
- Investment control
- Self-audit
- Joint venture accounting

These components offer enhanced best-in-class application functionality integrated with R/3 Release 4.0. These financial components are separate business components of the SAP *Business Framework* architecture that permit you to easily and quickly deploy business functionality components without disrupting your current R/3 environment.

Providing Functionality

These financial components provide you with several benefits since they capture a great deal of R/3 functionality into independent applications for improved flexibility, simpler maintenance, and much quicker deployment. These components can be updated independently from the remainder of your R/3 implementation. Therefore, whenever regulations change or new functionality is added, new component releases become available. The power to upgrade individual components will ease and refine your upgrade process and allow customers to add increased functionality as needed.

New organizations gain enhanced functionality for particular corporate finance functions that are separate from the core finance functions. You gain benefits from easy, real-time access to data within your company.

There are several features included in these business components. The first involves consolidation. This component collects data from all areas of your R/3 system. Data collection can happen at the company, business, or profit-center level. Consolidation offers both valuation and elimination methods, and is the foundation for optimizing group reporting within your company. Consolidation also connects to the centralized R/3 *Executive Information System*.

The next area of functionality includes the *Treasury*. Features for this component include applications for managing money-market funds, foreign exchange, derivatives, securities, loans, and market-risk management. This type of management deals with interest and currency exposure analysis and portfolio simulation.

The *Investment Controlling* component allows global capital investment management. In this component, appropriation requests assist your company in managing the corporate approval process from conception through implementation. This effectively allows your users to rate requests with respect to their viability and priority.

The *Self-Audit* component enhances audit quality and makes the auditing process much easier and more direct. At the root is the *Audit Report Tree,* a comprehensive level of auditing functions and default configurations, including auditing procedures, documentation, auditing evaluations, and downloading audit data.

Joint Venture Accounting is a component that permits several organizations to link their monetary and personal resources for projects that are at high risk, as well as for extensive capital investment and extended payback periods. *Joint Venture Accounting* distributes revenues and expenses between partners with respect to specific working relationships. It then transfers material and assets among ventures and permits change management and suspense between groups of equity holders. It also permits expense and revenue netting by equity partners.

Availability and support exist for each of these financial components. Each component is compatible with R/3 Release 4.0 and can exist on its own release cycle.

Human Resources Component

SAP *Human Resources* components offer upgrade flexibility separate and distinct from the core of R/3. SAP has received a great deal of respect when they divided their core applications into components with R/3 Release 4.0. *Human Resources* and *Travel Management* are original core R/3 applications and stand alone as independent business components. These components incorporate several workflow, Internet, and Intranet enhancements. They also offer country-specific versions.

These enhancements in R/3 *Human Resources* provide the majority of comprehensive global solutions for human resources planning, benefits, administration, payroll processing, and travel management.

These benefits are realized through the R/3 component *Human Resources*. SAP offers you both increased flexibility and agility. R/3 Release 4.0 has a *Human Resources* solution that can be upgraded on an independent release cycle that effectively allows you to deploy *Human Resources* functionality quickly and simply to satisfy changing regulations and business rules in all countries. It is an independent component that can be deployed individually from your R/3 system.

There is also a great deal of expanded support for new countries, as well as for the euro currency. The SAP *Human Resources* component offers global companies the most consistent best practices available on a global basis. It also enables decentralization of human resource systems to support country-specific requirements.

Human Resources Functionality

R/3 Release 4.0 offers significant human resources functionality in several areas. Globalization meets the individual needs of more than 30 countries' legal requirements and business procedures. There are also new versions available for personnel administration in Mexico, Taiwan, and Sweden. New versions for payroll include Mexico, Brazil, Argentina, Venezuela, Indonesia, Malaysia, and New Zealand. Trip cost accounting is now available for Great Britain, the Netherlands, Belgium, France, and Denmark.

Employee self-service (ESS) solutions and outsourcing interfaces are critical elements to R/3 functionality in this area. The *Interfaces* toolbox is used to establish the interfaces needed for outsourcing. R/3 Release 4.0 offers an interface to ADP PC/Payroll for Windows through a master extract so you don't need to configure gross payroll schemes and rules.

Integrating Third-Party Components

SAP offers an enhanced development environment that permits integrating third-party components into the R/3 enterprise system much more simply. ABAP objects are elements of SAP's *Business Framework* strategy. They build on the foundation of SAP's ABAP programming language, as well as on its object programming technology. The new development environment offers individual and team development tools together with a virtual machine that offers cross-platform application portability. It incorporates both publish-and-subscribe and event-trigger mechanisms to support business application requirements.

Business Information Warehouse

R/3 Release 4.0 logistics functionality enhanced SAP's position within the Enterprise Resource Planning Market. The SAP R/3 system has often been seen as the leader within enterprise resource planning. R/3 Release 4.0 offers a great deal of enhanced functionality within its core *Logistics* applications to satisfy additional ERP needs that specifically deal with your individual industry requirements. R/3 Release 4.0 offers new functionality with respect to an ERP solution that offers best-practices. It offers new sales and distribution functionality, distribution resource planning (DRP), available-to-promise (ATP) server, flow manufacturing, and sequencing.

You can see some obtainable benefits through its comprehensive *Logistics* functionality that assists you in achieving the most efficiency and supply-chain innovation. It reduces cycle times and increases customer satisfaction.

The *Logistics* applications offer a great deal of enhanced functionality such as sales and distribution enhancements, distribution resource planning, credit and payment card payment processing, payment authorization processing, sales channel operations, and freight charge processing. In addition, it can employ an interface with respect to transportation planning and optimization of freight rates and agreements.

These tasks can be accomplished through the SAP condition technique manual and automatic release of freight charge documents. The purpose is for the settlement calculation of transportation costs at each stage of shipment. This is achieved through SAP pricing completion of settlements with service agents.

There are also BAPIs used for transportation, communication, environmental, regulatory, and the available-to-promise server. Each executes advanced available-to-promise order-processing transactions and decision-support activities. They yield multilevel product availability checks simply even with physically distributed systems and global sources.

External Catalog Integration provides a simple means by which to access external electronic catalogs through procurement. *Vendor Consignment* enhances the handling of vendor consignment stocks, while *Value Contracts* support the validity period, agreed total value, pricing, and rules. *Free Goods* automates promotion management.

Business Components

SAP offers several business components that supplement R/3 Release 4.0 *Logistics* functionality that incorporate the *Sales Configuration Engine* (SCE), *Product Data Management* (PDM), *Web-Based Catalog*, and *Purchase Requisition System*.

SAP R/3 Release 4.0 kills the trade-off from the best of breed and integration and provides advantages from them both. R/3 Release 4.0 delivers SAP's *Enterprise Solution* that provides best-in-class functionality, increased speed, flexibility, more rapid implementation and upgrades, and a very detailed extended supply-chain level of functionality.

R/3 Financial Capabilities

R/3 Release 4.0 financial components offer five components that increase its functionality as a financial solution. There is also a SAP euro-currency component that enables an organization for conversion and multiple currencies. The *Human Resources* components offer upgrade pliancy that separates from the core R/3. R/3 *Logistics* applications offers capabilities that enhance SAP leadership in the enterprise resource planning market

The SAP *Sales Configuration Engine* is a component written in Java. In addition the *Product Data Management* component is from SAP and connects engineering to manufacturing. R/3 Release 4.0 *Upgrade Strategy* provides a quick program that allows R/3 Users to utilize Release 4.0 with the least amount of downtime and to connect with a smooth element of business processes.

The R/3 *Business Engineer* is knowledge-based. There is also an interactive version of R/3 *Business Engineer* that greatly simplifies configuration.

The SAP *Web-Based Catalog* and *Purchase Requisition System* offers a new Web-based catalog and purchase requisition component that refines and simplifies purchasing.

Supply Chain Management

Advanced planning and optimization is completely integrated with R/3. In addition, there is memory-resident processing technology that gets real-time speed and performance.

The SAP supply-chain optimization, planning, and execution initiative (SCOPE) ties together both the power of the SAP R/3 enterprise resource planning solution along with advanced planning and scheduling (APS) products and technologies, third-party products, Internet capabilities, and a total level of business intelligence solutions.

In the SAP *Business Information Warehouse,* you will notice that the SCOPE project allows SAP to directly support your requirements for a cost-effective, high-performance, real-time planning and optimization solution. The SAP *Advanced Planner and Optimizer* (APO) component is completely integrated into the core R/3 enterprise applications. It allows you to directly perform your optimized plans. This solution offers you a significant market advantage via increased responsiveness as well as reduced costs and increased efficiencies in your business processes.

SCOPE offers you a great deal of cost and business benefits from when you use R/3 including the power to optimize performance and costs throughout your complete supply chain through the combination of *APO* and *Business Information Warehouse*. In addition, you can lessen your cost of ownership and reduce complexity via the elimination of third-party integration and interfacing expenditures.

You gain a great deal of both speed and performance through new or enhanced SAP technologies such as *liveCache. LiveCache* is a memory-resident data-object processing entity that has the functionality of offering real-time cross-system, cross-company Internet simulation and decision support. This is all achieved from synchronized data and tight integration between the *APO* component as well as the R/3 execution backbone. You can significantly reduce costs and effort through the automatic creation of a supply-chain model.

Conclusion

This chapter emphasizes the importance of your accelerated project preparation. This section has examined your needs for all decision makers to agree on your R/3 implementation. At this point, the text guides you to the point where you can collect all of your internal and external implementation team resources and complete your final preparation. At this point you can test all of your interfaces, complete the training for all of your end users, and finally migrate your business data to your R/3 system.

Business Architecture

Introduction

SAP has worked diligently to produce the AcceleratedSAP program on a broad scale both domestically and internationally. However, developing a fast implementation scheme is highly dependent on creating several other features and functionalities within the SAP business architecture. Some of the enhancements include the improvement of their ALE features. SAP relies on specific enhancements in their technology, including messaging technology to improve integration of R/3.

SAP is maintaining a high level of tight integration for its R/3 client-server suite as it gears its product toward a distributed development architecture.

Integration

A high level of integration permits big SAP customers to synchronize various business operations across several locations. Integration is the cornerstone of SAP's success in the client-server arena. In order to sustain the exact same level of integration, SAP modified its R/3 root architecture to adopt an Intranet distribution model. SAP produces extended functionality for their ALE messaging technology. ALE is the most important connection between R/3 and its future of segmented components.

Enhanced ALE code was first available in SAP R/3 Release 3.1. This was the first version of SAP's business applications that incorporated a set of components for performing business processes over the Internet or an Intranet.

SAP originally developed ALE in R/3 to let organizations execute R/3 tasks separately, while keeping track of information. ALE is enhanced to incorporate consistency checking, audit checking, and logistics checking features. ALE has benefits that extend above R/3 to software from other companies. In terms of other third-party packages that can be used with SAP, ALE is a crucial tool to execute specific functionalities.

The consistency check, in particular, is connected to the SAP workflow, so it can be used as a monitoring tool in a distributed system. If it detects inconsistencies between data created at two different points, it signals an alarm and furnishes the different data for analysis.

SAP also offers an *Employee Self-Service Intranet Application* component—a collection of 10 Internet and Intranet tools that interface with

Figure 10-1
SAP Training Courses.

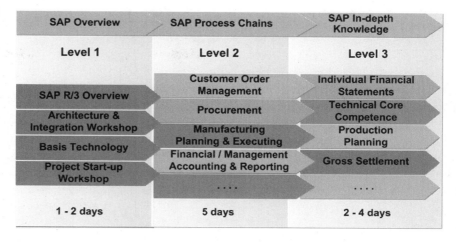

SAP Overview	SAP Process Chains	SAP In-depth Knowledge
Level 1	**Level 2**	**Level 3**
SAP R/3 Overview	Customer Order Management	Individual Financial Statements
Architecture & Integration Workshop	Procurement	Technical Core Competence
Basis Technology	Manufacturing Planning & Executing	Production Planning
Project Start-up Workshop	Financial / Management Accounting & Reporting	Gross Settlement
	....	....
1 - 2 days	**5 days**	**2 - 4 days**

R/3. These tools include *Personal Information, Benefits, Time Entry, Time Off, Travel and Expenses, Purchase Requisition, Electronic Paystub, Employee Directory, Employment, Salary Verification, Change Password,* and *Training Courses.* In terms of cost, these new components are priced on a license-fee basis for identified users. One of the most important assets you can have in learning to use these applications includes SAP's training courses shown in Fig. 10-1.

Business Client

The R/3 *Business Client* adds a customizable component-based GUI as well as providing broadcast technology to decrease maintenance costs. In an effort to ease enterprise application deployment and establish new standards for ease of use, SAP has integrated support for user-interface client components, including controls and applets in its next-generation *Business Client,* called *SAPGUI.*

The new interface changes the essentials method by which users interact with the R/3 system. It links the power of standard PCs to graphical interfaces. It then preserves network performance, scalability, and client-administration efficiencies of thin clients. Integrated components can effectively utilize the client workstation's computing power.

These user-interface components are small, specialized, front-end applications. A text editor or 3D graphics engine exemplifies these application types. SAP enhanced its *Business Framework* (shown in

Figure 10-2
Business Framework.

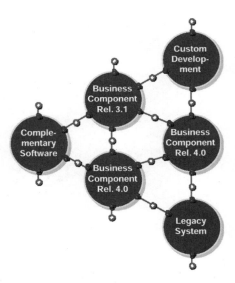

Fig. 10-2) to the presentation layer by using the integration of the client-component empowering technology into your R/3 user interface. The client-component empowering technology acts as a repository for executing various types of controls and components, including those implemented in *JavaBeans* and *ActiveX*. The *Business Client* introduces a self-upgrading software environment that allows simpler application maintenance.

Advantages

The R/3 *Business Client* offers you benefits in that it is the first GUI for enterprisewide standard applications, which can be personalized to satisfy your individual or corporate needs. In utilizing *JavaBeans* applets and *ActiveX* controls, customers have a great deal of pliancy together with complete Internet integration.

When you install an HTML component, your *Business Client* is open to the Internet. This is indicative of your business' desire to process pertinent information on the Internet (for example, stock quotes) so it can be accessed directly from within an R/3 transaction screen through its interface. It assists R/3 end users in becoming more productive.

The client-component empowering technology also eases maintenance and administration tasks. Components are recorded in an R/3 database and sent automatically to the client workstation when requested. This decreases the cost of client maintenance by breaking down client administration and making certain that components are easily updated through simple database updates.

Functionality

Besides using standard components (that is, text fields, input fields, or buttons), the new interface offers frame features that can execute client components to enhance functionality. Initial components incorporate a new editor component, an HTML component, an explorer component, an SAP graphic component, and an SAP matchcode component.

Client-component empowering technology is composed of three main elements:

1. Client-component container on the front end
2. Self-upgrading software environment (SUSE) on the R/3 application servers
3. Data provider responsible for converting various data formats used by R/3 and its associate client components

The client-component container handles the integration of client components into R/3 screens. This incorporates publish and subscribe communication between client components, as well as R/3 applications operating on the application server. SUSE automatically offers new components that are implemented in *ActiveX* or *JavaBeans* to the PC, or Net PC (NC) clients, as required by an R/3 application. In addition, it also supports component upgrades and distributes new customer-specific client components. The data provider automatically converts data, based on the MIME standard, and, in offering this service to all components, it significantly eases deployment of new client components.

DCOM Components

SAP offers BAPI-to-DCOM integration, which permits rapid enhancements and extension of your R/3 system. Due to the continuous joint development between SAP and Microsoft Corp., SAP offers customer and third-party developers a smooth distributed component object model (DCOM) integration into R/3 business processes and applications within *Business Framework.* The DCOM component connector offers DCOM-based integration between business application programming interfaces and the full array of Microsoft development and run-time technologies, such as the Microsoft Transaction Server (MTS). This is acceptable for large-scale applications, and the DCOM component connector greatly enhances the existing BAPI control and offers single-user COM support.

It provides you with several advantages together with seamless development and run-time access to BAPIs from the Microsoft environment, from your current developers, and from a diverse pool of developers knowledgeable in Visual Basic, Visual C++, or Visual J++. As a result you can instantly improve your R/3 solution and reduce the need for new development tools and disciplines.

If you have already deployed DCOM-based applications, you will find that the new DCOM component connector significantly reduces the work required to access R/3 business processes through BAPIs. In addition, it also supports reusing COM and DCOM components and simplifies access to BAPIs and leveraging them with new applications.

In terms of DCOM access for R/3, it is important to balance Microsoft Transaction Server Transparent access to BAPIs through direct DCOM connection or remotely over networks. Centralized installation and administration of DCOM component connector security and individual log-on compatibility with Microsoft Transaction Server permits a two-phase commitment between MTS and R/3. It provides the capability to operate under Windows NT and on other platforms as well. It allows easy, simple installation as an installer shield under Windows NT.

Java-Enabled BAPIs in R/3

As an SAP customer, you can benefit from Java Openness and utilize development tools and components through both BAPI and Java integration.

SAP has allowed business application programming interfaces to be used with the Java programming languages. This allows customers and partners to create totally pure Java applications through creation of development tools that leverage R/3 business processes.

It provides you with significant advantages when you need to deploy applications across multiple platforms that deal with everything from UNIX graphics workstations to Windows PCs and Macintosh computers. Java offers the ability to write-once, operate anywhere, and have the functionality to significantly reduce software development and maintenance costs while enhancing system agility and stability.

Developers can utilize these new tools in Java to create applications compiled solely in Java that have total BAPI access to R/3 applications. Java-enabled BAPIs preclude the need for developers to exit their Java development environment to enhance your R/3 solution.

In combination with SAP, either you or information partners can create add-on applications for R/3, while utilizing your organization's investment in Java. This is illustrated through custom components that are written as Java applets and then distributed on the Internet or an Intranet to permit your company's independent dealers to obtain order information from R/3-based systems.

In terms of functionality, there is no distinction between either native *JavaBeans* or Java BAPIs that are completely integrated. Applications can operate on any Java VM that is solely in Java.

Web-Enabled *Business Workflow*

Several organizations are responding to the increasing level of competition through a flexible transformation of business processes. SAP *Business Workflow* provides Web-enabled workflow management on the enterprise level. It enhances workflow features over the Internet/Intranet. You also have a simplified workflow functionality available to you at anytime on a global basis.

SAP *Business Workflow* functionality offers true development with respect to Web-enabled workflow management at an enterprise application level. SAP *Business Workflow* is a crucial element of your *Business Framework* integration technology. It permits active process control of business processes that deal with non-R/3 and desktop software components. It has close integration with Internet application components, and makes certain that business processes in the Internet are workflow-enabled too. Additionally, any BAPI can cause a workflow that is actively controlled by the SAP *Business Workflow*.

Business Application Programming Interfaces

BAPIs have experienced significant industry growth and support. Business application programming interfaces (BAPIs) are growing significantly in terms of their acceptance because they easily integrate the best practices and useful business processes of the R/3 solution into new and current business applications. BAPIs offer object-oriented access interfaces to R/3 business rules and methods. They are used to create advanced or specialized business solutions.

SAP has developed the Open BAPI Network to offer widespread BAPI adoption to its customers because of new business components that are part of R/3 Release 4.0. In addition, there are several available BAPIs that deal with practically all areas of R/3. Furthermore, BAPIs can be invoked both synchronously and asynchronously.

The first practical utilization of BAPIs came with SAP's introduction of 25 Internet and Intranet application components and 10 employee self-service components. At this time, SAP is using BAPIs extensively in establishing its supply-chain solution too. In order to offer greater support for the development activity encompassing BAPIs, SAP has created the Open BAPI Network to offer software developers at customer sites access to BAPI experts as well as online information and activities. In addition, complementary software partners requests are also supported by the SAP Complementary Software program.

Significant benefits can be achieved from these business entities. BAPIs were created to offer a stable interface between business applications and components. Since the interface is stable and long-term, individual components can be modified extensively without disrupting other components. This allows a simpler method of adding new applications, as well as enhancing current applications or utilizing the advantages that new technologies have to offer, including 64-bit processors or improved programming languages (for example, Java). This level of technology independence assists in the rapid customer and vendor modifications that allow you to gain the adaptability of custom-developed applications with sophisticated business processes offered by enterprise applications.

BAPIs are available in the majority of R/3 application areas because their number has increased two-fold. The Open BAPI Network has been created to assist in the open sharing of BAPI-related technical information. Development environments support BAPIs to a greater extent. IBM and Borland are also embracing full BAPI support in their VisualAge and Delphi/Connect environments.

Several training courses are now offered by SAP and its partners to help you use BAPIs in several specific environments, including Microsoft Visual Studio. BAPI training courses offer you and SAP partners detailed information on BAPI usage. There is a significant increase in the amount of BAPIs and the amount of SAP business objects structuring the BAPIs in R/3 Release 4.0.

SAP is producing new BAPIs for its data warehouse solution that allows a simpler form of integration for both complementary data and tools.

Business Information Warehouse

The SAP *Business Information Warehouse* links modern data warehousing technologies together with SAP's business expertise to produce a comprehensive solution. It incorporates all the components necessary for installation, use, continuous changes, and maintenance of a data warehouse. The content of your *Business Information Warehouse* establishes a benchmark for speed and ease because it is preconfigured with intelligence regarding your organizations business processes. It offers a much quicker return on your information investment. This modern solution offers your users a detailed view of data throughout your organization that incorporates R/3-based data in addition to that of other systems.

The *Business Information Warehouse* is an independent component of the SAP *Business Framework* architecture. It permits you to rapidly deploy business functionality or components as they become available without interfering with your current R/3 environment.

The *Business Information Warehouse* was created as an open solution that provides new business application programming interfaces (BAPIs) for non-SAP data integration and complementary third-party analysis tools. SAP works in combination with well-known extraction tool providers, including Evolutionary Technologies International (ETI) and Software AG, in order to test and make certain you receive a quality interface with BAPIs that will provide external data to the *Business Information Warehouse.*

BAPI's availability allows SAP to function with its partners in the Complementary Software program to make certain that customers can select from a wide variety of third-party products. This allows you to simply create a powerful data warehouse that relates to your data and information requirements.

Rapid Benefits

Many organizations find that implementing SAP's preconfigured *Business Information Warehouse* helps support their specific data requirements. The *Business Information Warehouse* will greatly reduce data load time and as a result, it provides global access to your data on a real-time basis. Additionally, it increases data accuracy and greatly reduces maintenance and overhead costs for your data warehouse.

The *Business Information Warehouse* gives you several distinct benefits, not the least of which is a rapid solution. When dealing with a business component of SAP R/3 *Business Framework,* the *Business Information Warehouse* can be implemented rapidly at a reduced cost. The smooth integration of decision-support functionality into the existing business applications environment does not jeopardize the performance of those systems.

The *Business Information Warehouse* is not restricted to R/3 and offers an open architecture. By utilizing open interfaces, the *Business Information Warehouse* can be linked to non-SAP data sources, as well as to data access tools. There is also a great deal of functionality with the *Business Information Warehouse.* It offers a large array of robust reporting and analytic features for effective investigation and explanation of data. It provides a very flexible solution designed to adapt to modifications executed in business processes or the IT environment during continuous system operation.

The *Administrator Workbench* offers effective support for simple maintenance of the *Business Information Warehouse* and rapid implementation of modifications. It provides a very powerful, business-centric solution that is rooted in SAP expertise and R/3 client-server technology using real-world business processes. The *Business Information Warehouse* is created to respond to the specific information requirements of decision makers in all industries in an efficient manner. These industries are illustrated in Fig. 10-3.

Figure 10-3
Industry List.

Program Management And Industry Experience

Experienced professionals have helped lead teams to transition from multiple financial centers to shared services environments in a variety of global industries, including:

▶ Pharmaceutical   ▶ Telecommunications

▶ Financial Services   ▶ Manufacturing

▶ Insurance   ▶ Petroleum and Chemical

▶ Travel Services   ▶ Consumer Products

The advantages of functionality seen within the *Business Information Warehouse* server involve an online analytical processing (OLAP) engine in combination with a metadata repository. They are both preconfigured with business content, and they save you time and money in creating a data warehouse. The *Business Information Warehouse* server was created to offer rapid retrieval, interpretation, and preparation of the information recorded in the data warehouse. The *Business Explorer* offers you a simplified three-dimensional access interface. The *Business Explorer's* creative navigation functionality permits you to create a personal catalog of reports for continuous or recurring queries and reports that import data from Microsoft Excel 97. In addition, automated data extraction and loading capabilities feed the *Business Information Warehouse* server with data from R/3 applications, R/2 applications, as well as any other data source. The *Administrator Workbench* is a feature of the *Business Information Warehouse* that offers a centralized point of control for creating, monitoring, and simply maintaining the entire data warehouse environment. It effectively reduces the total cost of ownership to you, while open BAPIs tie together external data sources and applications.

The Very First BAPIs

SAP is working to increase the openness of its R/3 enterprise application suite. BAPIs are open, standard business-process interfaces that form the foundation for converting R/3 to the component-based *Business*

Framework architecture. BAPIs will allow SAP to create an industry standard, which will work in the long term to increase the usage of SAP. SAP will have a great deal more work created by having an open set of standards on the market. These BAPIs will work to enhance R/3's customer base into a midsized market. It allows you to use only the software links that you need. Therefore, you do not need to use all of the SAP functionalitiies.

SAP is doing more than simply publishing the interfaces to work its way into the midsized market. It is important to note that BAPIs were an important tool; however, SAP is also handling several other issues involving both distribution and selling channels prior to breaking into the midsized market. There is a large gap between SAP and other companies in this market segment. BAPIs will essentially make it simpler for software vendors and customers to connect applications to R/3.

You don't require the same amount of customer effort to interface with a custom application written or an older application being migrated to SAP. You won't have to create these interfaces by yourself. The existence of an open interface simplifies developer tasks, so they can now write in several languages, including Visual Basic, as opposed to just ABAP (which is SAP's proprietary language). In fact, you can greatly decrease the level of skill you need to bring in-house to achieve those tasks.

Customer Management Corporate Profile

CrossRoads Software is producing a creative solution for the enduring problem of integrating specific, complex enterprise application solutions. They are created with modern object technologies, which lends a solution that offers a simple application collaboration environment.

Most enterprises now operate with a variety of applications, including legacy, client-server of multiple generations, and increasingly Internet-capable. IT departments have found it difficult to create or obtain cross-generational and cross-functional application systems. Modern enterprise application portfolios don't integrate or communicate efficiently and they have been found to be very expensive to operate.

The difficulties involved in integrating crucial enterprise business systems or offering preintegrated solutions is so complex that multibillion dollar Services and Enterprise Business Applications (EBA) industries have grown to meet the increasing market demand. As technology increases in complexity, so do the problems of integration.

CrossRoads offers solution in combination with the industry-leading EBA suppliers. They offer out-of-the-box, prebuilt, partner-certified application-integration functionality. These functions are produced as collaborations and connectors. CrossRoads' method concentrates on business methods and processes that need multisystem integration founded more on a middle-ware method.

This business-process orientation permits your organization to establish a drag-and-drop environment that allows your application administrator to visually develop and implement significant cross-application functions in very little time. The first release collaborations include:

- Account status
- Order fulfillment and status
- Product configuration
- Field-service logistics
- Service billing

CIS + ERP = Customer Management

The two most significant areas within the Enterprise Business Application market include Customer Interaction Software (CIS) and Enterprise Resource Planning (ERP) systems. CIS solutions deal with front-office automation of sales, marketing, customer service, and support. ERP systems typically support the financial, manufacturing, and logistics requirements of organizations serving those customers.

You will often find value in integrating these functions to attain superior end-to-end management and customer value. These projects have been dealt with wholly on an expensive, customized basis.

While CIS-EBA integration is the first component of an effective solution, CrossRoads created a technology and business base that needs to extend to several additional, potential integration combinations.

The CrossRoads solution was created through object-oriented methodologies and technologies that provided a component-based, highly distributable application integration environment. The CrossRoads' core elements include collaborations, connectors, and the interchange server.

Collaboration objects are composed of the application-independent business methods that permit cross-application functional execution, such as service billing, while connectors are the application-aware intermediaries that connect collaborations to the native interface environment of the supported EBA system. Finally, the CrossRoads Inter-Change Server exploits Java, DCOM, and CORBA distributed object models in order to permit application systems that were not intended to operate in distributed environments to acquire that precious functionality together with collaborations and connectors.

Conclusion

This chapter details your progress to the point that you are now prepared. This section has examined the importance of your company's business requirements. Your *Business Blueprint* is essentially a model of your future environment once you have completed your R/3 implementation. Your efforts conclude with your project team defining its scope and concentrating on the R/3 processes required to run your business effectively.

It is important to get as much as possible out of your environment. Timing will help you utilize AcceleratedSAP and other SAP components in your enterprise applications. The result is that you will have an environment that can take advantage of the preconfigured tools and standards and use the tools that work for that information to speed your implementation effort.

You can tie together existing production applications and integrate your business system implementation to provide a very smooth transition into your SAP-inspired ERP solution. As technology advances, it is important to note that small and midsized companies can now take advantage of all of the functionality R/3 can deliver. The growth in future years will be fostered by startup organizations who can utilize high-level functionality to produce a growth spurt that can effectively pay for itself with increased business and customers who are satisfied with the extended functionality R/3 can provide quickly and efficiently.

GoingLive and Getting Support

Introduction

When you Go Live, you want to reduce your risk as much as possible. In order to accomplish that task, you need a very cost-effective deployment to take advantage of your acceleratedSAP R/3 implementation. The SAP R/3 Concept Review Service, illustrated in Fig. 11-1, eliminates the risk of having to adapt concept and implementation processes throughout your *GoingLive* and production phases.

Experience

SAP collects information from users and documents their experiences, and then enters that information into their experience database on the Internet to increase the number of solutions to possibly prevent problems early in the SAP R/3 Concept Review Service before they actually occur. The SAP *GoingLive* check makes certain you receive an uneventful transition from the implementation phase to utilizing R/3 in production. As an R/3 customer, you can benefit from SAP's *GoingLive* check. SAP experts log on to your R/3 system via a remote data transfer connection to examine the configuration of individual system components. At that point, they can offer recommendations for optimizing your system.

Figure 11-1
SAP Concept Review
Service.

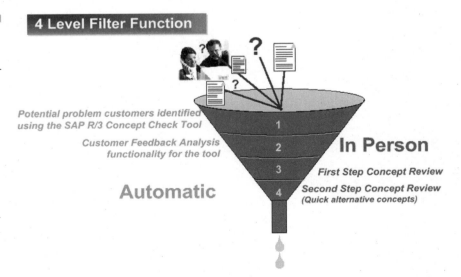

Figure 11-2
Performance to Manage Your Business.

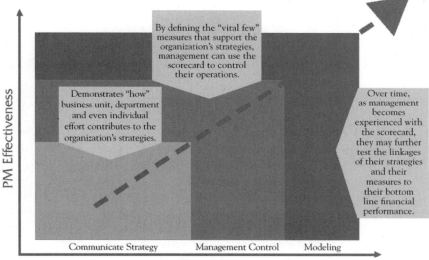

Utilizing Performance Management To Manage The Business

Evolution of the Performance Management process: How to utilize Performance Management to manage the business.

By defining the "vital few" measures that support the organization's strategies, management can use the scorecard to control their operations.

Demonstrates "how" business unit, department and even individual effort contributes to the organization's strategies.

Over time, as management becomes experienced with the scorecard, they may further test the linkages of their strategies and their measures to their bottom line financial performance.

PM Effectiveness

Communicate Strategy   Management Control   Modeling

Time

Your primary objective is to get your R/3 system ready for live production. Your productivity is often crucial to managing your business. This level of business management performance is shown in Fig. 11-2. You can inspect your system components prior to starting production. At that point, SAP can significantly enhance the availability and performance of your system.

SAP's extensive experience with R/3 projects indicates that the majority of performance problems can be identified and fixed before production begins. It is important to be able to identify your performance problems to ensure your productivity, as seen in Fig. 11-3. SAP experts have access to a detailed knowledge base that allows them to support and analyze your R/3 system to determine individual solutions for optimal system functionality. The SAP *GoingLive* check is composed of three extensive system inspections that are executed at regular intervals throughout the *GoingLive* phase.

Figure 11-3
Assistance for Performance Problems.

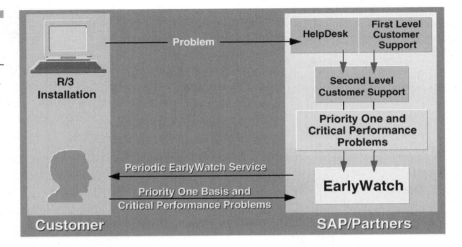

Figure 11-3
Assistance for Performance Problems.

GoingLive Check

The *GoingLive* check is completed as part of three tests. The first test looks at the major components in your R/3 installation for system consistency and reliability. This check focuses on your operating system parameters, database configuration, configuration of the *Basis* system, distribution of SAP processes across your individual servers, and the relationship between hardware structure and quantity. This test takes place about 2 months prior to your planned *GoingLive* date.

The second test deals with system optimization, which provides support for your system environment. This test goes beyond simple analysis of integral transactions from a technical standpoint. It looks for transactions with high resource utilization. The results are used to determine if specific adjustments are required to modify either your system configuration or database and system sizing. This test is best completed about 2 weeks prior to the beginning of your production phase.

The *GoingLive* check is completed by the final test, which involves verification of your system components and validates changes recommended by the two previous tests. This inspection is completed when the system is in production operation.

In order to make certain you don't have any problems with your operation, you need to have these checks completed 2 weeks after the start of your production phase. Following each system inspection, you need to acquire copies of the detailed report of each of the tests and the recommendations for optimizing your R/3 system.

Difficulties discovered in your system may require extensive recommendations for solving them. *GoingLive* experts will designate logistics with respect to their service session activities in combination with your primary personnel prior to, during, and following each service session. SAP experts utilize standard settings for each comparison. Attempts to deviate from these predefined standards are reviewed by your team to make certain that the knowledge and experience they have acquired in reviewing your environment is seen by your management team.

The level of R/3 installation is dependent on two different SAP service strategies. When dealing with either small or standard R/3 installations, the *GoingLive* check will act as a remote service. It will be offered through integrated tools and standard check procedures. These results are transmitted to customers as a standard service report. When dealing with more complex R/3 installations with several application modules (that is, more than 500 users, extensive modifications, or in-house solutions), you will find it is difficult to perform remote analysis effectively.

Optimization

In order to ensure your R/3 system optimization, two SAP service engineers actually go on-site for 2 to 3 days to analyze and document your core business processes that deal with volume, dependencies, time schedule, performance goals, performance analysis, and optimization potentials. This team will develop a checklist of optimization tasks to obtain the necessary performance goals for complexity, impact, necessary skills, and resources that are defined by SAP's teams of service engineers. They offer remote support for the implementation of your system optimization tasks.

The SAP *GoingLive* check is executed remotely, while on-site security procedures protect your data. *GoingLive* sessions are executed with a user copy and user password. You have complete control of the data link that exists between your R/3 system and SAP's Regional Service Center. You also have the ability to monitor your screen for each operation executed by a *GoingLive* specialist.

SAP *EarlyWatch*

The SAP *EarlyWatch* service makes certain you don't have problems with your R/3 systems around the world, and regular remote diagnoses will accomplish this. This process entails detailed analyses of SAP applications and configurations and includes your database, operating system, and network components. When you monitor your system environment on a regular basis, SAP *EarlyWatch* provides the foundation for a significant level of system availability and performance.

Data Security

SAP *EarlyWatch* offers a form of preventative maintenance that performs an initial analysis and allows you to institute safeguards before problems occur. Monitoring your R/3 operation is done by evaluating statistics on the various system components. This data is prepared by a special SAP tool called the *Computing Center Management System* (CCMS), which is offered in combination with your R/3 system. As a customer, you are supported individually by SAP's team of experts.

SAP personnel have a great deal of expertise to offer you on various platforms, databases, networks, and applications, which allow you to analyze specific problems and create safe solutions. As you and your partners work together, you can make certain that you receive the highest level of technical support. SAP also performs regular system checks to make certain you don't have any trouble in the business operations of your R/3 installation.

System Component Checks

Since no expensive travel costs are involved, the SAP *EarlyWatch* service is executed remotely from Regional Service Centers. On-site system checks are restricted to individual system components. SAP *EarlyWatch* provides a detailed examination of your total R/3 system, including preventative checks of your SAP applications, system configuration, and the load on your application servers and databases.

You receive an SAP applications analysis for each system component, which identifies serious errors in your SAP system log, suspect events in the SAP kernel, and any termination of ABAP/4 programs.

In addition, you can utilize the SAP configuration analysis which details the effectiveness of various SAP buffers, memory requirements compared to hardware configurations, and recommendations that deal with the SAP configuration modification. The remaining analyses involve workload analysis, which deals with average response times per SAP task type; workload distribution across several SAP services; and workload data sorted by days, weeks, and months. Server analysis deals with CPU utilization, memory utilization, swap space size, and recommendations that deal with server configuration modifications. Finally, database analysis deals with missing database indices and backup and archiving procedures so long as the backup utility is supported by SAP.

As a customer of *EarlyWatch,* you regularly receive an extensive status report on your productive R/3 installations composed of the analysis results and recommendations for optimizing your specific system performance.

Training Courses

One of the most important elements of a successful R/3 implementation project is the extent to which R/3 competence has been created at your site. Thorough comprehension of R/3 functionality and integration will get you the most from new technology advancements. Your objective is to learn the most you can from SAP's training courses and then have the ability to demonstrate the tools provided by R/3. These courses are geared toward business processes and interprocess links in your company. These links are based on greater than 800 business processes within R/3.

These training courses deal with project groups and consultants in both SAP and SAP's partner companies. They provide three training categories to satisfy your requirements:

Level 1 courses are 1-day seminars that offer you an overview of basic topics, including system architecture and integration of *EarlyWatch* services. Business process knowledge transfer is part of all Level 1 courses. These courses concentrate on management and members of project teams.

Level 2 courses take from 4 to 5 days, and they concentrate on business processes utilized by R/3 and how they are integrated. They are of special interest to members of the project teams responsible for implementing R/3.

Level 3 courses offer project teams a much more detailed view of specific business functions. These R/3 self-teaching units are used for ongoing knowledge transfer following the completion of an organized training activity.

The *Basis* seminars concentrate on transferring basic knowledge and information. However, the self-teaching units assist seminar participants in increasing their knowledge. SAP can also provide training for special topics such as system administration, performance analysis, and database management.

An alternate method of obtaining and transferring knowledge is through TechNet, which is an effective modern platform created to optimize learning within the range of SAP's total SAPNet information propositions. This training service for R/3 *Basis* and application-related topics is encompassed in up-to-date discussion forums via the Internet. It allows both its customers and partners to ask questions of SAP's experts. Furthermore, all questions and responses are documented and can be seen at any time by any TechNet user, which gives you instant access to the information you need.

The main element of this new training concept is IDES, which is SAP's International Demonstration and Education System. This model is integrated into the R/3 system and, in a practical way, depicts business application functionality of applications and the way in which they work with each other. In terms of a completely integrated system covering all applications, such as IDES Level 2 courses, Level 3 courses, R/3 Knowledge Products, and SAP TechNet, IDES offers an enhanced perspective into business processes and relationships. It simplifies your understanding of R/3.

When you take an SAP course, you benefit from training examples and exercises, based on the IDES model company. You then acquire hands-on experience and utilize the theoretical knowledge you learn in the classroom by applying it to your own R/3 system. IDES is offered at no cost. Furthermore, SAP workshops offer you a great deal of SAP knowledge that has been acquired from many years of experience with customer projects. Specifically, they satisfy your requirements throughout each of your R/3 project phases.

These workshops stress knowledge transfer, and this transfer is accomplished by you and your instructor working through the material as a team. Workshops are held at SAP or at your organization, depending on the specific topics, workshop structure, your regional service, and support structure. The System Administration Workshop and Implementation Workshop are taught at your company site and are organized to meet your individual needs. Whenever you register for in-house workshops, you are provided with a list of possible topics. You then choose which topics fit well with your project. You can schedule the workshops based on your needs and time frame.

Another benefit is that you can specify the limit of students within the workshop. The in-house workshops are taught by experienced SAP consultants who use both examples and practice sessions to demonstrate issues using your R/3 system. You can use that information to establish initial settings. Furthermore, in addition to the workshop, you get consulting and a preconfigured system tailored to meet your organizational needs. In-house workshop offerings include the System Administration Workshop which deals with all the primary concepts associated with R/3 administration.

Each idea is discussed and thoroughly explained to each student. At that point, you receive checklists that illustrate associated administrative tasks. Together with the consultant, you can execute all of these concepts on your R/3 system. This combination provides you with a great deal of expertise that allows you to establish important settings within your R/3 system.

The in-house workshops cover several key issues, including the client-server architecture, user concept, profile maintenance, printer configuration, background processing, operation modes, system monitoring, database, correction and transport system, memory management, and finally troubleshooting.

Then, discussions are held on issues relating to your specific system configuration and organizational requirements. This is a 4-day workshop, but before you can take it, your R/3 system must already be installed. While basic SAP knowledge is not necessary, this workshop prepares its students for specific *Basis* technology courses. The Implementation Workshop covers very important concepts and tools that permit you to customize your R/3 system efficiently.

Your implementation procedure is made evident through system examples. In addition, specific SAP R/3 concepts are covered, including the integration of the R/3 system, the SAP *Business Engineer* (Implementation Guide IMG, SAP Procedure Model, SAP Business Navigator), R/3 Analyzer, business processes mapping, project management, authorization concept, profile generator, and modification as opposed to parameter configuration. This type of SAP R/3 support cycle is shown in Fig. 11-4.

This 4-day workshop can be lengthened to incorporate additional topics that you need such as Internet/Intranet, R/3 *Business Workflow,* and data warehouse topics. The OSS (Online Service System) Workshop is offered at SAP, and it discusses several functions available to you in SAP's Online Service System. This workshop deals with OSS functions, including problem management, online availability of training informa-

Figure 11-4
R/3 Support Cycle.

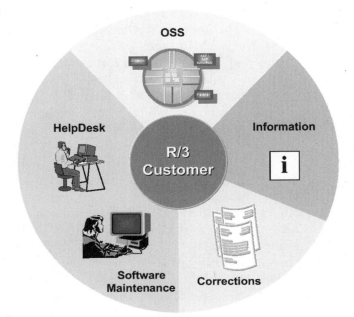

tion, administration, Hot Packages, and service connection. It also deals with SAP Software Change Registration, and OSS within the Customer Competence Center (CCC) whose functions can be seen in Fig. 11-5. This workshop is 1 day in length.

The Network Workshop offers crucial information on how to develop your internal network and establish a remote connection to SAP that is necessary in order to use several online services. This workshop deals with the communications requirements of the R/3 client-server application, IT network infrastructure needed to use SAP R/3, TCP/IP as a communications protocol for SAP R/3, systems management, network security, and SAP R/3 Online Services. The CCC support infrastructure is illustrated in Fig. 11-6.

The International Demonstration and Education System (IDES) is a comprehensive R/3 system that operates with data from a multinational model company. It is available at no cost when requested. The IDES Workshop offers general information with respect to using IDES and covers corporate organization of the IDES group, strategic benefits of various applications, and utilization of the online help created expressly for IDES.

The *GoingLive* workshop offers you crucial elements for going live. It responds to questions from various application areas, such as service

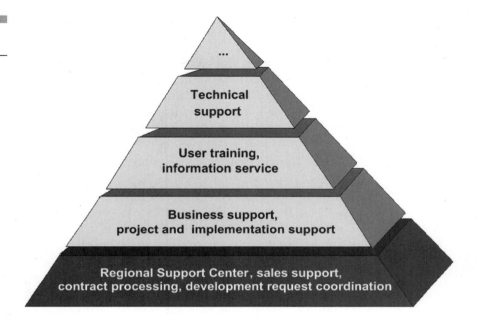

Figure 11-5
CCC Functions.

and support for customers going live. This includes SAP R/3 support, SAP *GoingLive* check, SAP *EarlyWatch,* Online Correction Support (including Hot Packages), printer administration, strategies for data backup and recovery, client copy, repository switch, system administration, and the Computing Center Management System (CCMS). This workshop is 2 days in length.

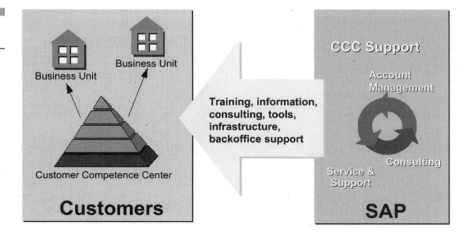

Figure 11-6
CCC Support.

Consulting Services

Partnering with SAP consulting provides you with access to high-quality, on-site assistance throughout your R/3 implementation and throughout the productive operation of your R/3 system. For questions that do not need on-site consulting, SAP offers a Remote Consulting Service that allows you to grow with respect to your changing business requirements in your live R/3 system. The variation between the levels of assistance that are done in-house or remotely is illustrated by Fig. 11-7.

On-site consulting activities are rooted in the customer's need to use SAP software effectively. Even though the R/3 system provides a great deal of functionality and integration, proper implementation of the software allows your business processes to take advantage of the system to the full extent. Consultants work with you as your partners in your R/3 implementation project. Use of your R/3 software to its fullest extent is your primary objective. SAP consulting works closely with your implementation team to locate a solution for every individual project. Utilizing efficient tools increases the speed of your implementation process, while offering a higher level of quality with respect to the analysis of goals, requirements, and business processes at your corporate site. It provides you with specific implementation concepts, methods, and standards for defining, planning, and controlling your implementation project.

SAP consulting works closely with you to carry out an extensive analysis of your organization's core business processes. At that point,

Figure 11-7
On-site versus
Remote Consulting.

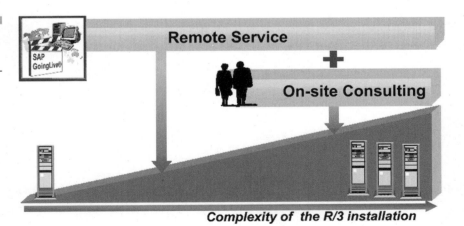

you can design and develop proposals for improving your organization and implement business processes commonly referred to as *business reengineering*. This process encompasses the use of best practices that result from years of experience in various consulting projects.

Solving Problems Efficiently

Successful problem solving can be achieved via SAP's experienced staff and the complete range of skills they possess. The continuous creation of specific knowledge, together with the constant development of the personal strengths of SAP's employees, allows you to work toward your ultimate objective. Partner success is often seen through partnership consulting departments in close contact with other areas of SAP, such as development and sales. This effort makes certain that your current standards and quality are maintained and enhanced.

You will benefit from communications between your consulting and customers' qualification and SAP consultants' cooperation with other departments. It is important to work closely together with selected qualified consulting partners to make certain you can respond to your needs in the most effective manner possible. SAP consulting helps you look for partners, and supports you in a variety of tasks.

Remote Consulting

SAP remote consulting offers you consultant assistance on short notice. It helps you with all phases of your implementation project and production operation. Over the course of your R/3 project, you may require the assistance of specialists during implementation and afterward. Because these situations cannot be planned, it may be necessary for you to wait for the service you require. Short consulting visits and unproductive travel expenses can be eliminated with remote consulting. Remote consulting services offer you the necessary short-term support with the assistance of new procedures and technologies. It allows you, essentially, to gain fast, competent support from SAP experts.

Remote consulting can be your qualified, knowledgeable partner for all questions regarding your R/3 system. In addition, you can get assistance from either SAP or consulting partners. Expert teams will answer your questions quickly and reliably. In addition, small program changes can be executed rapidly and efficiently in this manner.

Traditional project work that includes strategy or design consulting still requires on-site consulting. However, there are several occasions where remote consulting can solve your problems. Cooperation with external partners includes parameter configuration, questions regarding ABAP/4 Development Workbench, database reorganization, SAP upgrades, questions about SAPscript, and pricing. In addition, remote consulting can be utilized in several other methods, such as consulting by telephone, remote connection via an X.25 connection, and through personal video conferencing.

On-site versus remote consulting benefits include more rapid consulting, superior access to comprehensive consultant expertise about all applications and *Basis* technology, lower costs by eliminating unproductive travel time, and enhanced dialog using new video communications technology. Several benefits can be achieved through this level of consultation, as seen in Fig. 11-8. As a result, you can always obtain excellent assistance for your installation regardless of location.

SAP's Special Conversion Service is used where companies are subject to changes in the business environment in which they operate; internal organizational structure changes, corporate divisions fold, and new companies are purchased. In order to standardize business processes, existing numerical systems, including charts of accounts or

Figure 11-8
Consulting Benefits.

Benefits

Experience
from many successful projects

Effectiveness
through the use of efficient tools and performance-oriented procedure models

Competence
from concentrating on your products

Qualification
through the continuous training of employees working in the SAP environment

Know-how
from continuous discussion with your development department

Global cooperation
through consulting skills available worldwide in SAP subsidiaries

Reliability
through long-term cooperation that continues after production startup

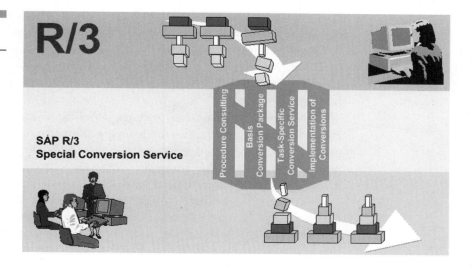

Figure 11-9
Conversion Service.

material masters are modified to meet requirements throughout corporate groups. The SAP R/3 Special Conversion Service, illustrated in Fig. 11-9, offers you a detailed solution that allows you to execute modifications to your R/3 production systems to compensate for changing business requirements.

The Special Conversion Service is appropriate for all questions concerning the R/3 system that result from changes to your corporate environment. The SAP R/3 Special Conversion Service offers you a detailed level of support in procedure consulting. This allows you to schedule appointments with consultants who offer information and advice regarding various approaches you can select. Modifications to your corporate structure are best illustrated through modifications to business area structure, company code structure, or sales structure. Procedure consulting is available as an individual service that can be chosen in combination with other components of the SAP R/3 Special Conversion Service. The *Basis* conversion package is the technical foundation for all procedures employed for any type of field conversion in an R/3 system. Examples of simple field conversions include renaming currency keys or changing a base unit of measure.

The *Basis* conversion package involves a specific transaction, which allows you to use a menu to execute modifications required for each conversion task. You can utilize the *Basis* conversion package separate from the other components of the SAP R/3 Special Conversion Service. Special conversion packages are available to support tasks that can be standardized and initiated by business requirements. This is best illustrated by the type of task that includes switching to a new fiscal year after a shortened fiscal year, changing a chart of accounts, or merging controlling areas.

Task-specific conversion packages include components such as the *Basis* conversion package which forms the technical foundation for all procedures, predefined task-specific parameterization of *Data Dictionary* objects, conversion programs, and table entries. In addition, it also deals with conversion algorithms needed by specific tasks, a technical prerequisite checklist, checklist documentation for each conversion package that is used. Finally, it deals with documentation of specific conversion packages and with the procedure consulting or implementation conversion services. If you do not wish to implement a conversion or have a consultant implement it, you can request that the SAP R/3 Special Conversion Service support it as part of its service offering. This results in it being a special project.

There are several methods for implementing conversions, however, these methods are dependent on whether existing, task-specific conversion packages are available, or whether you have any specific requirements that must be handled. R/3 services offer a variety of packages to assist your R/3 system, including check and monitoring services that make certain you have the best system functionality. In addition, training services assist you in creating a good knowledge base within your organization. Finally, consulting services offer you an extensive array of individual support.

Since you are an SAP customer, it is reasonable to think that you are investing in a technology that will maximize the return on your information investment. SAP provides a preconfigured solution in AcceleratedSAP to implement your R/3 services as quickly as possible. In order to supplement your R/3 support, each package offers solutions specifically created to satisfy your requirements throughout each phase of the R/3 product life. This offering makes certain that you can depend on straightforward productive operation of your R/3 system without difficulties.

Essentially, you gain significant advantages that promote rapid R/3 system implementation, enhanced system performance, customized support, and cost advantages. All of these factors work in concert to provide you with an accelerated and successful R/3 project implementation.

R/3 Service Packages

R/3 service packages provide an integrated service solution regardless of whether you are implementing your first R/3 system or already using R/3. SAP offers service packages tailored to meet your individual needs. SAP professionals guide you through the expansive capabilities of R/3 for the purpose of illustrating the advantages gained by refining your business processes.

There are specific benefits you should expect to see from these service packages, including special workshops and guidelines for the best possible knowledge transfer, preventative examinations and monitoring services, simple access to all services, professional advice, and the right service at the right time.

Selection of your R/3 service package solution is based on different elements. You can pick the package that best suits your corporate requirements. When you install an R/3 system, you can enhance your solution by gaining detailed assistance. The R/3 Standard Service Package will satisfy your requirements throughout all phases of the R/3 life cycle, including:

1. Installation

2. Implementation

3. Going live

4. Productive operation

These packages also incorporate workshops, R/3 knowledge products, system checks, and remote consulting. When combined, they essentially offer you all the services that you need for quick implementation of your R/3 system. SAP then offers assistance for going live and makes certain you achieve productive operation without difficulty.

The package includes specific training that deals with all of the important aspects, including production start-up, detailed system checks (before and during productive operation), and high-quality consulting services. Your goal is to use R/3 productively and have the ability to implement additional applications easily. The R/3 *GoingLive* Service Package guides you effectively through the start-up phase of your new applications. Helpful consulting services and detailed system analyses specifically meet your *GoingLive* phase. You want to make certain you have the best project start possible. In addition, you gain optimal performance of your live R/3 system while avoiding possible malfunctions. Furthermore, the R/3 Productive Operation Service Package utilizes regular system examination and consulting professional SAP assistance.

Overcoming Problems

Possible system constrictions are identified and prevented at an early stage to make certain you have continuous system availability. The R/3 Standard Service Package offers you benefits in its Optimizing Service Package, *GoingLive* Service Package, and R/3 Productive Operation Service Package. It is important that you make certain that the applications of your R/3 system are configured for the highest level of performance.

Package Benefits

The R/3 Concept Review Service Package assists you in performing a detailed examination of your R/3 implementation from a performance perspective. The package incorporates the *Concept Check* tool, as well as a professional analysis completed by two SAP specialists. This effort is supplemented by remote personal assistance. In addition, you will wish to utilize the International Demonstration and Education System (IDES) as a training and decision-making tool. IDES is a comprehensive R/3 system that functions by using data from a model multinational corporation. The R/3 IDES Service Package provides important information on how to use IDES and allows you to rapidly understand your R/3 functionality.

All services that assist you in using IDES are components of the R/3 IDES Service Package. SAP workshops offer extensive information on all topics that relate to R/3 implementation and configuration. These workshops are taught either at the customer site or at SAP's Regional Service and Support Centers. In any point in your R/3 project, the R/3 knowledge products offer you a great deal of SAP expertise for self-study and reference purposes.

The SAP Concept Review examines your R/3 implementation foundation and stresses relevant issues that affect your system's performance. During the SAP *GoingLive* check, SAP professionals execute a precise analysis of your R/3 system architecture. The main focus is on determining whether your R/3 system is ready to start productive operation. Your productive R/3 system is examined periodically to make certain you have constant system availability.

SAP's remote consulting services supplement the services listed in this chapter to support you and help you Go Live. The remote consulting allows SAP consultants to offer advice on the R/3 *Basis* system, R/3 applications, and International Demonstration and Education System. Remote consulting is accessible through phone consultation, remote logon, or personal video conferencing. If you have any questions about the R/3 service packages, simply submit an information request in the OSS or call your local SAP *Help Desk* for answers. The R/3 services that you need are bundled into R/3 service packages. The packages contain services that are specifically designed to meet the different phases of your R/3 product life cycle. These services permit personal training, workshops on R/3 products, preventative maintenance examination, monitoring services, remote consulting services, SAP's *GoingLive* examination, and SAP's *EarlyWatch* remote consulting services.

Service and Support

Both service and support are crucial elements of the customer competence centers. When you enter into an agreement with SAP (for example, a volume contract, outsourcing contract, value contract, or general license), large customers establish a Customer Competence Center (CCC) at their site. The CCCs offer an interface between large corporate customers and SAP. Furthermore, they are the primary local sources for questions pertaining to SAP, R/3 software, and R/3 accelerated implementations.

Active partnerships between SAP and the CCCs make certain you receive the best possible deployment and operation of SAP products at all global and domestic corporate locations. When you optimize R/3 usage, you reduce R/3 implementation time and accelerate your entire process.

CCC functions incorporate the development of standards for individual company units. CCC then provides technical support for R/3 installations within your company. In addition, CCC provides the resources for technical issues, including system upgrades, getting involved in the reengineering of business processes, and performing reviews. You also benefit from information management and user training within your company's Customer Competence Centers.

You can establish a customer *Help Desk* to assist end users in your organization solve problems with SAP software. The main source of information involves the error notes database in the OSS. Functionality is also achieved by supplying your company units with sales information. However, it is important that you remain responsible for R/3 license administration and license processing for your organization. You must also handle all of your development requests in your company, and then communicate with SAP regarding these requests.

The partnership between SAP and CCC allows SAP to provide CCCs with an extensive level of global support from the setup phase through productive operation. This can then be segmented into support and service offerings that include organizational support, as well as content of the CCCs and the necessary infrastructure. You also gain back-office support from SAP's Regional Support Centers and support from SAP Account Management. You are provided with tools and systems that include the Online Service System (OSS), the International Demonstration and Education System (IDES), and the R/3 *Business Engineer* (BE). You have support from the SAP Global/Customer Support Manager as well as SAP consulting services.

An added level of expertise is achieved through support from SAP R/3 services including *EarlyWatch* service and remote consulting service. Training is important for CCC employees, including on-site training and standard training courses that take place both at SAP, as well as through an SAP training institution. CCCs can also organize their own training through SAP's R/3 information database. The most significant benefits you gain from establishing a CCC include experience and expertise gained from various implementation projects. This information is collected in the CCC to be used in your company as standard solutions and is available for all company units through what is called the *synergy effect*.

It is important for your organization to clearly define problems so that your users gain a detailed level of assistance and get quick responses to their R/3 questions. As a result, they can solve any problem that occurs. It is important to work closely with SAP to reduce your risk throughout your SAP software implementation and bring your projects to productive operation as quickly as possible. Customer Competence Centers (CCCs) act as the interface between corporate customers and SAP. CCCs work together with SAP to provide R/3 service and support for your corporation.

Building Partnerships

Creating customized solutions is an important factor, and it allows SAP to create an ERP solution that meets specific needs and goals for your corporate goals. SAP has created partnerships with global and domestic organizations to provide you with a specific level of pliancy in your SAP installation. You have access to partners that offer a comprehensive range of products and services that support SAP projects, including business case development, hardware sizing, end-user training, system monitoring, and support.

SAP's service and support partnerships supplement SAP's own service offering and make certain that you can access the resources you need on a global basis. The different tasks in SAP's R/3 support area allow you to make certain that all areas have complete support. When partners' employees don't work at SAP Support Centers, SAP has access to its partners' support infrastructures. SAP's R/3 services can be offered by SAP, SAP's partners, or by SAP and its partners. SAP *EarlyWatch* is illustrative of this fact because it can be carried out by partners.

Partner Integration

SAP works in combination with several partner firms including Goal Support Service. Consulting partners are business and technology consulting firms that offer assistance in all stages of an R/3 implementation project. They maintain a great deal of expertise and utilize best practices for effective business process redesign, managing change, and using technology for business benefits. SAP's consulting partners offer a great number of services, including planning, developing customized documentation, and end-user training. SAP's consulting partners utilize their expertise with SAP systems to accelerate the implementation process, reduce cost, and optimize the return on your information investment. SAP solution centers are dedicated to specific industry and business requirements.

SAP groups consulting partners into three classifications related to the type of business at hand. The first involves Global Logo Partners which is the biggest and most experienced consulting partner firm that has multinational and multiindustry R/3 service capabilities. The second involves National Logo Partners which involves selected firms that have resources and capabilities that offer R/3 service throughout a particular country. The third involves Implementation Partners which involves firms offering more localized or specialized R/3 service dealing with a specific industry or functional area.

R/3 hardware, logo, and implementation partners offer the computing hardware required to satisfy a customer's system requirements. They work closely with SAP, you, and hardware partners on an ongoing basis to establish SAP service and support. The result is that you gain an optimized product that satisfies real-world requirements for operating business applications with SAP software. Hardware partners have created dedicated organizations to offer high-level SAP assistance that assists with every stage from production selection to system setup and installation, and finally continuous performance tuning. Each hardware partner has at least one competence center devoted to making certain you have the correct computer systems, as well as full compatibility with SAP software.

Technology partners bring together database manufacturers, operating systems, networking, and other information technology products. SAP works with these partners to make certain you receive a smooth integration of products with SAP's software. SAP's relationship with technology partners assists in the coordination of activities to integrate product advances and decrease the time to market for new products, releases, and applications. This effectively protects and enhances the value of your SAP investment.

Development partners are organizations that work with SAP in the development of future releases of SAP software. These organizations offer distinct business, technical, or industry expertise that enhance the internal functionality of SAP's development centers around the world. They also help SAP integrate the most recent best practices and technological improvement into their suite of products and services.

Value-Added Resellers

Value-added resellers are turnkey system vendors who offer comprehensive support for SAP's R/3 product for both small and midsized companies. These partners are authorized to sell the R/3 system and offer all the R/3 service and support necessary in order to implement and use SAP's business solutions. Value-added resellers are chosen with great care, so you can be certain that they have the extensive experience needed. In addition, they will have the ability to provide definite solutions for your specific industry.

Complementary Software Program

SAP's complementary software program permits independent software vendors to integrate their products with SAP's product line. Since SAP is known as a comprehensive integrated software solution, you need additional features to meet your specific business requirements. SAP has created an infrastructure to support the integration of independent software vendors' products with SAP's R/3. SAP's open technology foundation offers several possible interface avenues.

SAP updates a catalog of products and firms who have interfaces that are certified or provide complementary solutions. This complementary software program offers you a resource for increasing the performance and value of your SAP systems.

Partner Expertise

The basic element that forms the root of the relationship between your partner consultant and SAP is locating experts to help you implement an effective R/3 solution. Consultants have the greatest amount of SAP knowledge and applications expertise with the result that they are an important resource that offers skilled support and consistency around the world.

Consultants receive in-depth training in all of the latest SAP systems, tools, and implementation techniques. Quality training provides important benefits for you by increasing implementation effectiveness and business performance.

Five application instructional tracks are provided for new consultants. These process-orientated tracks incorporate 5 weeks' intensive instruction in R/3 capabilities and applications. Classes start with the basic R/3 concept and the way in which components effectively integrate to your advantage.

These classes deal with the best business practices and how you can implement them with SAP. They also deal with all of the specifics for configuring R/3 systems to execute specific functions. Training is completed with a 1-week case study in which a cross-functional team of students is formed for the purpose of creating a company in a simulated environment.

It is important to successfully complete academy training to gain the necessary level of achievement. Consultants need to complete this detailed course of instruction and demonstrate that they fully comprehend the subject matter by getting a passing grade in SAP's certification exams.

This release-based certification verifies comprehensive, up-to-date SAP knowledge. The result is that it is an important measurement of your consultant's knowledge. These exams are often given in combination with Academy courses, however, any consultant with enough SAP experience can complete these exams for the purposes of acquiring certification. These tests help to maintain high standards via a program of continued education. Certified consultants are linked into the SAP information network and are offered advanced courses on particular subjects. Periodic exchange of information makes certain that consultants know about the most recent SAP technology and can implement all of the newest best practices in your computing environment.

Conclusion

This chapter examines the point at which you are ready to proceed with your implementation. This section establishes a specified time to finalize your implementation. However, the most important factors when you Go Live is to make certain you can effectively solve any problems arising from snags that had not been foreseen during your implementation process. We end this section by providing information on how you can contact SAP's support and services program to obtain support so you can stay live and realize your implementation investment. Ultimately, this effort pays off when you have the power to fine-tine your R/3 system to fit your individual business processes.

CHAPTER 12

Cost versus Time

Introduction

Several consultants have concentrated on the implementation of SAP R/3 business applications. In order to achieve rapid implementations in the past, consultants charged very large fees for projects that took a significant toll on senior management. In order to prevent your implementation from running over in terms of schedule and cost, you need to prevent this type of situation by carefully documenting your business case and your return on investment (ROI). These estimates will help you manage your spending and satisfy upper management. Some organizations feel that SAP was more at fault than the high-priced consultants. However, SAP has taken to policing its consultants and implementors and has them convert SAP applications into simpler components that can be configured much easier. This permits your organization to implement software over a longer period of time as opposed to a single big bang.

In order to speed up your implementation in a cost-effective manner, SAP has introduced a well-received accelerated implementation program called AcceleratedSAP (ASAP). This program allows them to cut costs and still implement R/3 in as little time as possible.

Managing Expectations

Spending unlimited amounts of money for SAP consultants is not an effective move for many organizations. SAP put together a program that takes all of the best practices observed from prior implementations and offers that expertise to organizations who wish to implement R/3 in as short a time as possible. In terms of management, you will find that most executives have specific ROI projections. These estimates allow you to manage the expectations of upper management with respect to what seems to be growing implementation costs.

SAP's move to police its implementation consultants keeps costs at a controlled level. In addition, SAP is creating components from its applications, so that they are configured to order as opposed to being built to order. The concept is to move away from the "all at once" principle and regulate growth over time so that it is more of a steady stream. This component strategy utilizes the BAPI (Business API) strategy that permits your organization to write its applications to constant APIs. This protects you from changes and upgrades that are executed in your root R/3 software.

Accelerated Programs

SAP's introduction of their accelerated implementation program, called ASAP, is a step in the path to build on the client-server platform with the goal of embracing Intranets. SAP is also embarking on an Intranet strategy that incorporates global support of Java and *ActiveX*.

This strategy has helped SAP to maintain their large customers while, at the same time, eliminate barriers that have prevented many smaller customers from implementing R/3. It is important to reduce the complexity of these programs and increase the number of customers in order to stay competitive. Smaller businesses need the same functionality as their bigger rivals but don't have the money or time to wait. ASAP allows them to compete in a growing marketplace at the same level.

Implementation and consultant costs, however, will not decrease with respect to the need for additional computing hardware and disk storage. These areas are more than just software and consulting; they deal with the cost of more processing power and disk storage. These requirements only increase with time and are very important ingredients in faster processing. Training costs will not decrease either. Many organizations often develop their own computer-based training methods. Your company may choose to investigate an alternative to cut costs. However, SAP training is a valuable tool that cannot be easily replaced.

AcceleratedSAP

AcceleratedSAP is SAP's global technique for rapid deployment of the R/3. AcceleratedSAP ties together all of the benefits from past implementation best practices collected from the experiences of thousands of SAP customers. AcceleratedSAP is a worldwide program that deals with multinational companies and offers a centralized method of deploying R/3 across global operations. AcceleratedSAP offers you a faster return on your information investment. The real benefits you observe early in your effort include cost savings and operational efficiencies.

AcceleratedSAP's objective is to plan backward by scheduling from the objective Go Live date. It makes certain that all of your tasks result in adding value and help you in meeting the goal.

Partnership is an important aspect for SAP consultants and implementation partners who are trained in the AcceleratedSAP methodology. These people are dedicated to your success, and they work as a tightly integrated team with you from project launch through your final Go Live date.

The *Implementation Assistant* is a toolkit of templates, forms, questionnaires, and checklists that assists your ASAP program by giving you a lead on your implementation strategy. The most time-consuming task is trying to start from the very beginning. Instead, you can simply fill in the blanks to gain a better perspective on your efforts by employing an automated tool to help you throughout the entire process.

Process orientation offers you the ability to configure your core business processes. It involves looking at cycles across departments to make certain you receive a cross-functional, integrated solution. Quality assurance is elementary to any process. It works with the AcceleratedSAP *Roadmap* to make certain you achieve a complete, steady route of project deliverables. It specifies exactly what needs to be done at each phase of your implementation.

The reusable approach is used once your implementation has been completed. As an AcceleratedSAP customer, you gain standard procedures and customer-specific documents for deploying R/3 more diversely throughout your organization. In addition, role management works within your ASAP program to designate and coordinate your project team roles for application design, technical installation, and project management across all stages of implementation. This makes certain that all activities function correctly.

AcceleratedSAP Ingredients

The AcceleratedSAP *Roadmap* provides a detailed description of all of your implementation tasks with a detailed project plan. The SAP toolkit is an integral part of your R/3 *Implementation Assistant*. It is composed of tools that prevent you from having to create each process from scratch. You can use predefined business processes to cut costs and save time during your implementation effort.

The R/3 *Business Engineer* is the foundation for your system configuration. It offers you automated configuration capabilities and support

▇▇ ▇▇ ▇▇ ▇▇
Figure 12-1
Remote *GoingLive*
Check.

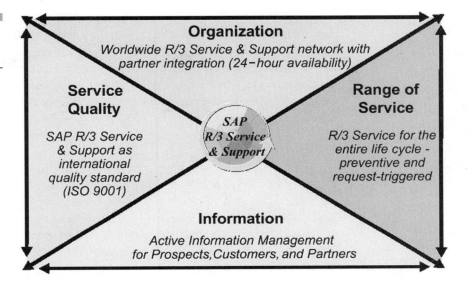

for the continuous enhancement of your business processes. In terms of both service and support, SAP consultants, together with implementation partners, work to form a close bond with you throughout the entire implementation project. Increased support is given through *EarlyWatch, GoingLive* checks, and Online Service and Support. The remote *GoingLive* check is illustrated in Fig. 12-1.

ASAP Stages

Project preparation is the first step to gain executive commitment. You can choose a project team to make critical decisions and then you can complete your high-level project plan. Your *Business Blueprint* allows your project team to work together with AcceleratedSAP consultants to establish a comprehensive blueprint of your business on R/3. You may then give that plan to your company executives for approval.

Simulation allows both your consultants and the project team to configure and install four-fifths of your basic R/3 systems using the *Business Blueprint* to emulate business transactions with real master data to refine and establish your blueprint. Validation is the stage that allows your project team to work with consultants to allow your system to grow into a totally integrated and documented solution.

At last, final preparation is the stage where you complete system testing, train end users, and plan a Go Live strategy. Then you can finally Go Live and reach the stage where your organization starts using its newly productive R/3 environment. Both consultants and project team members make certain that the business environment is totally supported by verifying the accuracy of transactions and making certain users' needs are met.

R/3 *Business Engineer*

SAP's R/3 *Business Engineer* is a strong configuration tool for quicker, more effective implementation of the R/3 enterprise business solution. It allows you to achieve ongoing improvement in business processes. The R/3 *Business Engineer* Release 4.0 gives you the power to configure R/3 more quickly and simply. It offers a detailed level of support for your entire R/3 environment. R/3 *Business Engineer* allows you to implement changes quickly at any point within your existing enterprise system.

It offers you benefits of a comprehensive, interactive configuration of R/3 that permits rapid implementation; support for ongoing business growth; and it gives you a quick, continuous return on you information investment by offering you an open configuration environment.

The R/3 *Business Engineer* has improved significantly in Release 4.0. It makes implementation much simpler and adds another level of interactivity with a question-and-answer–based configuration process. This process guides you through the R/3 configuration and defines problems, while activating R/3 process chains to depict how configuration decisions impact business processes throughout your integrated system. It also emulates operation of the live R/3 solution. It links traditional enterprise modeling together with the live R/3 system, while simultaneously connecting business models and deployment. *Business Engineer* makes certain that process design integrity is maintained, so that the decisions made during system configuration are compatible and supported. R/3 features a standard interface that opens the R/3 *Business Engineer* to partners, consultants, and customers. It permits each of these parties to enhance industry solutions and create corporate rollout templates.

Easier Configuration

R/3 *Business Engineer* Release 4.0 significantly simplifies configuration with its tools. It incorporates 100 business scenarios that tie together R/3's 1000 business processes into manageable pieces of best business practices. Industry templates offer a rapid project start with a custom-made R/3 solution. SAP offers templates for all its target vertical industries separate from the R/3 *Business Engineer* release cycles.

Ongoing enhancement of the R/3 *Business Engineer* permits you to manage change and continuously execute system improvements by supporting nine-tenths of your daily business changes, including the addition or removal of components within your corporate structure. These components include business units, production plants, warehouses, new staff, promotions, reallocation of work tasks, and maintenance of authorization profiles. This enhancement also includes both new and current currencies and the conversion to the Euro, adding international business partners. It must also deal with modified legal requirements, including the new tax rates and employment legislation.

R/3 *Business Engineer* provides you with a great deal of flexibility by allowing you to configure several versions of R/3. It provides benefit in new releases. It also allows you to introduce new projects into the operating system. Standard APIs to R/3 *Business Engineer,* in combination with support for major standard interfaces (for example, COM/DCOM and *ActiveX*), permit integration with third-party software, tools, and methodologies. The Web-browser front end, as well as the HTML-based documentation, makes R/3 *Business Engineer* independent of any one platform, with the result that it is easy to use and access. This meets the requirements set out by SAP's *Business Framework*. R/3 *Business Engineer* supports component-oriented implementation and is updated with the delivery of R/3 components.

Aerospace and Defense

SAP's Service Network for the SAP Aerospace and Defense Industry provides a complete network of high-quality services for the entire life cycle of your R/3 system. It provides services that are reliable, effective, and available globally.

SAP's objective is to offer utilities with a professional service infrastructure to make certain you have easy implementation, optimization, and growth of the SAP utilities solution. This should be accomplished in the quickest, least expensive, and most secure method available. SAP's extensive experience in the utilities industry has been achieved from numerous R/3 installations in each IT industry. This experience is gained from partnerships with the industry's leading consulting companies together with a varying array of services. They make certain that you obtain the best possible level of support to obtain your goals.

Information Services offer you the very latest information about SAP, their products, and their partners. SAP's information and communications service is called SAPNet. It deals with SAP's home page on the World Wide Web (WWW), as well as the Online Service System (OSS), and offers you recent information on SAP and customer and partner information about the utilities sector.

Education Services

SAP's professional education services offer your implementation teams several tools to promote quick R/3 knowledge transfers that form the basis for more rapid, cost-effective implementation and more effective on-the-job performance in your utilities company.

Knowledgeable R/3 instructors and SAP consultants provide you with high-quality, business process-based training, and interactive workshops to support your utilities company. This support is acquired during the planning, implementation, and customizing stages of your R/3 project. The specific planning table is shown in Fig. 12-2.

IDES

The International Demonstration and Education System (IDES) is a complete, preinstalled R/3 system. IDES was designed for testing, demonstration, and training purposes. It offers complete online and printed documentation in addition to SAP Knowledge Products (CD ROMs). The information offered is important and easily accessed on the R/3 system, along with the implementation.

The most important benefit is that there is always profession assis-

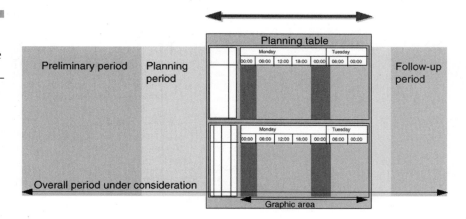

Figure 12-2
Planning Table as a
Window on the Time
Axis.

tance available to you from SAP's *Help Desk,* remote consulting service, and SAP Utilities Industry Center of Expertise (ICOE). All are available to provide expert assistance on your specific utilities or general R/3 issues. In addition, they also offer practical support to refine your R/3 installation. The *EarlyWatch* system monitors your installation, while the Online Service System (OSS) records and processes your R/3 queries.

Cost-Effective Implementations

Rapid and cost-effective implementation is something that SAP has invested in significantly to provide you with the elementary ingredients you need for a refined, time-efficient implementation of SAP's utilities solution. The ASAP implementation process itself is shown in Fig. 12-3. Experienced consultants, best-practice implementation processes, and powerful implementation tools are required to achieve your goals.

Professional Consulting Support supplements SAP's consultants. These people form the partnerships created with industry-leading consulting firms. SAP has created a large network of global, regional, and national business partners to offer you professional support in satisfying the functional and budgetary requirements for your utilities company. SAP's consulting and implementation partners are chosen for their professional expertise and industry experience with SAP utilities.

The combination of an expert team of experienced SAP consultants offers you high-level support at each stage of your R/3 project, including

Figure 12-3
AcceleratedSAP
Implementation
Process.

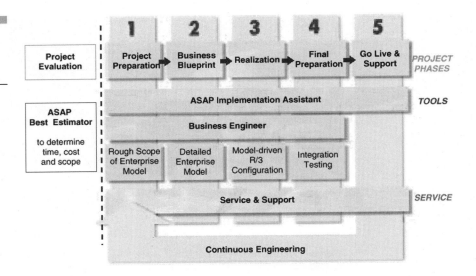

Figure 12-3
AcceleratedSAP
Implementation
Process.

requirements planning, implementation, customizing, and going live. They can assist you with your business process reengineering projects in order to make certain that your R/3 implementation satisfies specific corporate requirements. Their goal is to implement ROI investigations to quantify your project's results.

Implementation Assistance

The *Business Engineer* offers a complete set of graphical models, business processes, and implementation guide tools for rapid comprehension and customization of SAP utilities. It allows you to plan your project step by step. It guides you through all project activities while SAP provides you with an R/3 *Procedure Model* in combination with the AcceleratedSAP *Roadmap*. These elements provide you with extra tips and tricks, templates, and questionnaires to support each step of your implementation. These elements are based on the experience gathered from several thousand successful R/3 implementation projects. Ernst & Young offers a high level of implementation assistance to their customers, as illustrated in Fig. 12-4. These services all fit together to create the ideal foundation for scheduling your R/3 project activities.

The R/3 *Reference Model* helps examine and provide details on your needs. It is a set of graphical business process models that represent

Figure 12-4
Implementation Assistance offered by Ernst & Young.

Implementation Assistance	
Infrastructure Support	**SAP Functional Support**
▸ Hardware Acquisition and Sizing	SD
▸ Systems Software Implementation	MM
▸ Telecommunications	FI/CO
▸ Networking	HR
▸ Help Desk Support	PP
▸ Disaster Recovery	PR
▸ Desktop Services	Change Management
▸ Security	Package-Enabled Reengineering
▸ Hardware/Software Tuning	Training
SAP Evolution Support	

utility-specific best-business practices in the R/3 system. The *Implementation Guide* sets configuration parameters and serves as an active tool with direct links to status fields, resource assignment, and project documentation, so that you can customize all R/3 system settings. In order to further automate and optimize your business processes, you can use a completely integrated SAP *Business Workflow*. When individual enhancements are required, the ABAP/4 *Development Workbench* offers simple and flexible development tools for your R/3 company-specific enhancements.

SAP's Automotive Industry Service Network

SAP provides a detailed network of high-quality services for the complete life cycle of your R/3 system. Its services are globally available, reliable, and effective.

SAP's objective is to offer its automotive customers a professional service infrastructure that will make certain you receive a very orderly implementation. In addition, it offers the most rapid and cost-effective solution possible. SAP's detailed automotive experience is accumulated from several R/3 installations throughout the IT industry. This expertise is gained from partnerships with industry-leading consulting companies and the vast array of services they offer to make certain you obtain the best possible level of support to achieve your objectives.

Services

In addition to SAP conferences, there are several automotive-specific events and customer visits that provide you with a wide range of media that includes the most recent information about SAP, its products, and partners. SAP's information and communications service is called SAP-Net, and it incorporates SAP's home page on the World Wide Web (WWW) as well as the Online Service System (OSS) which offers you the most recent information on automotive-specific customer and partner information.

In terms of education services, SAP's professional education services offer your implementation team a plethora of tools for the quick R/3 knowledge transfer that forms the basis for rapid, cost-effective implementation. This speed translates into a more effective on-the-job performance level in your automotive organization.

Experienced R/3 instructors and SAP consultants provide you with an exceptional level of quality in their business process-based training and interactive workshops. These components work together to support your automotive company throughout the planning, implementation, and customizing stages of your R/3 project.

The International Demonstration and Education System offers you a complete, preinstalled R/3 system with automotive-specific data for your core business processes. The IDES was created for testing, demonstration, and training purposes. There is also a detailed level of online and printed documentation and SAP knowledge products (CD ROMs). These components add valuable, easily accessible information on your R/3 system, throughout it's implementation.

Essentially, you gain a great deal of expertise and assistance in your accelerated R/3 implementation. SAP's 24-hour-per-day, 7-day-per-week *Help Desk,* remote consulting service, and SAP Automotive Industry Center of Expertise (ICOE) offer expert advice on your automotive-specific and general R/3 issues. There is also dedicated support to refine your R/3 installation illustrated by the *EarlyWatch* system, which monitors your installation, and by the Online Service System, which records and processes your R/3 queries.

ICOEs

The SAP's Automotive Industry Centers of Expertise concentrate on your resources in order to make certain they create enhanced integrated solutions that support specific automotive industry topics as well as your business processes. They link SAP professionals with automotive industry expertise in an effort to function as one unit with industry partners and automotive companies in order to establish a detailed, fresh solution to satisfy your needs.

The automotive ICOE philosophy is to work together with industry organizations, automotive user and focus groups, and SAP design councils in an effort to determine new trends, designate automotive industry needs, and develop priorities that can be integrated into the basic design for R/3 development.

Chemical Industry

SAP offers a detailed service network for the entire life cycle of your R/3 system and services designed for the chemical industry are available globally. SAP works to provide its chemical customers with a professional service groundwork that makes certain you have easy implementation, optimization, and development of your SAP R/3 solution as quickly and cost-effectively as possible. SAP's extensive experience in the chemical industry is achieved from several R/3 installations and from their partnerships with the industry's leading consulting companies. This experience allows them to offer a detailed range of services to help you meet your individual goals.

Information Products

In addition to SAP conferences, there are several distinct chemical-industry-related events and customer visits that provide you with several information about the latest information on SAP, their products, and partners. Their education services include professional education services that offer your implementation team several tools that promote quick R/3 knowledge transfer. This knowledge transfer forms the basis for faster, cost-effective implementation and more effective on-the-job performance.

Experienced R/3 instructors and SAP consultants provide quality business process training in interactive workshops designed to support your company throughout the R/3 implementation and customization processes. The International Demonstration and Education System offers you a complete, preinstalled R/3 system that incorporates industry specific data for your core business processes.

Support Services

SAP has placed a great deal of effort into its refined, cost-effective implementation of SAP's solution for the chemical industry. They achieve this goal with experienced consultants, best-practice implementation processes, and strong implementation tools.

Professional consulting support supplements SAP consultants with partnerships established with industry-leading consulting firms. SAP has created a large network of global, regional, and national business partners to offer professional support in order to satisfy your chemical company budgetary requirements. SAP's consulting and implementation partners are chosen for their expertise in the chemical industry to help you achieve your goals.

Chemical customers benefit from experienced SAP consultants who help you with each stage of your R/3 implementation project. This assistance extends to each of your business processes, including reengineering projects to make certain that your R/3 implementation meets your particular requirements. You know exactly what the return is on your information investment, so that you can see realizable results from your accelerated R/3 implementation project.

Assisting Your Implementation

The *Business Engineer* offers a complete GUI environment with models, business processes, and implementation guides that allow you to customize R/3 chemical solutions and involve a sample project plan and step-by-step guide for all of your project activities. The R/3 *Procedure Model* and the AcceleratedSAP *Roadmap* provide important tips, templates, and questionnaires to support each step of your implementation process. These steps are based on the collective experience from thousands of successful R/3 implementation projects. These experiences form the foundation for scheduling your R/3 project activities.

In order to examine and outline your requirements, the R/3 *Reference Model* offers a collection of graphical business process models that explain chemical-specific best-business practices in your R/3 system. The *Implementation Guide* serves as a set of configuration parameters and is an active tool that has direct links to status fields, resource assignment, and project documentation for customizing all R/3 system settings. You can automate your business processes with the SAP *Business Workflow*. However, if you need specific improvements, the ABAP/4 *Development Workbench* offers an easy set of development tools for your R/3 specific requirements.

The R/3 *Reference Model* provides a detailed set of R/3 chemical-specific business process models that deal with sales order processing, batch and continuous manufacturing, process costing, and personnel management. These graphical models utilize best-business practices and illustrate the R/3 business processes that meet chemical industry requirements. These processes permit your implementation team to wade through your R/3 system easily, so they can rapidly comprehend R/3's business processes and integrated information flow. This flow gives you a detailed perspective enabling you to recognize opportunities that allow you to refine your routines and procedures throughout departmental boundaries. The R/3 *Reference Model* provides the basis blueprint needed for your chemical company to determine the correct resources and implementation strategy necessary to meet your specific needs. It assists you in reducing required planning, customization effort, and associated costs.

Business Consulting Partners

SAP's ICOEs concentrate on your business processes while providing resources to make certain you obtain integrated solutions that satisfy your particular chemical industry issues and business needs. It connects SAP professionals with chemical industry expertise who work together with industry partners and leading chemical companies to establish detailed industry solutions. ICOE works together with your organization, its chemical users, focus groups, and SAP design councils in order to determine emerging trends, designate chemical industry requirements, and create priorities that are integrated into total design plans for R/3 implementation.

Pharmaceutical Industry Service Network

SAP provides an extensive network of services for the complete life cycle of your R/3 system. SAP works to provide its pharmaceutical customers with a professional service foundation that makes certain your implementation, optimization, and growth occur as efficiently and cost-effectively as possible. SAP's extensive pharmaceutical experience was acquired from many R/3 installations which helped them create a vast array of services to provide you with the support you need to meet your implementation goal as fast as possible.

SAP's goal is to provide you with a refined implementation with strong tools and best practices to implement R/3 effectively. An area that is particularly helpful is professional consulting, which supplements SAP's consultants with partnerships gained through industry-leading consulting firms. SAP has created a vast network of global, regional, and national business partners to offer professional support to satisfy your budgetary needs. SAP's consulting and implementation partners are chosen specifically because of their expertise in the pharmaceutical industry.

SAP works together with experienced SAP consultants to offer its pharmaceutical customers the best level of support for each stage of your R/3 implementation. In essence, you can accelerate your requirements planning, implementation, and customization. Then you can Go Live sooner. You gain an increased level of assistance with your business process reengineering projects so you can be certain your R/3 implementation will satisfy your specific company requirements and produce a decent ROI.

The *Business Engineer* offers you a detailed set of graphical models, business processes, and implementation guides that provide you with a sample project plan and step-by-step guide to accelerate your solution. SAP provides an R/3 *Procedure Model* and an AcceleratedSAP *Roadmap* which has tips, templates, and questionnaires to support you through each phase of your implementation. Best-practices experience helps your R/3 implementation projects to create a solid foundation that helps you schedule your R/3 project activities.

Analysis of your requirements can be enhanced by the R/3 *Reference Model,* which offers a broad set of graphical business process models that reflect the specific pharmaceutical best-business practices in your R/3 system. The *Implementation Guide* sets configuration parameters and acts as an active tool with a direct connection to status fields, resource assignment, and project documentation for customizing all of your R/3 system settings. In addition, the SAP *Business Workflow* automates and accelerates your business processes. Specific enhancements are achieved through the ABAP/4 *Development Workbench* which offers simple, but flexible, development tools for your R/3 specific industry enhancements.

The R/3 *Reference Model* offers a detailed set of R/3 pharmaceutical business process models, including batch and continuous manufacturing, process costing, and personnel management. These graphical models utilize best-business practices and reflect the R/3 business processes specific to your pharmaceutical organization. They enable your implementation team to easily navigate through the R/3 system and understand R/3's business processes and integrated information flow. It essentially offers you the ability to better identify opportunities you can use to optimize your routines and procedures throughout the departmental entities within your organization. The R/3 *Reference Model* provides the blueprint you need to make your pharmaceutical company realize the best resources and implementation strategy necessary for your specific needs and assists you in required planning, customization effort, and associated costs.

Plant-Focused Consulting Partners

SAP's Industry Centers of Expertise (ICOE) concentrate on the development of tightly integrated solutions that satisfy pharmaceutical industry business processes by linking SAP professionals with pharmaceutical industry expertise. These professionals work together with industry partners and pharmaceutical industries for the purpose of developing detailed industry solutions. The ICOE foundation involves working together with pharmaceutical users to determine emerging trends and designate pharmaceutical industry requirements. At that point, you can develop priorities and integrate them into your R/3 development.

Public Sector Service Network

SAP provides a detailed network of services for the entire life cycle of your R/3 system. SAP offers public sector customers a level of professional service that makes certain you have an easy implementation that is accelerated and completed at the lowest cost possible. SAP's extensive public sector experience is acquired from many R/3 installations in this industry as a result of their partnerships with the industry's consulting organizations. This is supplemented by several services to supply public sector customers with global support to achieve your implementation objectives.

Accelerated Implementation

SAP offers you accelerated, refined, cost-effective implementations for public sector solution by using experienced consultants, best-practice implementation processes, and extensive implementation tools. Professional consulting support supplements SAP's consultants. SAP has created an extensive network of global, regional, and national business partners to offer you professional support that satisfies the needs and budget of your public sector organization. SAP has a great deal of expertise and public sector industry experience.

Together with experienced SAP consultants, you gain public sector expertise and support for each stage of your R/3 project, including planning, implementation, and customization. You can then Go Live with the assistance for your business process reengineering projects to make sure that your R/3 implementation satisfies your corporate needs and provides a good return on your information investment.

The *Business Engineer* is an excellent implementation tool that provides a detailed set of graphical models, business processes, and implementation rules to assist you with an effective R/3 public sector solution.

The R/3 *Reference Model* provides a detailed set of R/3 public sector-specific business process models, including sales order processing, budget planning, approval, budget execution, controlling, and personnel management such as position management. These graphical models are founded on best-business practices and reflect R/3 business processes that are specific to the public sector. They allow your implementation team to navigate through your R/3 system and comprehend R/3's business processes and integrated information flow. You then gain a better perspective which allows you to optimize the routines and procedures in each department. The R/3 *Reference Model* is the model by which public sector organizations can identify required resources and implementation strategies that will assist in reducing planning, customization, and costs.

SAP's Industry Centers of Expertise (ICOE)

SAP's public sector ICOEs concentrate on developing high-level integrated solutions that satisfy public sector business processes. They link SAP professionals with public sector industry expertise who work together with partners and public administrations to establish detailed solutions.

The public sector ICOE fosters tight integration with public sector users to designate emerging trends, identify public sector industry requirements, and develop priorities that are integrated into your R/3 design plans. The public sector ICOE, based on research and development, makes certain your current R/3 solution will grow as technology evolves.

The public sector ICOE fosters a complete solution that includes industry-specific partners. In order to make certain you receive the most effective and efficient integration of R/3 into your existing environments, special support in the areas of hardware, software, systems engineering, and implementation allows you to speed up your implementation efforts.

SAP's Retail Service Network

SAP offers its retail customers a professional service foundation that makes certain you benefit from easy implementation, optimization, and growth of your SAP retail solution. SAP's extensive experience in the retail industry is acquired from numerous R/3 installations. More information is gained from partnerships with leading consulting organizations and several services that make certain you gain the support you need to obtain your implementation objectives in the time allotted.

In order to gain the most rapid, cost-effective implementation, SAP offers a refined retail solution with help from its experienced consultants, best-practice implementation processes, and implementation tools. Professional consulting support supplements SAP's consultants. SAP has developed a large network of global, regional, and national business partners to offer professional support to satisfy your needs and the cost restrictions of a retail company. SAP consultants offer its retail customers a high level of support for each stage of the R/3 project, including assisting you with your business process reengineering projects. It makes sure that your R/3 implementation meets your specific company's needs and obtains the desired project results.

The *Business Engineer* offers you a set of graphical models, business processes, and implementation guides for rapid understanding and customization of your SAP retail solution. SAP offers the R/3 *Procedure Model* and the AcceleratedSAP *Roadmap* to provide support at each phase of your implementation. Accumulated best practices from SAP's previous R/3 implementation projects allow you to create the foundation for scheduling your R/3 project activities. The R/3 *Reference Model* examines your requirements and offers you a set of graphical business process models that illustrate retail-specific best-business practices in your R/3 system.

SAP's Telecommunication Service Network

SAP provides a detailed network of services for the entire life cycle of your R/3 system that provides its telecommunications customers with a strong foundation that ensures an easy implementation of an AcceleratedSAP telecommunications solution in the most cost-effective manner possible. SAP's extensive experience in the telecommunications industry is a result of its partnerships, services, and best practices which make certain you achieve your implementation on time and on budget. Information services are available as conferences, telecom events, and customer visits. SAP provides you with the newest information through SAPNet and OSS.

Conclusion

This chapter deals with the overall cost to implement R/3. Then, we try and determine if that cost is justified by the amount of time it will take to implement R/3. Many organizations believe that ASAP can effectively produce a quick implementation, but they are unsure of whether the quality will be there. In this section we have illustrated examples and programs that help to identify the amount of resources a typical implementation will require and show that this type of implementation can be effectively achieved without sacrificing quality for speed.

CHAPTER 13

AcceleratedSAP
Benefits

Introduction

There are several benefits from using the AcceleratedSAP program. ASAP improves time, quality, and efficient resources utilization throughout your implementations. Its primary benefits include quicker R/3 implementation and improved business results. It offers a standard approach to R/3 implementation for your partners and consultants, so that you are confident in the quality and guaranteed implementation knowledge. It results in more effective use of available resources, and these results can be used in future implementation stages to decrease your overall implementation costs for a better return on your information investment.

Accelerated R/3

The largest drawback to R/3 has been that it takes far too long to implement. The AcceleratedSAP program was designed specifically to refine and produce a standard implementation approach to cut the implementation time to less than 2 years and reduce costs, making it an acceptable solution for smaller businesses.

The ASAP program implementation of R/3 has six stages beginning with collecting and assessing your resources and ending with the final Go Live and support stage. This program reduces the time it takes to learn the system, and places you in a distinct advantage in terms of time, so that everyone within your organization is working together as a cohesive unit.

When dealing with CBS, the process is further shortened. The CBS version ties together some stages to offer an even shorter, less-labor-intensive start-up process for organizations that must work within daily work hours. The CBS implementation program is founded on the premise that its customers are too busy for a full system analysis.

The CBS program offers a complete process and ASAP speeds implementation. This system includes a questionnaire as part of the planning process, but the most disturbing fact is that many people simply don't define their project requirements before starting. This is an important step that ensures your success.

The best program benefit is that it defines a course of action prior to implementation, however, you don't receive any documentation as to how your system works after you Go Live with the product. SAP's average time to implement is approximately 6 months, a time frame that can vary either way, depending on the size and complexity of your organization. It is important for your project team to have an understanding of how a business works. Implementations are managed successfully when a company knows and can communicate its business needs.

This program neither resolves all implementation issues nor deals with reengineering issues. Therefore, if your company has just migrated from legacy systems, you need to deal with issues that this plan doesn't support.

Realization of ASAP Benefits

According to customers who have implemented SAP R/3 or are evaluating using R/3 for their business, upper management needs to realize the benefits from SAP R/3 at the fastest rate possible. AcceleratedSAP offers you a quick implementation option that is designed for enterprises that are ready to utilize the significant values of R/3 quickly, while establishing the technology foundation for future business improvement.

The return on your information investment remains the primary goal of any enterprise implementing SAP's integrated R/3 client-server software. It is important to make your business investment viable to accumulate a high return on your investment in the shortest time possible. One of the methods to assure you receive the best possible ROI is to investigate the integrated service solution shown in Fig. 13-1.

The ASAP program was created and tested at customer sites by SAP to satisfy the demand for faster returns for companies implementing R/3. The project team responsible for its development examined the collective experience from several years of R/3 implementations. They then defined successful accelerators in business processes and eliminated redundant implementation efforts. Once this was accomplished, they could benefit from the growth of automated configuration capabilities in R/3's *Business Engineer* as seen in Fig. 13-2. The end product was an efficient R/3 implementation option for customers whose main goal was to achieve critical business functionality from an R/3 investment in 4 to 10 months.

AcceleratedSAP was created originally for North American customers whose annual revenues were between $200 million and $2.5 billion. However, the ASAP program is not utilized domestically or globally by

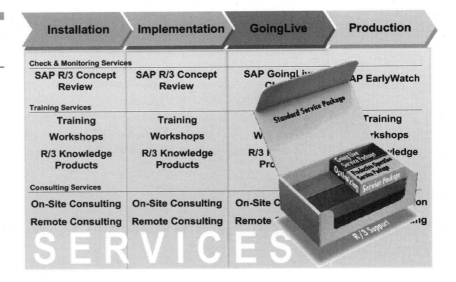

Figure 13-1
Integrated Service Solution.

multibillion dollar customers who need to gain more rapid returns on an SAP investment. SAP and several of their implementation partners use this program. It is an option for enterprises that need to complete their tasks, migrate from legacy applications, and at the same time meet year 2000 compliancy.

AcceleratedSAP is not effective for all R/3 implementations. Enterprises that require a great deal of operational improvement via large-

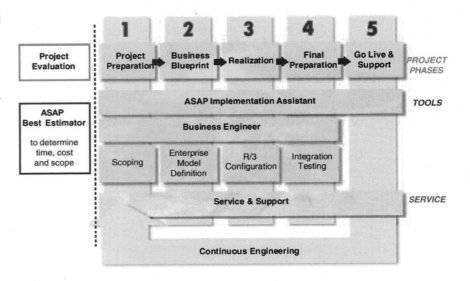

Figure 13-2
Business Engineer—An Enabling Technology for Accelerated-SAP.

scale reengineering can benefit from a more standardized R/3 implementation effort that stresses process improvement over rapid deployment. However, the factors of accelerated implementation are what AcceleratedSAP is about as it applies to almost everyone across many different R/3 implementations.

ASAP Differentiators

ASAP is the first implementation solution created and supported directly by SAP. It provides you with a straightforward SAP-derived preliminary estimate of resource requirements. It ties together elements that lead to success. It reduces time, cost, and people to form a solution that relies heavily on your needs. ASAP can be used by any of SAP's implementation partners that wish to offer this accelerated methodology. AcceleratedSAP is used as the foundation for R/3 customers around the world, as they can utilize a standard method for their R/3 implementations throughout any department, region, or country. The best goal is that it provides an excellent foundation for future R/3 upgrades, due to the fact that the ASAP program has only small software modifications. In that way, you are in a superior position to utilize the benefits from SAP's research and development from current and future releases.

Business Engineer Benefits

Significant improvements have been made in SAP's R/3 *Business Engineer* (BE). BE is a configuration, modeling, implementation, and ongoing improvement tool that provides distinct advantages in speed for any organization that wishes to compare specific business requirements to R/3's capabilities. The *Business Engineer* is the foundation tool for AcceleratedSAP, as it permits rapid implementation and ongoing process improvement.

AcceleratedSAP is different from any other traditional software implementation efforts due to the fact that executives need to be ready for rapid software deployment, which is of significance to any enterprise resource planning (ERP) package implementation that includes R/3. This preparedness requires that you are highly motivated to make effective decisions about business processes, execute definable business objectives, and agree to carry the project to completion in the most timely manner possible.

Upper management needs to be ready to estimate the level to which their business can utilize R/3's best practice processes as opposed to the possible modifications needed for their own operational needs. For executives who are confident that their enterprises do not need a great deal of change management, reengineering, or R/3 modification requirements, AcceleratedSAP provides a great deal of time and resource savings as it forms the foundation for ongoing operational improvements.

AcceleratedSAP: Six Phases

Before your business selects AcceleratedSAP as an implementation program, SAP consultants help determine the suitability of this program for your particular location. Consultants utilize the SAP *Project Estimator* kit that incorporates predefined questionnaires to interview upper management and operating managers regarding their expected results and objectives from using R/3 for their business, and the level of speed they need for their deployment. Their responses are compared with a database of past implementation information, and the responses should be similar to those in the database. After the analysis of the responses, the consultant will develop a potential plan, resource utilization chart, and cost estimates for your entire implementation process.

The result is several initial estimates that are very important due to the fact that the amounts often form the foundation for discussion, opposition, and enhancements at the beginning of your R/3 implementation. Often, the R/3 implementation starts with implicit and incompatible expectations by both the customer and independent professional services consultants. This 2-day process adjusts expectations and permits SAP consultants to suggest the best AcceleratedSAP approach, so that you will be prepared to implement R/3 quickly with the fewest system changes. This action assists SAP consultants by recommending the level and type of R/3 consulting support the customer requires.

Phase 1: Project Preparation

This step determines how ready your organization is to proceed with its implementation effort. When your organization selects AcceleratedSAP as its implementation path, it is ready to learn about business solutions within R/3. This first stage allows your organization's management to come to an agreement as to which R/3 best practice processes work to support the majority of your business requirements. In addition, the major modifications to R/3 are reduced, which leads to a much smoother implementation. This acceptance of R/3 integrated processes will allow you to save a great deal of implementation time.

Upper management can feel more confident in the fact that a thorough decision-making process is being used to confirm your project's objective with the least amount of change and a written agreement to refine the scope of your project. When your project guidelines are developed, an implementation team of managers throughout your organization come together to complete the preparation phases and begin your implementation effort. The project start involves executive overview training about the product as well as the process for the implementation team members.

Phase 2: *Business Blueprint*

In order for you to define your business needs, the next phase of your ASAP implementation is perhaps the most difficult. SAP consultants utilize several very detailed questionnaires collected from individual interviews, group discussions, and executive sessions to determine your core business and to list the specific processes that your company uses. Throughout a typical 6-month implementation, this phase will take 3 to 4 weeks of very focused work. The result will be a detailed blueprint of your business needs. At the same time, your implementation team members attend a week of training to distinguish between different types of business systems.

This process defines your business requirements and provides you with several benefits, including a clearly defined project scope for your implementation team. You also have the opportunity to acquire R/3 solutions and benefits without knowing R/3 tables. Implementing R/3 will provide you with enhanced efficiency. Figure 13-3 shows the change before and after implementing R/3. Finally, as an R/3 customer, you will see what your business will look like after your accelerated R/3 implementation.

The *Business Blueprint* phase doesn't require you to make a major reengineering effort. AcceleratedSAP concentrates on meeting busi-

Figure 13-3
Before and after
Implementing R/3
Improved Efficiency.

Before R/3	After R/3
● **Very limited shop floor control capabilities**	● **Fully automated, integrated shop floor control**
● **Only one bill of material per item, company wide**	● **Bills of material maintained by plant**
● **No facility for tracking raw material substitutions**	● **Full-cycle tracking of substitutions**
● **Trouble reports prepared manually and faxed to buyers**	● **Schedulers and buyers have online access to shortages and scheduled receipts**

ness requirements so that superior advancements to processes can be determined by SAP consultants and highlighted for you to use. AcceleratedSAP doesn't offer a great deal of reengineering capabilities, however, it provides the cornerstone for ongoing business process improvement.

Phase 3: Simulation

When you have agreed on a *Business Blueprint,* the members of the AcceleratedSAP team start to focus their training on your R/3 system to transfer knowledge directly to your project team. At the same time, AcceleratedSAP consultants begin to configure your R/3 system, based on your *Business Blueprint.* As an AcceleratedSAP customer, you realize that your implementation project should use as many of R/3's integrated processes as practical so that your system can be configured when your project team members complete their training.

The benefits from the simulation phase include continued knowledge transfer of the software and technology to the customer, as well as an initial R/3 system configuration that must resemble your enterprise's business processes. The simulation phase permits your AcceleratedSAP team of internal managers and consultants to demonstrate the proposed system for your entire user community. Then you can start the critical communication and buy-in regarding the reason why these changes will improve each worker's individual work environment.

Phase 4: Validation

In an attempt to finalize your configuration, knowledge is continually transferred to your project team. The *Business Blueprint* permits the configuration of most of your R/3 system. In addition, there will always be distinct business scenarios that must be handled. This is the critical, detailed work where the AcceleratedSAP team must make certain that your final R/3 configuration best supports your organization's business processes. Your employee team members are sent for additional technical or module training on an as-needed basis while all these events are taking place.

Throughout the validation phase, your implementation team concentrates on the time and available resources for any business exceptions that were not configured in the simulation phase. It is at this point that the AcceleratedSAP technique permits your project team to focus on and customize areas where your organizational business processes are unique. During this process, your team members learn the R/3 system that your business is deploying.

Phase 5: Final Preparation

Once you have completed testing and have trained your end users, it is time to see how AcceleratedSAP is designed to test your system throughout the implementation. The results from this phase concentrate on testing interfaces and get end-user approval. Complimenting end-user approval is end-user training. The final preparation phase offers the skills that your users need to best operate and utilize R/3 for their jobs. ASAP concentrates on speed, but that focus does not negate the need for training end users in order to make R/3 successful. As an Accelerated-SAP customer, you need to work with your SAP consultants to make certain that training is done in a complete and timely manner so that you achieve your goals. However, while that process is often complex to coordinate, it offers you a chance to satisfy your enterprise resource planning requirements in an effective manner, without wasting time.

Phase 6: Go Live and Support

In order to quantify your ERP investment, you need to determine if the employees within your organization are self-sufficient enough to operate their own R/3 system. SAP consultants must be available for specific additional work, including the financial close at the end of each year. The AcceleratedSAP program offers your business the system, tools, and skills to operate and quantify the benefits of your R/3 investment. This leads to a productive system with a team that is trained for future AcceleratedSAP module implementations run by trained personnel.

TeamSAP and ASAP

TeamSAP defines SAP and its large, global structure of customers, partners, and suppliers that SAP has put together through its years of operation. Linking together a team of the best in many industries offers you complete SAP solutions. As an R/3 customer, you trust SAP staff for direct support and advice regarding specific implementation needs. The creation of AcceleratedSAP is part of an ongoing effort to make certain that you have both the partner resources and SAP support necessary to achieve your business objectives. TeamSAP, in relation to AcceleratedSAP, specifies SAP's partners, as well as Global Logo Partners, National Logo Partners, National Implementation Partners, and customer representatives that all have an important sense of urgency and direction on your R/3 implementation team.

Global Logo Partners

SAP's Global Logo Partners are made up of the largest of consulting firms who provide business and technology functionality that deals with reengineering assistance, change management, and education in cross-platform expertise. These firms provide the best implementation options for bigger R/3 customers who are proceeding with core business changes. Current Global Logo partners offer comprehensive implementation services to help you achieve your accelerated business objectives successfully.

Global Logo Partners find that AcceleratedSAP provides them a chance to supplement continuous enterprisewide efforts where there is a need for a rapid roll-out in a particular region, business unit, or pilot project. This program can provide time-sensitive services that are required for you to achieve a successful conversion effort in the year 2000.

The designation "AcceleratedSAP Inside" is provided by the Global Logo Partners to identify the use of this SAP-sponsored implementation program. SAP's Global Logo partners offer their own programs to meet customer demands for quicker returns on their R/3 investments. These partners hasten R/3 deployments by using preconfigured industry templates, tools, and techniques that complement the modeling functionality of the *Business Engineer*. They also expand their knowledge of Intranets to quickly share best-practice information on a global basis. In addition, implementation decisions must offer you a set price and time and risk-sharing options. You also gain the benefit from SAP consultant teams in SAP Solution Centers. AcceleratedSAP offers extra options so that Global Logo partners can satisfy your implementation requirements.

Implementation Partners

SAP's National Implementation Partner Program participants first see advantages from utilizing the AcceleratedSAP program with its customers. Consulting firms often function as the primary R/3 implementor for businesses with revenues below $1 billion. AcceleratedSAP was designed to deal with the requirements of small enterprises. In contrast to its bigger industry competitors, smaller businesses examining R/3 have less resources to deploy, however, they need to rapidly create an information infrastructure to support development. Therefore, midsized organizations were the initial target for utilizing AcceleratedSAP. Currently, SAP's National Logo and National Implementation Partners include:

- Affiliated Computer Services
- Holland Technology Group
- Applied Integration Services
- Intelligroup
- ARIS Corporation
- Honeywell
- Arthur Andersen
- IDS Prof. Scheer, Inc.
- Bureau van Dijk

- IMI Systems
- Card America, Inc.
- Kurt Salmon Associates
- CCAI
- MultiVision Consulting
- Chaptec Group
- Osprey Systems, Inc.
- CISCorp
- Plaut
- Clarkston Potomac Group
- RCG Information Technology
- Computer Aid
- RSA
- Comsys Information Technical
- SAIC Services
- D.A. Consulting
- Seltmann, Cobb & Bryant
- DDS
- Softline, Inc.
- Decision Consultants, Inc.
- Software Consulting Partners
- Deno Morris Group, Inc.
- Software Consulting Services
- EMAX Solutions Partners
- Spearhead Systems Consultants
- Global Core Strategies
- SPO America, Inc.
- Grom Associates
- Technology Solutions Company
- Hewlett-Packard
- Waypointe Information Technologies
- HJM Consulting, Inc.
- Whittman-HartMost

National Implementation Partners has been successful with AcceleratedSAP and plan to integrate its service offerings. It is important to choose the right TeamSAP partner for your AcceleratedSAP implementation. You may wish to examine your AcceleratedSAP program in order to locate consultants working for SAP, however, you may find that SAP does not have sufficient consultants to directly support all its customers. Furthermore, SAP will not integrate this service because there are several partners that have over 25,000 SAP consultants globally for each IT industry.

SAP focuses on its own consultants' efforts to support the AcceleratedSAP program with respect to assisting customers with the size and scope of their project before and during the preparation phase. They also make certain that there is always an SAP manager available for customers and consultants during all six phases. They offer specialized SAP product knowledge and quality assurance for continuous implementations. The result is that the majority of AcceleratedSAP customers are in a position where they can evaluate potential professional service providers to enhance their internal capabilities and the support that SAP consultants offer.

The majority of R/3 implementation customers choose their R/3 implementor on the basis of how much confidence they have in that person. This confidence is based on a past relationship or on the confidence of strong colleague references. When an organization is not familiar with the market or is looking for additional information about implementation partner options, SAP can recommend certain consultants that satisfy unique implementation requirements for your organization.

AcceleratedSAP and TeamSAP Support

AcceleratedSAP is fostered by centralized SAP support for training, software, and SAP consulting support. SAP offers several programs that support both the AcceleratedSAP and TeamSAP program.

SAP has a professional services organization. When AcceleratedSAP was initiated in 1996, it paralleled the development of a new professional services organization at SAP America. There are more than 1200 consultants within SAP's professional services organization. This number will continue to grow to make certain there is extensive coverage and continued contact with customers and partners implementing R/3 rapidly.

There is dedicated SAP field support for you. SAP makes certain there is continuous customer support via a field services organization. In larger organizations, there is a senior SAP manager who acts as a full-time liaison on your project. In smaller organizations, there is a similar senior SAP manager who supports several customers, resulting in direct, continuous customer communication of both SAP experts and resources.

SAP also provides technology and applications consulting that involves technology planning, knowledge transfer, execution, and quality assurance meant to assist your implementation of R/3 as quickly as possible. It also makes sure that you are self-sufficient during your productive operations. This group also works hand in hand with SAP development groups to transfer knowledge on changing customer requirements.

AcceleratedSAP Training

In order to support the initiation of AcceleratedSAP, SAP offered what is called "spring training" classes for implementation partners as an overview of the people, tools, and processes that make up this program. Although spring training is no longer offered, SAP still offers partners classes in the AcceleratedSAP techniques.

These classes lead to partner certification. SAP is on track to certify implementation partners to effectively utilize AcceleratedSAP. Certification will indicate that specific training and SAP experience conditions have been satisfied before certification is granted.

Business Engineer configuration functionality is further increased by R/3 version 4.0. This enhanced functionality continues to improve the ability of AcceleratedSAP to quickly configure, deploy, and constantly modify R/3. As the foundation tool for AcceleratedSAP, *Business Engineer's* improvements will continue to enhance the AcceleratedSAP program.

Customer benefits from AcceleratedSAP are increasing exponentially. While AcceleratedSAP was designed for companies with revenues between $200 million and $2.5 billion, it was believed that these organizations would have the greatest need for a rapid implementation option that didn't require as many resources. However, the result was that customers from all sized companies and locations discovered advantages in using the AcceleratedSAP techniques. The reasons for the broad acceptance of ASAP was seen in benefits that allow customers to achieve significant goals in a shortened period of time.

ASAP produced much quicker returns on their R/3 investment. It acquired rapid returns for each R/3 investment and was the motivating factor for the creation of AcceleratedSAP in the first place. Many customers found that they benefited from this program with a quick return on their investments. This often meant restricting an implementation to three or four modules in order to make certain that rapid deployment could be met, while the remainder could be deployed in either the second or third AcceleratedSAP phase. The results indicate realizable returns in a shortened time frame.

ASAP for Accelerated Year 2000 Transitions

The year 2000 problem is growing in complexity, and the time for dealing with it continues to diminish significantly each day. One way to counter this problem is to transition your computer systems from legacy applications. Once you accomplish this goal, you can replace many non-compliant, older systems with new systems that offer enhanced functionality. The largest factor against deploying R/3 involved satisfying your year 2000 functionality which, under a normal implementation time frame, would sacrifice too much time to accomplish your compliance goals. The utilization of AcceleratedSAP permits any size organization to rapidly replicate existing functionality.

Standard Global Production

There are several large businesses that have deployed R/3 globally only to find that each R/3 implementation was managed by a leading consulting firm that varied from site to site. In this sense, you would not acquire sufficient benefits from reusing or learning from one implementation site to another. However, this standardization permits a much simpler enterprisewide production of R/3 functionality. AcceleratedSAP provides a common technique that can be used by various consulting firms throughout various geographic or business boundaries in simultaneous implementations.

Reusable Technique for R/3 Deployment

When you reuse techniques, as either a pilot or a first-phase R/3 production, the knowledge of AcceleratedSAP and R/3 exists within the client organization. Customers who initiate a second phase through an AcceleratedSAP implementation require less external resources for their next implementation phase.

One of the benefits is that it offers an optimal basis for R/3 upgrade. One of the most important lessons acquired from different organizations who have implemented R/3 is that the more modifications executed on the R/3 system, the more challenging it is to benefit from its advanced functionality in R/3 upgrades. This is due to the fact that SAP spends several hundred million dollars in research and development every year to enhance its R/3 solution. At that point, customers often believe that they have modified R/3, but instead become upset because they lack the ability to easily migrate from one version to another. The functionality of AcceleratedSAP rests in the fact that it can help you find solutions within R/3. It can successfully result in an optimal foundation that allows you to upgrade from one R/3 version to the next.

Deploying R/3 Effectively

Regardless of whether AcceleratedSAP is chosen, the process that enterprise management uses to make this determination offers a great deal of information on the R/3 implementation path that is selected. AcceleratedSAP does not optimize all R/3 implementations, however, making that decision makes executives deal with compromises between a rapid R/3 deployment and the efforts necessary for fundamental business changes while deploying R/3.

Conclusion

Until the release of ASAP, R/3 enterprise implementations often were directed only at large businesses. Time was the largest limiting factor, and was estimated at anywhere from as little as 1 year to as long as

3 years or more as an investment in R/3 performance. It often took a long time for a implementation, based on the complexity and size of each particular organization. The additional time needed was often due to the fact that many organizations used the business change effort in R/3 without specifically documented expectations of what was to be achieved and what needed to be changed in the process. In the absence of a clearly expressed business plan, R/3 implementation teams often attempted to deploy a software package under enormous challenges caused by the constant changes in the business' operational infrastructure.

AcceleratedSAP has made it possible for any size business to have the option of realizing R/3 returns in only 4 to 6 months because SAP and SAP's implementation partners continue to refine and improve their R/3 service offerings to meet growing customer demand for rapid R/3 investment returns. The biggest difficulty in rapid implementation of R/3 is initiating the attempt with realistic and specific expectations at both the executive and project level about what needs to be accomplished. When these items have been set, the best procedure for implementing R/3 depends on your objectives.

When dealing with rapidly duplicated functionality (for example, year 2000 efforts), you may vary from each path to move your enterprise to a dramatically different operational infrastructure.

The capability of meeting expectations is formally integrated in the AcceleratedSAP methodology to make certain that the project begins with clear objectives that can be successfully achieved in a shortened project time frame. When combined with accelerators, such as SAP R/3's *Business Engineer,* the *Project Estimator,* and the collaborative resources of SAP's partners, then AcceleratedSAP provides R/3 users with a program that allows them to realize the value of their R/3 investment quickly and cost effectively.

This chapter looks at the benefits of using AcceleratedSAP. It focuses on time, quality, and efficiency using implementation resources. The main elements of this section involve how you can produce a more rapid R/3 implementation, develop a uniform approach to R/3 implementation with both partners and consultants, obtain quality and guaranteed implementation experience, use resources efficiently, reuse results for future implementation phases, and finally reduce implementation costs and obtain a faster return on your investment.

Business Engineer

Introduction

AcceleratedSAP is designed to help you compete and gives you the ability to execute change quickly and effectively. This effort depends on your transition from traditional function-centric architectures to a much more flexible, process-specific organizational structure.

Business Software

Business software plays a very important role in your organization. It should support your transition and provide you with flexible business operations that form the foundation for successful and ongoing engineering, process orientation, and competitive edge. SAP's R/3 offers a great deal of functionality that helps you gain a competitive advantage due to its reputation as a leading ERP platform. SAP is software that offers a cost-efficient method of achieving increased efficiency and process orientation.

When a standard solution is insufficient for your individual needs, it becomes necessary to refine the R/3 systems for your individual corporate and organizational requirements. R/3's *Business Engineer* helps you configure to order since it permits you to configure R/3 more rapidly, easily, and efficiently than before. It can support phased implementation and permit you to execute changes to your existing configuration at any time, without disrupting continuous business activities.

Some of the main factors that the R/3 *Business Engineer* offers is a powerful R/3 configuration tool that supports quick implementation and ongoing change. These factors assist you in reducing costs and maintaining your competitive edge.

The R/3 *Business Engineer* gives you the ability to designate your organization's infrastructure, business processes, and business requirements using everyday language through an interactive, step-by-step technique. It permits you to create R/3 workflow that matches the way in which your organization functions, as opposed to changing your needs to fit your solution. In short, R/3 *Business Engineer* clarifies initial and continuous R/3 configuration.

In addition, it also offers a knowledge-based configuration that gently moves you through implementation and automatically makes you aware of any problems to make certain you achieve a consistent solution.

There are more than 100 industry-specific business scenarios and templates available, which lessens R/3's functionality to manageable views and accelerates implementations significantly. Industry-specific business scenarios or templates are not required, however, existing configurations can be altered or extended effortlessly at any time as new business goals and needs occur. Furthermore, offline configuration and support for distributed working indicates faster, simpler implementations and a much more rapid return on your information investment.

R/3 *Business Engineer* is a component of your R/3 system and is the motivating tool of SAP's complete consulting program for rapid R/3 implementation, AcceleratedSAP.

Designed to Be ASAP

R/3 *Business Engineer* was created to be used by business professionals, IS departments, consultants, and partners. R/3 *Business Engineer* is the R/3 configuration and implementation tool founded on the R/3 *Reference Model,* shown in Fig. 14-1, which empowers you and your consultants to refine your implementation of R/3, as well as to adapt your current configuration to new needs or modified circumstances.

Figure 14-1
R/3 *Reference Model:* Prototypes for Vertical Industries.

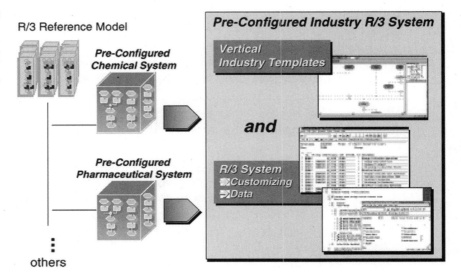

R/3 *Business Engineer* is much more than a viewing tool. It offers you an interactive hierarchical structure of your business scenarios, organizational units, processes, and functions. This allows you to configure your own enterprise model, or *Business Blueprint,* through an interactive guidance system of questions and answers. That R/3 functionality is automatically linked to the enterprise model you have created.

It is unnecessary to recreate the configuration inside R/3. Integrated validation checks make certain that configuration decisions are compliant with appropriate business rules and R/3 functionality. Configuration decisions are verified and documented, and the enterprise model is saved in the R/3 *Repository.* It is a metadescription of your R/3 configuration that can be modified at any given time.

R/3 *Business Engineer* assists you in creating a high-level R/3 solution rapidly and easily. In addition, it assists you in modifying that solution with the same simplicity for your changing needs and goals. R/3 *Business Engineer* is a basic part of your R/3 system, as well as its scope of supply. The *Business Engineer* can be installed and maintained as a stand-alone application that is not dependent on the presence of your R/3 environment. R/3 *Business Engineer* guides you through configuration via an easily understood system of questions and answers.

AcceleratedSAP Defined

AcceleratedSAP has now become an established tool for faster implementation. AcceleratedSAP is a complex program that deals with consulting services, tools, and proven techniques for rapid implementation and continuous optimization of your R/3 solutions. AcceleratedSAP's efficiency has been illustrated frequently within organizations worldwide. The R/3 *Business Engineer,* outlined in the previous section, is a key component in AcceleratedSAP projects that are used for scoping, configuration tasks, and integration testing.

AcceleratedSAP's greatest strength is offered through its *Roadmap* tool, which consists of project preparation, and the *Business Blueprint* for realization, final preparation, and finally going live and support.

The *Roadmap* also incorporates descriptions of general information and best practices. Its toolkit has all of the tools employed in AcceleratedSAP, such as the R/3 *Business Engineer* and software products (for example, Microsoft Project). AcceleratedSAP's *Best Estimator* tool gives you the ability to correctly determine your required resources, the costs, and the time needed for your implementation.

The AcceleratedSAP *Implementation Assistant* is a how-to guide that assists you through the distinct phases of implementation, such as the checklists and project plans. Service and support provides you with expert support from initial planning to achieving a successful implementation. Services incorporate consulting and training. ASAP utilizes the service and support that covers all areas pertaining to your SAP environment. *EarlyWatch,* concept reviews, and *GoingLive* checks are components that ensure a total quality check and allow you to actively refine your R/3 system.

These components benefit you by giving you:

1. Much quicker R/3 implementation and business results

2. A standard technique for your R/3 implementation

3. A common implementation guide for consultants

4. A common implementation guide for business partners

5. Assured quality

6. Knowledge through implementation

7. Effective resource utilization

8. Reusability of results for future implementation phases

9. Reduced implementation costs

10. More rapid ROI

Business Engineer and Simplified Implementation

The R/3 *Business Engineer* simplifies implementation at the start of each project. However, it is critical that you outline your company's needed structure and operations. You must then designate specific problems within the current structure and determine a method for achieving increased performance.

One of the ways in which you can enhance your performance is by development of an accurate enterprise model or business blueprint. Then you can learn about R/3 functionality and the ways in which it can support your evolving business processes. The purpose is to create an accurate business blueprint that explains how your organization functions, its processes, and structures. The features of your blueprint can either improve or degrade your implementation. This particular stage of your implementation consumes a great deal of resources and time.

R/3 *Business Engineer* gives you the ability to create a high-quality blueprint that assists you in defining your specific needs and determining how R/3 can meet them sufficiently. When you employ the R/3 *Reference Model,* you can define (in a short time frame) specific opportunities for optimizing routines and procedures throughout departmental perimeters.

R/3 *Business Engineer* is the tool that is the motivating factor within AcceleratedSAP. ASAP has a well-established method for providing quick R/3 implementation. It allows you to establish an accurate business blueprint that forms the foundation for your R/3 solution. In addition, it gives you the significant advantage of achieving a knowledge-based interactive configuration that is fostered by business-oriented questions. These questions can be asked directly, or you can utilize an animated model that guides you through all of the specific question levels. These answers form the foundation of the enterprise model of your R/3 system. Often, these selections can be made with the click of a mouse, however, this method relies on your specific answers. Otherwise, additional questions may be required. R/3 *Business Engineer* knows how to determine which questions are needed and to verify the consistency of the configuration.

R/3 *Business Engineer* divides the work of creating a business blueprint and configuring R/3 into workable steps. It begins at the top with the overall structure of your business and progressively works down through the broad areas, including sales, distribution, production to business scenarios, processes, and individual functions.

It is important to note that simplification and acceleration of implementation using this top-down approach, as shown in Fig. 14-2, also accelerates your configuration work. You need only choose the business processes you need, then R/3 *Business Engineer* takes you to the associated configuration tasks. You can also emulate processes that have already been configured.

There is also a level of flexibility in configuration and migration because the *Business Engineer* environment offers you the ability to establish new configurations and to adapt your R/3 solutions to satisfy changing business requirements without disrupting production systems. A detailed guide leads you through a comprehensive library of established business scenarios. These scenarios provide your project team members with the flexibility they need to work with several versions of R/3, so that they can plan and schedule the introduction of new releases and multiple versions of R/3, which can be configured at any given time.

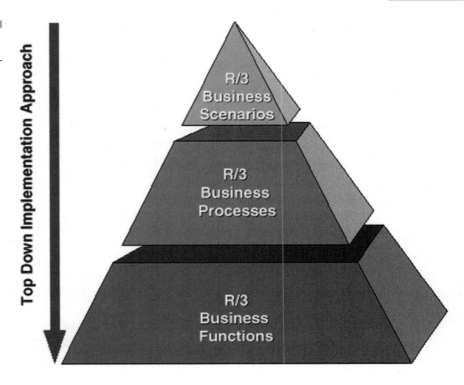

Figure 14-2
Top-Down Approach.

R/3 *Business Engineer* accelerates implementation by offering two different starting points that eliminate a great deal of the work affiliated with industry-specific configurations, including comprehensive industry-specific business scenarios and preconfigured templates. Typical business scenarios and preconfigured templates are available that save you time and simplify your configuration.

These templates are simple to comprehend and use due to the fact that they use industry-specific business practices and familiar terminology. These business scenarios and preconfigured templates are meant for real-world conditions, and are developed together with customers, consultants, and partners.

Detailing Your Business Processes

The best practices for businesses involved in R/3 *Business Engineer* offer several industry-specific business scenarios created by leading industry executives. These scenarios illustrate proven solutions meant for everyday use that have been acquired from real-life businesses. They represent specific industries by employing basic concepts and language, resulting in a preconfigured process where you don't have to create every scenario from scratch. Essentially, you can select the methodology that represents your type of business. In addition, you can use the aspects you like, and modify them to meet your requirements.

The R/3 *Business Engineer* offers numerous business scenarios that illustrate the best business practices. The business scenarios explain key business practices, including business scenarios that examine all standard production types, such as material replenishment, repetitive manufacturing, continuous production, and business plans that deal with the typical procurement of stock material and external services.

Business Scenarios Revenue

The industry-specific *Reference Model,* together with business process areas and business scenario value chains, reflect the integration of business scenarios and processes across departmental boundaries. They provide the best opportunity to optimize encrusted structures and routines.

Business Engineer incorporates several complete templates that assist in accelerating implementation even further. These templates consist of preselected business scenarios and processes, and were created by consultants and customers. They are flexible and can be modified to your specific organization by deleting or adding scenarios or processes. They may also be modified by changing existing selections.

SAP offers preconfigured industry templates for all SAP-defined industries. However, the template concept is not restricted to the models offered by SAP. Consultants and customers can develop their own models for specialist needs or markets, by using shortcuts for accelerated implementations.

Templates

R/3 industry prototypes support ongoing change from the start of your implementation project. Many organizations are constantly changing their business objectives. Therefore, their mission-critical applications must adapt and grow at the same speed. If software is not able to expand with the needs of your organization, then your company will find it is unable to cope with new situations or business processes.

When you implement an ERP application, you can execute changes quickly, and change can be instituted easily and continuously. R/3 *Business Engineer* enables your business to grow and increase its production capacity while reducing costs. The enterprise model and the associated R/3 implementation created with R/3 *Business Engineer* can be modified to permit customers to support up to 90 percent of their daily business changes at any given time. Modifying your organizational structure is easily accomplished by accessing the method by which functions are assigned to organization units.

These changes include adding or deleting items in your corporate structure, such as business units, production plants, and warehouses. You can deal with new personnel and associated issues, including promotion, reallocation of work tasks, and maintenance of authorization profiles.

R/3 Functionality

Business processes can be optimized to support new versions of R/3. *Business Engineer* simplifies change management and permits modifications to be executed at any time, which allows you to make certain that you achieve change compatibility, while other configuration decisions are executed smoothly, resulting in an easy transition to your live system. The R/3 *Business Engineer* gives you the opportunity to emulate possible situations that can move your innovation forward.

The R/3 *Business Engineer* consists of the following components:

- Interactive configuration of R/3 models:
  1. Selection
  2. Reduction
  3. Combination
- Creating enterprise models
- Maintaining enterprise models
- Knowledge-based integrity validation of all configuration decisions
- Animation of business processes
- Automatic top-down guidance through R/3 *Reference Model*

- Automatic generation of lists of customizing tasks, views, and, profiles (settings) with respect to process models and functions chosen
- Question-and-answer–driven customizing of R/3:
  1. Functions
  2. Organizational entities
  3. Authorization profiles

Components

The R/3 *Reference Model* is a complete metadescription of R/3 functionality from various perspectives. The R/3 *Business Configurator* utilizes the R/3 *Reference Model* to create enterprise models and drive implementation. The R/3 *Reference Model* incorporates the organization model, process model, data model, and the distribution model (which examines distributed functionality within a shared enterprise organization model). It also continues the business object model that examines objects, including customers, vendors, employees, and cost centers. The business objects are similar to links between the model and implementation levels.

The R/3 *Repository* is a main component of the R/3 system. It is made up from the R/3 *Reference Model,* industry-specific models, and the enterprise models. In addition, it also logs alterations made to models and specifies all of the versions of R/3 being utilized. The R/3 *Repository* is the core for ongoing continuous engineering, as shown in Fig. 14-3.

Figure 14-3
Continuous Engineering.

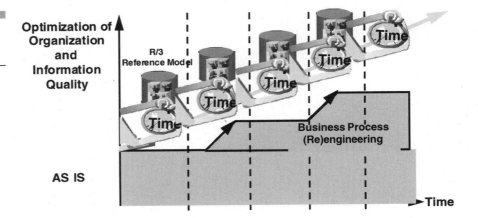

Open R/3 *Repository* interface offers an API (COM/DCOM) that permits non-SAP applications (modeling tools) to communicate with the R/3 *Repository*. The API allows you to both read and write various information from the *Repository*. This includes extracting and reloading the R/3 *Reference Model*. The result is that third-party tools can be used to extend the R/3 *Reference Model*.

This extended model can then be returned to the *Repository*. Both consultants and partners can use the R/3 *Business Engineer* as an independent configuration tool together with their own R/3 implementation technique.

The R/3 *Repository* interface opens up the R/3 *Reference Model* to partners and consultants. However, the R/3 *Business Engineer* was designed for anyone who wants to implement an R/3-based solution. When you simplify the configuration, it makes R/3 more accessible. In addition, it will help your organization reduce its dependence on expensive specialists or outside consultants. The user friendliness of R/3 *Business Engineer* is beneficial to business professionals who are required to join discussion groups, create prototypes, and create business blueprints.

Phasing in R/3

Departments of companies that need the ability to customize R/3 applications more efficiently and more quickly include small- to medium-sized companies. These companies have not been open to the idea of implementing R/3 due to the complexity and time involved in creating this type of project. Since the creation of the AcceleratedSAP program, these organizations can now phase in R/3 far more easily.

Consultants and SAP partners who need a rapid method of implementation find the ability of customers to configure-to-order or create customizable R/3-based solutions for their markets very appealing. R/3 was developed for emerging technologies. It was designed to be open and can use a Web browser as its front-end together with HTML online documentation. R/3 business objects act as real-world items that are increasing in number, which allows your enterprise to design parts of its business processes by using objects.

The R/3 *Business Engineer* will support object-oriented processes by offering object-oriented configuration and customization. R/3 *Business Engineer* also supports major standard interfaces, including

COM/DCOM and *ActiveX,* which makes it compatible with several third-party modeling tools and software packages, including Microsoft Excel. R/3 *Business Engineer* is an element of SAP's *Business Framework,* which acts as the foundation for emerging technologies. In addition, it will completely support the R/3 component architecture.

R/3 *Business Engineer* is more than just a means of visualizing the enterprise; it also acts as a powerful configurator. It permits you to tailor R/3 to your needs simply and effortlessly. *Business Engineer* was the first tool to offer this type of comprehensive knowledge-based configuration and to support continuous R/3 configuration. It offers you a total solution to configuration and implementation that deals with the full range of R/3 functionality.

The *Business Engineer* helps you achieve an efficient R/3 implementation as well as continuous engineering. *Business Engineer* permits model-driven R/3 configurations where business model processes provide predefined functionality as a foundation, so that your organization can change model parameters without programming. This allows you to set up an information system that meets your individual needs.

The *Business Engineer* offers a new architecture for business process modeling by giving you tools created to support rapid initial implementation of integrated process chains and permits postconfiguration. This functionality allows for step-by-step enhancement and extension of your business application areas during your entire R/3 life cycle. *Business Engineer* has complete comprehension of R/3 implementation, and suggests the best method of proceeding, what you need to do, the order in which you should go forward, what to order, and why to choose one business case over another.

Procedure Model

The *Business Engineer* is a business application repository that contains tools that assist the interaction between business users and the live R/3 system.

The R/3 *Procedure Model* offers you a technique for developing procedures that yield structured direction for all implementation and system maintenance stages. The R/3 *Reference Model* offers a complete *Business Blueprint* for all of your functions, process models, components, and business objects in R/3 for individual selection.

R/3 customization is an active system-driven process that offers individual customization of R/3 applications without programming by a detailed standard for all business activities that the R/3 system supports. This facilitated configuration incorporates easy-to-use graphical maintenance of organization structures, rapid creation of individual menus, and authorization profiles.

The SAP *Business Workflow* offers separate adaptation, automation, and optimization of business processes. However, *Business Engineer* offers you much more than a rapid implementation tool. Once you have completed your initial implementation, it permits you to make continuous adjustments within a live R/3 system, including enhancements, release upgrades, modification, and the integration of non-SAP products.

The goal of the *Business Engineer* is to reduce implementation time significantly by concentrating on your most critical elements. This improves your comprehension of R/3 through basic industry-specific models, value chains, and group industry scenarios. You can remove unwanted details and expedite continuous engineering and change management throughout releases across your complete R/3 life cycle. It essentially yields a complete business repository in active business *Reference Models* in combination with configuration options.

Implementing Network Configuration

SAP's management software is called the *Business Engineering Workbench* (BEW). It ties together more than 800 business description/specification processes and more than 170 core business objects that integrate with a running R/3 application to facilitate implementation. BEW offers a business repository found in the R/3 *Reference Model*. The *Reference Model* forms a set of predefined processes and interrelationships that expedite your system setup. Your users will find it necessary to customize R/3 for their specific needs. In addition, individual department managers must make certain that their needs are satisfied.

IntelliCorp is one organization that provides PC modeling tools for BEW that allows users to emulate their model in a system. *LiveModel* for R/3 is the tool used to perform transactions and find out how specific corporate situations would run on a real R/3 system.

R/3 provides a great deal of functionality, however, that power is tempered with the incessant challenge for implementors of working with a great deal of complexity. This difficulty has let R/3 consultants work strenuously to link business processes. The advent of AcceleratedSAP has improved this process somewhat by allowing the implementation of R/3 to proceed more smoothly. However, it is important to use its inherent preconfigured best practices to speed implementation.

Whenever a consultant tries to implement systems such as R/3, they are often confronted with numerous CD-ROMs with extensive documentation. Individuals within your organization must usually learn everything possible in order to stay alive during this complex installation. Acceleration is highly dependent on the consultant's ability to use all of the situations from other installations to institute a solution quickly and effectively. However, that consultant has to have a great deal of experience in order to identify the right best-practice situation that will apply to the specific needs of your organization. In essence, constant attention must be paid to your specific business processes in order to succeed with your R/3 implementation.

The biggest difficulty for R/3 users is locating and understanding the system information they need for any given application. However, that process can normally consume an overwhelming amount of time for both the consultant and the R/3 customer, as shown in Fig. 14-4. R/3 customers need to better understand what is in the R/3 system and how they can make better use of the system.

SAP's *Business Engineering Workbench* (BEW) is an aggregate of 800 business processes and more than 170 core business objects. When all of

Figure 14-4
R/3 Customer.

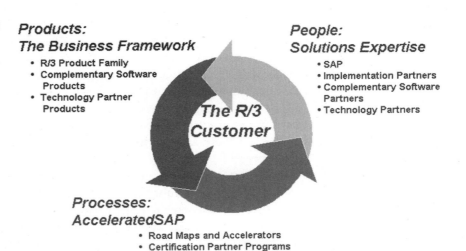

Products:
The Business Framework
- R/3 Product Family
- Complementary Software Products
- Technology Partner Products

People:
Solutions Expertise
- SAP
- Implementation Partners
- Complementary Software Partners
- Technology Partners

The R/3 Customer

Processes:
AcceleratedSAP
- Road Maps and Accelerators
- Certification Partner Programs
- Support, Services and Education Programs

the components are integrated with a functioning R/3 application, it simplifies your system implementation.

BEW works similarly to your *Business Blueprint*. You need not start from the beginning without advanced planning. Instead, you can utilize a core business *Repository* that supports the R/3 *Reference Model*. The *Reference Model* itself is a set of predefined processes and interrelationships that act as a starting point for any implementation. At that point, you can utilize SAP's experience represented by hundreds of working business scenarios. Each process can be used as is or customized with online graphical tools and high-level views of the enterprise. That versatility becomes useful as you find that your organization must constantly redefine its business processes to satisfy its constantly changing business environment.

Most organizations find that a standard R/3 implementation would take a great deal longer to complete in the absence of someone to coordinate the logistics of the entire migration effort. Many companies find that BEW is useful for determining methods of individualizing its business processes to take advantage of R/3's power and functionality.

Increasing Departmental Productivity

The *Business Engineering Workbench* offers a great return on productivity, however, gaining the cooperation of each department within your organization guarantees an efficient SAP model. Although a great deal of business processes are possible within BEW, users will often find it necessary to customize the tool to satisfy their own business environments.

This customization often takes place by departmental managers sending recommendations back to the IT department. Often this procedure results in a solution that doesn't quite satisfy your needs. As a result, it becomes necessary to reimplement a solution (a very costly process) or just reorganize your organization to utilize software that you have. New PC modeling tools for BEW permit users to emulate their model in a system. *LiveModel* for R/3 allows users to move through each business process quickly. They have the ability to perform transactions and determine how they would operate in a real R/3 system.

These tools allow you to validate your design and make certain that the rollout and implementation will move quickly and be accepted without any problem whatsoever.

R/3 to Windows

Porting the R/3 application suite to a Windows environment is something that SAP and Visio Corp., have been working on. They have developed a process model visualization tool based on Visio's independent diagramming and flowchart program. The new tool has OLE compatibility, a syntax checker, drag-and-drop capabilities, annotation, and layering capabilities for graphics. These tools make the *Reference Model* available and affordable to all users.

SAP offers an improved R/3 *Business Engineer* in Release 4.0. This makes it the most detailed knowledge-based configuration tool for more rapid and effective R/3 implementation, as well as for continuous business process enhancement. R/3 *Business Engineer* is the core-enabling tool of AcceleratedSAP. ASAP is SAP's proven method for developing rapid R/3 implementations. R/3 *Business Engineer* for Release 4.0 allows you to configure R/3 more rapidly and easily by utilizing an interactive system of questions and answers. It also allows you to use integrated validation checks that make certain your configuration decisions are compatible with applicable business rules and R/3 functionality.

R/3 *Business Engineer* also eases initial and continuous R/3 configuration by using new business scenarios and vertical industry templates that collect R/3 functionality into simply managed views. R/3 *Business Engineer* permits you to implement changes quickly at any point within your existing enterprise system. It allows you to support continuous business process improvement and modifications.

Benefits

R/3 *Business Engineer* for Release 4.0 offers you configure-to-order functionality that accelerates and simplifies R/3 implementation so you have an instant initial solution. You can forget about the old trial-and-error technique for enterprise application configuration. *Business Engineer* allows you to support continuous business enhancement and ties together traditional enterprise modeling with your live R/3 solution. It links business models directly to deployment. It provides quick-start, preconfigured R/3 systems for various industries. It also offers a flexible, open configuration environment that is rich in both features and functionality.

These features include a knowledge-based, question-and-answer-driven configuration process that guides you through your R/3 configuration and determines any possible discrepancies that would interfere with your implementation. The whole idea is to make your implementation process more interactive and simple. There are also integrated validation checks that make certain your process design integrity is maintained, so that decisions are made during system configuration that are consistent and supported by R/3.

Preconfigured industry systems connect preselected business scenarios, processes, functions, and system settings for particular industries. They were first available for the chemical, consumer products, and steel industries, however, the preconfigured industry systems offer you a quick-start solution specifically geared toward the IT industry. One hundred business scenarios are collected for the 1000 business processes in R/3 to create a more manageable view of best business practices. Its goal is to offer you a top-down implementation approach in enterprise process areas, including production, procurement, sales, and distribution. R/3 process chain animation shows how configuration decisions influence business processes within your integrated system. In addition, it also simulates the live R/3 solution.

The standard interface opens the R/3 *Business Engineer* to partners, consultants, and customers. It permits you to enhance your industry solutions and create corporate rollout templates. It also has high-level support for major standard interfaces, including COM/DCOM and *ActiveX,* that foster integration with third-party software, tools, and technique. A Web-browser front-end and HTML-based documentation make R/3 *Business Engineer* platform-independent and simple to use. The R/3 *Business Engineer* supports the SAP *Business Framework* and guides you through a component-centric implementation that is updated with the R/3 component production.

R/3 *Business Configurator*

The R/3 *Business Configurator* offers the interactive configuration of R/3 models:

1. Selection
2. Reduction
3. Combination

It fosters the creation and maintenance of:

- Enterprise models
- Knowledge-based integrity
- Validation of all configuration decisions
- Animation of business processes
- Automatic top-down guidance through R/3 *Reference Model*
- Automatic generation of lists of customizing:
  1. Tasks
  2. Views
  3. Profiles
- Selected question and answer
- Customization of R/3
- Functions:
  1. Organizational units
  2. Authorization profiles
- Viewing of R/3 models

Conclusion

This chapter discusses *Business Engineer* and how it provides an efficient R/3 implementation, as well as an uninterrupted engineering effort that allows model-driven R/3 configuration. These business process models provide established functionality as the foundation for your organization. It can change parameters of its models. These models include the R/3 *Procedure Model,* R/3 *Reference Model,* R/3 customizing model, and the SAP *Business Workflow*.

System Performance

Introduction

SAP has placed a great deal of emphasis on the speed of your individual R/3 deployment. SAP relies on its partner certification programs to help customers speed up the implementation of SAP products. The most important programs are AcceleratedSAP Practices Partner and Powered By AcceleratedSAP, both of which are part of SAP's TeamSAP ambition. These programs are designed to verify national and local consultant agencies that are extremely familiar with SAP's AcceleratedSAP implementation technique.

Speed in Implementation

AcceleratedSAP is SAP's rapid implementation program that combines experienced consultants and SAP's accelerated implementation methodology to simplify and refine deployment of SAP software. Organizations certified as AcceleratedSAP partners need to have more than two-thirds of their consultants complete sufficient training in AcceleratedSAP, in addition to adopting the AcceleratedSAP approach.

Powered By AcceleratedSAP

The Powered By AcceleratedSAP program necessitates that companies utilize distinct AcceleratedSAP techniques and concepts together with their own.

Three companies were selected by SAP to initiate its Powered By AcceleratedSAP certification efforts:

- Ernst & Young LLP
- Deloitte & Touche Consulting Group/ICS
- Price Waterhouse LLP

More than 10 companies have committed themselves to the AcceleratedSAP program and additional companies are joining every quarter. AcceleratedSAP represents a high level of system performance and the ability to embrace the fastest implementation method possible.

What Is Ernst & Young?

Ernst & Young LLP is a member firm of Ernst & Young International. They are a global leading professional services organization whose member firms offer advisory business services, tax services, and consulting solutions for domestic and global clients. These organizations have over 72,000 employees in more than 600 offices in 130 countries. Ernst & Young's management consulting specialists work with global corporations and businesses in high-growth areas. They work to initiate business improvement and transformation programs that add real value to your organization's objectives.

The methodologies in this chapter include:

- SAP R/3 InfoDB (assembly storage and delivery)
- LEAP (courseware architecture)
- *Mentor* (implementation decisions)

Learning Solutions

In order for you to achieve the most benefit from Ernst & Young's SAP learning solutions, it is important to integrate functionality from their suite of courseware development tools based on instructional design techniques from Ernst & Young's extensive repositories. Distributed repositories are shown in Fig. 15-1.

The next step is to integrate this functionality into your knowledge bases and business process subject matter experience in an effort to develop a set of learning solutions that benefit from the effective reuse of knowledge. Ernst & Young's SAP learning center creates value-based solutions via knowledge reuse and enhanced learning techniques. The learning solution center concentrates on the development of technology-based solutions that utilize the SAP Information Database (InfoDB) together with Ernst & Young's knowledge of the R/3 application. The result is an enhanced level of personnel performance and business process capabilities.

Ernst & Young has created an integrated training and documentation toolset meant to expedite knowledge reuse, as well as automate the courseware development process, which is based on the SAP R/3 training and documentation tools. Both technology and knowledge management accelerate this training development process while curtailing

Figure 15-1
Distributed Repositories.

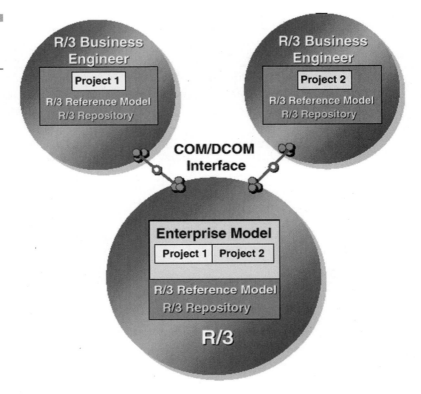

costs. Figure 15-2 provides details about the specific training and documentation tools involved in your implementation process.

Several important factors lead to a successful SAP R/3 implementation:

- Performance
- Change
- Perspective
- Role/function
- Learning-centered activities
- Learning objectives
- Knowledge and skills
- Competencies
- Measurement
- Approach
- Flexible packaging designed to foster knowledge and skills

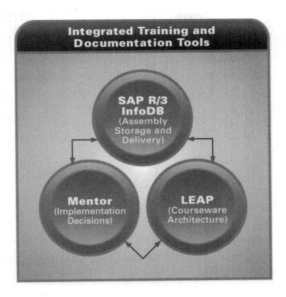

Figure 15-2
Training and Documentation Tools.

The purpose of Ernst & Young's learning solutions is to assist in your SAP R/3 implementation by developing the knowledge and skills required to meet your performance goals. Ernst & Young concentrates on business and performance needs with respect to your management team, project and technical teams, and end users. This effort extends across your entire process and includes everything beginning with the design, development, and implementation phases of an R/3 installation. These requirements are translated into SAP training goals. The goals include building organizational change management capabilities, creating SAP-specific technical and functional skills in the project team, and developing transactional and business process expertise in your personnel.

SAP's InfoDB

Ernst & Young has integrated the SAP InfoDB directly into their business framework objectives. InfoDB incorporates a comprehensive repository of educational information that can be utilized to establish customized training with functions that are part of a live R/3 system configured to your specific production screens. The SAP InfoDB training database has more than 150 courses created by SAP for technical and project team training. Besides a large amount of educational content, InfoDB includes course development templates that are used for interactive instructor training, multiple language support, presentation filters, as well as automatic SAP updates of training objects. All of these elements combine to offer functionality for effective assembly, storage, and delivery of SAP learning solutions inside InfoDB.

LEAP

Ernst & Young offers a program called LEAP that stands for Learning Environment to Accelerate Performance. This is an important collection of tools that incorporates applications for the quick creation of multimedia instructor-oriented or Web training and electronic performance support systems. LEAP supplements InfoDB by yielding high-speed access to several data sources, including:

- InfoDB
- Center for business knowledge (CBK)
- Internet and customer knowledge bases
- Project team knowledge bases

Content is stored and changed inside LEAP's database and built into courseware by project teams and subject matter experts using program templates created by instructional material designers. Courseware is created through LEAP, and can be delivered as part of an interactive instructor-oriented environment, throughout your corporate network, across the Internet, or via the InfoDB.

Value in Reusable Learning Solutions

The integration of this technology provides several benefits: faster training development, cost containment, and solution reuse. The training architecture permits your project teams to benefit from business process and implementation workflow knowledge, which helps them develop learning solutions that enhance performance as your systems Go Live. Ernst & Young's technique, instructional design knowledge, and technology offer you just-in-time learning solutions that are both cost-effective and extremely reusable throughout your entire corporate infrastructure.

Accelerators

Accelerators are crucial to effective, fast implementation of your SAP R/3 solution. For templates that will hasten your activities, look at Ernst & Young's industry life-cycle models. Ernst & Young offers a method that begins with efforts in your specific industry. Industry life-cycle models provide you with a combination of global industry knowledge, leading business practices, and an established methodology for tackling your SAP implementation to accelerate the delivery of benefits to your organization's implementation program.

Industry life-cycle models are far more comprehensive than any pre-defined industry template. Ernst & Young's industry life-cycle models are detailed industry-specific collections of dynamic, reusable knowledge objects that support process models, leading practices, exemplary deliverables, solution templates, preconfigured SAP solutions, and integration with Ernst & Young's best-in-class implementation methodology.

Each industry life-cycle model offers a continuous repository of pertinent solution objects that support the complete project life cycle from the design stage through end-user training and implementation. Ernst & Young's industry life-cycle models offer your implementation team significant competitive practices used together with established capabilities of the SAP R/3 package in a preconfigured SAP system. The base model can then be updated with client-specific information through the life of the contract. This offers you a centralized knowledge repository for the implementation team, as well as the foundation for knowledge transfer when your solution goes live.

Industry life-cycle models support SAP R/3 *Business Engineer,* so that you can utilize the SAP business model, as well as have a direct link to the SAP *Implementation Guide* (IMG) for extra customization for your specific needs. Ernst & Young has also included ASAP accelerators and sample deliverables as part of their solution objects in the industry life-cycle models to offer the best options from both SAP and Ernst & Young's implementation experience. Industry life-cycle models are available for the following industries:

- Automotive
- Consumer products
- Utilities industries

Accelerated Solution Environment

The accelerated solution environment (ASE) is the motivating factor for rapid business transformation. The ASE environment is an elementary component of your AcceleratedSAP implementation; it is an enzyme that catalyzes your planning and action, design, and decision-making process. It helps you refine both your long- and short-term goals and offers solutions at an accelerated level. This approach has a significant impact on the speed, quality, and acceptance of your solution design. Candidates come from an ASE DesignShop and have the capability of seeing and communicating their solutions across entire organizations. They have avoided the problems of traditional approaches with ASE's knowledge-based accelerated approach.

The customized environment of ASE's DesignShop was created to motivate creativity offered by its candidates with the knowledge, technical resources, and research ability to instantly explore a large number of business solutions onsite. These resources and work products incorporate rapid prototype systems, simulations, normative and industry process models, Internet sites, packaged systems demos, prototyping tools, a database of leading practices, and research tools and databases. ASE is a crucial catalyst and creative component of Ernst & Young's Business Solutions To Order.

Ernst & Young's *Mentor*

Ernst & Young's *Mentor* tool accelerates content development for their learning solutions. *Mentor* supports the SAP documentation and knowledge reuse function by permitting your project teams to collect and share crucial information regarding your business procedures, processes, and other implementation objects. This flexible tool also gives your personnel the ability to record details about non-SAP objects that include end-user roles and competency requirements.

Mentor's database is supported by a comprehensive categorized system. It is easily accessed by both InfoDB and LEAP. SAP project teams can analyze transactions and business processes that are impacted by SAP's R/3 system configuration. At that time, it is possible to record implementation decisions within *Mentor*. In addition, training documentation inside *Mentor* is automated through templates, standards, and guidelines developed by instructional designers and utilized by this tool. *Mentor* objects that support product development can be accessed by InfoDB and LEAP. It may then be fabricated into learning solutions.

Mentor is the cornerstone of knowledge management. While your project team is going through the many phases of your implementation, they will execute decisions that will have a significant impact on both the design and deployment of your Business Solution To Order. Seizing the framework of information and decision logic is crucial to your efforts in developing a scalable and maintainable solution. *Mentor* offers a powerful relational object-based architecture that accelerates knowledge organization by offering you customizable documentation templates and structures that can satisfy your specific project needs.

Mentor is connected to the SAP *Business Engineer* and to process modeling tools. It uses the tools to offer event-controlled process (ECP) diagrams such as the SAP R/3 *Reference Models*. These models can be engineered to depict the future state of your enterprise. When your project team is ready to configure the R/3 software, *Mentor* offers a direct connection from any process model in *Mentor*'s repository to its associated *Implementation Guide's* activities and transactions within the R/3 software. It gives you the ability to see and alter your R/3 processes to satisfy specifications as you record the complexities affiliated with their implementation.

All of these factors combine to make *Mentor* a powerful process engineering application and configuration acceleration tool within any R/3 project. *Mentor*'s functionality supports knowledge objects related to all aspects of your implementation, including policies, procedures, interfaces, software extensions, and complementary software products. *Mentor*'s knowledge repository is supported by powerful searching and reporting capabilities. These capabilities permit easy access to objects for reuse or modification.

When your project proceeds, *Mentor* becomes the cornerstone of knowledge management by offering you information on project tasks, including end-user training development and solution testing. *Mentor* is used to record a standard implementation approach and share the solution details to accelerate multiple site implementations. The Web-based version of *Mentor* can offer access to the repository from any global location.

Director

Director offers easy program management. *Director* is a Lotus Notes–based program management toolset that offers a comprehensive view into many projects and activities that compose your SAP R/3 implementation. This toolset was created to control daily program management, such as project planning and status reporting, risk and issue management, resource allocation and optimization, and impact analysis of decisions that deal with at least one project element within the program. Executives and team members can view the status of a team or of your entire program so they are aware of the location, skills, and availability of any assigned team member. This also gives them the ability to share lessons learned on a real-time basis. This information can be accessed and updated from any location. This remote access allows project management to execute informed decisions and manage geographically dispersed teams as if they were all located in one centralized location. *Director* provides program management with the ability to manage all components of your Business Solution To Order, as well as making certain that your project team achieves their goals successfully.

Fusion Methodology

Fusing together people, process, and technology is representative of Ernst & Young's fusion methodology designed to allow your project teams to benefit from leading practices and inventive solutions that have been integrated into a fused project approach. Fusion addresses the organization and implementation tasks required for a successful implementation. The SAP *Roadmap* navigates through fusion to concentrate on specific tasks and activities that are pertinent to an SAP implementation initiative. The *Roadmap* refines the process and concentrates on the enabling software and links the project phases and tasks to tools, techniques, and deliverables that are specific to your R/3 implementation. The people, processes, and technology involved in your implementation are shown in Fig. 15-3.

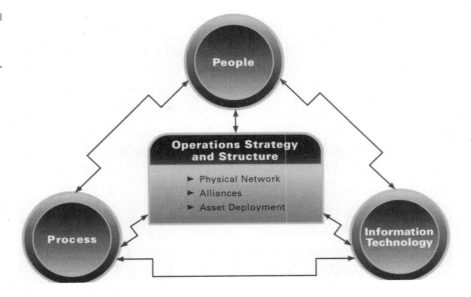

The fusion series methodology works to attain high value and rapid improvements through the effective leverage of SAP R/3 software supplemented by point solutions that enhance functionality. The focus is placed on cost, speed, and value for the integration of R/3 applications with associated people and process changes to enhance business performance.

Powered By ASAP

This AcceleratedSAP technique was developed to accelerate R/3 implementation delivery for your benefit. Ernst & Young has integrated ASAP components that include templates, project plans, checklists, and white papers into the fusion SAP *Roadmap*. All of these elements have been combined to create a powerful new method motivated by ASAP accelerators. Ernst & Young is one of the Powered By ASAP partners that can offer the power of fusion and the speed of ASAP to your Business Solution To Order.

You can achieve success with your enterprisewide SAP implementation. Retaining an implementation partner with the knowledge resources, tools, techniques, and methodologies is a smart method of accelerating your complete program dealing with everything from project start to *GoingLive* and more. Ernst & Young's tools and methodologies were created to specifically enhance access to proper resources, increase the communications level and flow of information within the implementation team, and make certain you achieve success within your accelerated implementation effort.

Transformational Outsourcing

Ernst & Young's transformational outsourcing method is highly effective and flexible for use in either small or large organizations that have the responsibility for enterprisewide business transformation. This process benefits from Ernst & Young's clients and their own core competencies. These techniques have evolved from their global experience in implementing SAP software throughout a wide variety of business situations and results from using their key vendor relationships and strategic alliances to avoid risk and emphasize implementation success. Because of the powerful aspects involved within the SAP solution, this implementation approach should also be dynamic and flexible in order to furnish the necessary amount of knowledge transfer. It is this transfer that allows your end users to become knowledgeable enough to operate the system on their own. It also allows them to adapt to the increased functionality in each new release of the software.

Ernst & Young's transformational outsourcing technique is sufficiently flexible to allow workers in your organization to learn at their own speed. However, this rate is sufficiently accelerated so that your end users can maximize your return on your information investment. This gives you the power to structure your implementation technique to take advantage of your specific business environment needs in order to achieve the most diverse set of options capable of supporting your SAP implementation and postimplementation requirements.

Several benefits can be achieved from Ernst & Young's transformational outsourcing approach that allow you to support a rapid SAP implementation. Ernst & Young has the responsibility of providing your organization with access to SAP software, and they can then accelerate your implementation time frame by up to 3 months. This permits you to concentrate on your core competencies and decrease the pressure on your personnel and financial resources throughout your entire implementation effort. Furthermore, you gain the ability to deal with the specifics regarding the changes in your information technology. In addition, your cash flow is maximized so that you spend only what is needed when necessary. Ernst & Young eliminates the problem of worrying about your corporate infrastructure with respect to performance, support, or obsolescence. Also, the constant improvement is part of your package instead of being an add-on.

The result of this activity allows your company to be transformed into a learning organization that can concentrate on the ongoing improvement through the utilization of the SAP R/3 software in combination with Ernst & Young's best practices. You are given the ability to focus on your core competencies while Ernst & Young works to develop the best method of using SAP software to achieve your competitive advantage while gaining the best return on your investment.

When your SAP configuration process is completed, Ernst & Young works side by side with you to create a long-term infrastructure and SAP evolution support method. Ernst & Young supports use of any hardware platform you select. They also function both in the short and long term to assist with your SAP functional and technical staff requirements using their own personnel. The objective is to develop a learning organization. The problem that most often exists in SAP implementation programs is the large amount of information involved can overwhelm your enterprise.

When you are confronted with large amounts of information, you can benefit from transformational outsourcing. This is where Ernst & Young can turn your company into a learning organization that can concentrate on the ongoing improvement by using SAP R/3 software. Their workers operate the new systems for you, which ensures that your personnel are not distracted from their current business responsibilities. Ernst & Young does more than do the job; they offer instructors and guides to work with your personnel at an appropriate pace. This effectively teaches your end users new functionality while offering SAP software functionality that increases your ROI. The focus of your SAP evolution support is to keep your workers at a level of SAP competency that facilitates the continuation of the transformation process for your business.

Where Do I Go?

Transformational outsourcing answers your organizational needs for implementing an SAP solution. Ernst & Young's method allows you to implement an SAP solution and reduce your problems. Ernst & Young utilizes its best-practice experience to satisfy your specific business improvement requirements. It offers complete implementation infrastructure support with its infrastructure support team to reduce the impact on your current technical environment and your immediate infrastructure costs.

After you have made your SAP configuration decisions, it helps you create a long-term infrastructure and SAP evolution strategy. This strategy can support your ability to take ownership of the infrastructure and SAP evolution for present and future objectives. You may also wish to transition these responsibilities to Ernst & Young. In addition, infrastructure cost is reduced by leveraging Ernst & Young technologies.

Core competencies are elementary to transformational outsourcing to provide you with an extensive level of SAP functionality in addition to your business expertise and core competencies. Ernst & Young's core competencies incorporate:

- Problem solving
- Education
- Training
- Expedited knowledge transfer

Expediting knowledge transfer requires that Ernst & Young be current in the technology and functionality of SAP software. In addition, you have the resources to operate SAP software because you have access to resources. Your current environment isn't going to be negatively impacted due to the fact that your people will continue to do business in your existing state as you manage your transition state by training your people to move forward when they are ready.

You can benefit from this move because Ernst & Young's task is to establish a business relationship that permits you to take advantage of SAP functionality, as required, and transform your business on a continuing basis.

Business transformation is constantly evolving. Therefore, when you deal with the future state and your SAP implementation is live, Ernst & Young stays to assist you in maximizing your SAP growth investments by offering you constant on-site functional and infrastructure support. Additionally, they can stay to offer you continuous functional support and ongoing training to satisfy your evolving SAP functionality.

Global Supply-Chain Management

One very crucial element to your business process supply-chain management (SCM) is the flow of materials and products, information, cash, and work from the point of first supply throughout the enterprise to the consumer and back. The most important business process for companies that buy, make, move, or sell products or services is SCM. SCM has grown into a true source of competitive advantage.

The cost, speed, and effectiveness of supply chains is distinguished by products, sales channels, and operating strategies that can impact business success. SCM consulting offers supply-chain–related consulting services that have been provided by Ernst & Young for more than 20 years. Your specific needs and opportunities are different from any other company in your industry. Knowing that is important to operating your supply chain and reflects on your suppliers, markets, products, and channels.

When you use these resources, as well as Ernst & Young's knowledge base and multiindustry experience, you gain the power to designate and quantify your supply chain, define your opportunities and targets, and outline a specific Business Solution To Order. This allows you to make certain that you achieve long-term business success. Building on the best supply-chain operating strategies allows you to execute and accelerate your strategic business, sales, and marketing plans. When you create the best operating strategy, you are essentially defining a very important success factor for your supply-chain transformation. These strategies define your mission statement, alignment, and the location of your operating assets, facilities, inventory deployment, and other capital that you use.

When you employ SCM to increase revenues efficiently, you effectively minimize cost through SCM. You have better tax rates by using SCM to reduce worldwide taxes. In addition, Ernst & Young's supply-chain strategy and industry experience permit you to function closely with your management to create the right strategy.

You gain the ability to utilize the accelerated solutions environment (ASE), as well as the computer-based supply-chain optimization models to create the best operating network for your specific needs. Your objective is to get the best assistance from your consultant to achieve the best strategic points of differentiation and new operating targets once SAP implementation begins. You can quantify the benefits when your supply chain is transformed. These benefits include cost minimization and profitable growth. Creating the right supply-chain strategies will offer detailed business benefits, key indicators to assist your decision making and measure progress throughout the program, and balanced scorecards to record and track operational performance.

Ernst & Young was one of the first organizations to quantify the effects of SCM on shareholder value by depicting the benefits of supply-chain transformation or improvements on free cash flow— a key measure of market value over time.

The Supply Chain

If your organization has a global foundation, your supply chains will be even more complicated. Ernst & Young's supply-chain process model depicts the primary business processes that comprise the value chain in your enterprise or global environment. The process model can be modified as needed for your specific company and industry.

A flexible supply-chain process model allows Ernst & Young to assist SAP implementations by accelerating the definition, measurement, and redesign of enterprise processes. They offer established industry process templates to gather the most crucial process objective, function, and variables. They also guide the implementation in cross-process issues such as logistics. Ernst & Young has utilized their supply-chain diagnostic method (RAPID Fx) in numerous corporate installations. Their extensive supply-chain experience and knowledge base contains several volumes of best practices, benchmarks, and established knowledge objects that can accelerate process designs, decisions on functions, and choices on variables.

Best practices provides you with a solid foundation for your accelerated SAP implementation. This permits you to gain extra time for redesigning processes or functions for the purpose of enhancing competitive business advantages.

Strategic Alliance Partners

The complexity of SCM often necessitates supplementary software products to improve the level of integration with SAP products. Ernst & Young supports strategic alliances as well as active partnerships with the leading SCM software companies. You can also hire completely trained consultants to work closely with you on your SAP implementations.

Ernst & Young's primary alliance partners include:

- Manugistics
- Technologies
- Red Pepper
- Numetrix for supply-chain planning and decision support
- InterTrans Logistics Solutions for transportation and network analysis products

■ EXE Techologies

■ BDM for warehouse management systems

In addition, Ernst & Young works side by side with third-party logistics (3PL) service providers who are skilled at supporting outsourced logistics functions, including transportation, distribution, and warehousing. All of these elements provide performance and lower costs. Ernst & Young maintains up-to-date knowledge of these 3PL companies, such as their IT and SAP integration functionality, to assist you with your outsourcing choices.

Networked Opportunities

E-Commerce in SCM is a rapidly advancing field that is used for business-to-business transactions performed via the Internet or other network. This type of transaction will more than likely become the standard operating procedure. Furthermore, the extended supply chains of most companies are electronically connected with their trading partners. Ernst & Young is a leader in electronic commerce strategies as well as accelerated implementations in SCM.

Ernst & Young's connected enterprise solutions create and deploy the ValueWeb. ValueWeb is a supply chain product channel that supplements SAP products by offering creative and comprehensive solutions.

The SAP-Enabled Supply-Chain Solution To Order offers a comprehensive SAP implementation environment that optimizes the potential for your supply-chain transformation and develops business advantages in your market. This comprehensive mix of software is accelerated in implementation, Ernst & Young experience, and knowledge, and is often an excellent SAP-enabled supply-chain solution for your business.

Conclusion

This chapter discusses techniques that you can use to maximize your system performance and availability. This chapter discusses SAP with respect to its preventative services and tools, as well as Ernst & Young's services that reduce the chances of random problems during your implementation effort. Finally, this chapter examines a typical system and indicates where checks should be executed to diagnose where bottlenecks are and determine how to effectively relieve them before they become critical and disrupt your services.

Adding Value and
Reducing Costs

Introduction

IBM offers the expertise and guidance you need to assist your SAP R/3 implementation to achieve a successful deployment. IBM offers a comprehensive range of solutions and experience with major system implementations and complex projects.

Benefits

IBM's experience offers you an excellent solution so that you can benefit from best-practice methods and decrease the risk of your accelerated SAP R/3 system implementation. You benefit from professional guidance that assists you in planning a successful business transformation with your SAP R/3 implementation. All of these components are further strengthened by access to a worldwide network of SAP experts and technical competency centers. The specific technical components of R/3 are shown in Fig. 16-1. In all, you get more than 3000 global resources that offer consulting and services for your R/3 solutions.

The most comprehensive consulting and technical services involve business transformation, SAP implementation, project management, client-server architecture and planning, basis consulting, education and training, industry solutions, business recovery services, and outsourcing. SAP consulting efforts are illustrated in Fig. 16-2.

Figure 16-1
R/3 Technical Features.

What are the main technical features of the SAP R/3?

The R/3 System, which is the basis for IS-B, features the following:

- openness

- client/server architecture

- relational database

- graphical user interface

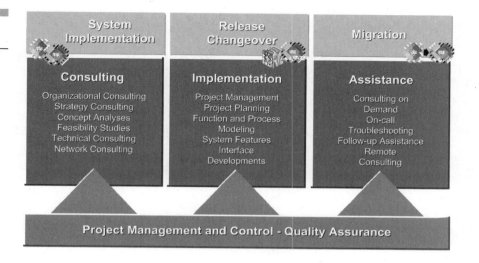

Figure 16-2
SAP Consulting.

IBM/SAP Relationship

IBM and SAP have a working relationship that has lasted for more than 20 years. This relationship involves development, marketing, and mutual customer aspects. IBM is a platform partner of SAP, and offers four server families for R/3. This provides a choice of high-performance, reliable, and available platforms for your corporate needs. IBM is a technology partner of SAP, and offers the high-performance DB2 database family to offer you consistent capabilities across multiple servers.

IBM offers a vast range of consulting and services for implementing, extending, and operating R/3 solutions. There are more than 3000 SAP experts and 74,000 IT specialists globally that can help to support your R/3 implementation. IBM provides complementary software and industry solutions that enhance R/3 solutions. A significant level of Internet application development, groupware, and systems management are also involved.

IBM is one of SAP's largest customers. As a result, they have implemented R/3 in many global business units and corporate processes.

Choosing IBM

It is often useful to explain why selecting IBM over a competitor can benefit your accelerated implementation project. One of the benefits from choosing a company with extensive experience is that you know what you are getting. IBM's efforts have always resulted in successful customers. IBM assists you in your SAP R/3 implementation projects. They work with you to accelerate your efforts and significantly reduce risk. The result is successful customers using IBM services, platforms, and technology to support their SAP R/3 project. There are more than 2500 SAP customers on IBM platforms and more than 2000 SAP implementations who have used IBM consulting. Many R/3 customers benefit from IBM products and services to achieve success. You can have confidence in your solution because IBM was awarded the SAP Award of Excellence for the third year in a row at the Sapphire '97 show held in Orlando, Florida. SAP bestowed this important honor because of customer satisfaction measured via a recent SAP customer survey. This award signifies IBM's continuing commitment to your success and the success of the IBM-SAP alliance. IBM is rich with resources to help your accelerated implementation efforts. IBM has nearly 5000 trained SAP consultants globally. The IBM Global Service Line ensures that all consultants have the same training, skills, tools, and access to information. In addition, it also stresses rapid implementation of industry-specific solutions. IBM Global Service Line provides you with a consistent approach to implementation, common methodology, and tools. You know you are dealing with certified, skilled consultants who have global resources at numerous locations.

SAP R/3 support is important, and IBM offers SAP skilled resources globally with coverage that is more extensive than any other SAP platform partner. The IBM SAP International Competency Center is located at SAP AG in Walldorf, Germany. They are responsible for offering the geographic centers constant, current information and providing second-level technical support. Other centers are located in Africa, Asia-Pacific, Australia, Europe, Latin America, and North America. Besides the global competency centers, there are more than 200 IBM engineers committed to the creation and improvement of SAP R/3 on IBM platforms. IBM has more than 30 development projects with SAP.

IBM also has the added benefit of offering integrated support. They provide a high-level integration between SAP's hotline support and IBM's support family for AIX and AS/400. This integration eases support procedures and permits both IBM and SAP software support hotlines to share information that includes IBM's operating system support databases. This results in a much more rapid, effective implementation.

Industry-specific solutions and expertise are very important in any

IBM industry solution as this works in combination with SAP ICOEs (Industry Center of Competence). These industries include manufacturing, petroleum, retail, health, automotive, telecommunications/media, process, and utilities. Other activities support cross-industry solutions integrated with SAP R/3, including IBM Product Manager, IBM Data Collection, IBM Factory Operations Executive, IBM Sales Force Automation, and Electronic Commerce.

IBM is one of SAP's largest customers. This is further illustrated by the fact that IBM signed a worldwide contract for SAP R/3. This makes IBM one of the largest customers ever contracted. IBM will have an estimated 50,000 SAP users by the end of the century. There will also be more than 100,000 employees of IBM and its business partners that rely on internal SAP R/3 implementations that use DB2. IBM customers can take advantage of IBM's experience with R/3 for implementation experience, project management, training, large-scale systems, increased availability, and systems management. IBM's San Jose facility is a dedicated SAP R/3 resource with over 1300 worldwide users in 36 countries.

There is a great deal of flexibility in selecting servers for R/3. As a result, you can choose the SAP R/3 server platform that is best for your needs. Your selection ultimately depends on the relationship of company standards with respect to availability and performance requirements. The advantage seen in selecting IBM as a platform partner for an R/3 installation is that IBM provides a comprehensive family of servers that can satisfy any combination of requirements and offer a great deal of scalability, high performance, high availability, and investment protection. IBM is the only SAP R/3 platform partner to provide this level of flexibility and choice, which ensures that your selection of a platform satisfies your individual corporate requirements.

IBM offers commercially available, high-performance, scalable solutions. The RS/6000 systems can be used as R/3 database and application servers from uniprocessor through symmetric multiprocessor (SMP) to scalable POWERParallel (SP) systems. The benefit is that they have PowerPC and POWER2 microprocessors. The RS/6000 is supported by AIX, IBM's version of UNIX that offers high-availability options.

The AS/400 Advanced Series provides enhanced technology with 64-bit PowerPC microprocessors and a 64-bit operating system. This allows SAP R/3 applications to function in full 64-bit mode. AS/400 is an integrated platform that offers a relational database DB2 on the OS/400. It offers security, systems management, and networking support. The end result is an integrated platform that facilitates easy system use, reduced

administrative costs, and benefits from your existing AS/400 investments in skills and technology.

There are also benefits in using Windows NT on your R/3 platform,
because PC servers provide a comprehensive, dependable solution for
R/3. IBM tools provide you with high availability, backup/recovery, distributed systems, and network management. In addition, IBM services,
including asset management and technology consulting, allow your Windows NT platform to function in a rigorous commercial environment.

R/3 and DB2

IBM and SAP made R/3 available on the S/390 server with OS/390 and
DB2 in order to produce a three-tier configuration. This solution permits
you to utilize your current S/390 skills, DB2 data, and network and systems management infrastructure. This provision allows you to acquire
an S/390 database server for R/3 that will link the strengths of SAP with
S/390's ability to support large databases and mission-critical operations
for several concurrent users.

IBM's R/3 certified DB2 database family offers well-established support
regardless of whether you decide to implement using a PC server,
RS/6000, AS/400, or S/390. The DB2 family offers extensive reliability,
integrity, and a reduced cost of ownership. DB2's cross platform compatibility makes certain that your solution is scalable and that your data and
skills are transferable across IBM platforms if your requirements change.

Finally, you can extend your network computing investment. IBM
assists you in enhancing your R/3 systems by giving you the opportunity
to enhance the reach of their R/3 data. This level of assistance allows
you to assist your personnel in working together with Lotus Notes and
SmartSuite. It also helps your systems work together with the MQ
Series (message queuing) and assists you in creating a powerful company on the Internet with the IBM Net.Commerce merchant server and
the CommercePoint secure Internet transaction technology.

IBM gives the power to be more productive by establishing a virtual
organization from your suppliers to your end customers. IBM's advanced
networking technologies allow you to create a scalable, reliable infrastructure for SAP R/3. You can then utilize your existing technologies,
including SNA networks, to achieve your goals. IBM offers an industry-
leading product for distributed systems, network, and applications management called Tivoli TME 10.

Tivoli TME 10 is integrated with R/3's CCMS function, and it assists you in the creation and management of a high-performance, reliable, available, and secure infrastructure to make certain you have both effective communications and total access distributed across your entire organization. IBM is the premier partner who can help you acquire a competitive edge by enhancing the reach of both your SAP system and your organization.

Technology Benefits

There is a global conglomerate for SAP systems called the *IBM SAP Competency Centers*. There are several benefits you can find in the SAP R/3 client-server business software that will help your company. Most organizations worry about how they can translate their current business systems to the advanced client-server model that allows them to implement R/3.

If your organization has sites in several regions and countries and uses different currencies, you need to determine the resources required to make certain that your system transition will be easy, effective, and successful on a companywide basis with reduced risk and maximum benefit.

IBM and SAP have established competency centers globally, so that these sites can be staffed by professionals who assist you in transforming your business, implementing business processes, and increasing your efficiency using R/3 and an important systems platform.

SAP R/3 Implementation

When you implement SAP R/3 as an enterprise resource planning (ERP) application, you will find that IBM offers several servers and a high-level database family optimized for R/3. IBM servers give you the performance and scalability you need to support a successful R/3 implementation. IBM's combination of servers, operating systems, and database family allows you to use them as a key vendor over a long period of time.

IBM's server and database products for R/3 include the RS/6000 servers for scalable UNIX performance, AS/400 Advanced Series for an integrated server and database platform, PC servers for a complete and reliable NT solution, S/390 database servers for powerful data integrity and reliability, and the DB2 family for database support and uniformity across servers.

Selecting an application package is only part of your complete ERP solution. You will need a server that emphasizes performance of R/3 for your specific business needs. When you select your system, you need reliability and support structure to make certain you can keep your operations functional. In addition, you will require the flexibility to upgrade your needs through your implementation.

IBM provides several platforms that support R/3 that includes everything from PC servers to mainframes. This offering includes a database family, operating systems, management tools, and a high level of technical expertise. IBM offers the best combination of hardware, software, support, and skills to bring your R/3 implementation to a successful completion.

RS/6000

The IBM RS/6000 offers performance for scalable UNIX systems and is one of the best R/3 servers with several thousand installations. The RS/6000 system offers R/3 database and applications servers that scale from uniprocessor through symmetric multiprocessor (SMP) to scalable POWERParallel systems (SP). They offer inventive PowerPC and POWER2 RISC technology. The RS/6000 is supported by AIX and has several options. The RS/6000 family can handle R/3 databases that include IBM's DB2, Oracle, and Informix. If your business has high-scalability requirements, then the RS/6000 SP also has the ability to support parallel databases through an Oracle parallel server.

AS/400

IBM's AS/400 offers an integrated platform that simplifies R/3 implementation and operation. This integrated system combines the hardware platform and OS/400 operating system with a relational database (for example, DB2 for OS/400). You gain security, systems management, and networking support in the process. SAP customers can buy the system with R/3 preloaded, which is a significant step in simplifying installation.

The AS/400 Advanced Series offers technology with 64-bit PowerPC microprocessors, a 64-bit operating system, and R/3 applications all operating in full 64-bit mode. The end result is a system that is simpler to use, reduces administrative costs, and leverages existing AS/400 investments.

Windows NT PC Servers

If you select Microsoft Windows NT as your platform, then IBM PC servers can offer you a detailed NT solution for R/3. IBM tools have high availability, backup/recovery, distributed systems, and network management. You also have the advantage of utilizing IBM services, including asset management and technology consulting. It is important to note that IBM can offer an NT platform that will support the load of a commercial computing environment.

S/390 Servers

The IBM S/390 has the reputation as the cornerstone of commercial computing environments. These servers act as mainframes for many global enterprises. They can support mission-critical applications for several concurrent users. S/390's high availability and reliability with respect to its network and systems management capabilities have made it an industry standard.

There are nearly 2000 SAP R/2 installations that use this platform in an SAP application environment. Both IBM and SAP have worked together to offer R/3 on the S/390 server with OS/390 and DB2. This joint effort provides the R/3 database server as a three-tiered configuration. This solution permits you to utilize your current S/390 skills, DB2 data, network and systems management infrastructure, and R/2 applications and data.

DB2 Family

IBM's DB2 for MVS/ESA has always been the most popular database for the majority of SAP R/3 implementations. IBM's R/3-certified DB2 database offers a high level of trusted support, regardless of whether you decide to implement on RS/6000, AS/400, or S/390. The DB2 family can supplement your SAP R/3 implementation by providing both reliability and integrity, while you have reduced cost of ownership. DB2 has cross-platform functionality and offers a level of compatibility that makes certain that your solution is scalable and that your data and skills are transferable if your requirements change.

IBM supports its DB2 family through extensive hardware maintenance and 24-hour-per-day, 7-day-per-week assistance that allows you to make certain that your systems stay in a productive mode. IBM gives you the power to enhance your R/3 solution by allowing personnel to function as one unit through Lotus Notes. This also allows your systems to work together with MQSeries. You can tie together Tivoli TME systems management with IBM's tools and operating systems in an effort to establish several options within your R/3 implementation.

Industry-Specific Solutions

IBM has developed an understanding of the application development and deployment requirements for each major IT industry. This development contributes to their ability to maintain a high level of industry expertise so they can provide the ability to produce industry-specific skills to satisfy your SAP implementation requirements.

IBM has several partnerships with industry-leading clients and has expanded its base of industry templates for SAP projects. These experiences (best practices) represent several business processes and application code that can reduce the cycle and refine the process for your SAP project. IBM and its business partners offer several integrated solutions that support the functional requirements specific to your industry. The method allows you to comprehend the business needs inside each industry segment and location. This information allows you to calculate the competitive benefits that IBM can offer you in meeting those needs with solutions, technology, and products.

The specific industry solutions are reflected within several key IT industries, including process industry, petroleum, chemicals, retail, utilities, manufacturing, metals, higher education, telecommunications and media, software industry, travel and transportation, forestry, and cross-industry solutions.

Process Industry

The IBM process industry method analyzes your business requirements within each industry segment and location. You can then decide the competitive benefits to bring to your customers to satisfy your needs in terms of solutions, technology, and products.

The IBM process industry solution unit is made up of several industry components, including metals and mining, chemicals, rubber/glass/plastics, textiles, and forest products.

The process industry segments are very capital-intensive and exhibit the cost factors of modern steel mill or paper that are greater than $750 million. The end result of such high capital-intensive industry segments is that the fixed cost segment of their product-cost structure is greater than the variable portion. In addition, high plant utilization is necessary in order to maintain a cost advantage.

Customer service, production, and delivery optimization have become very important aspects of maintaining a competitive advantage throughout the process industry. Often, prices are determined by the global marketplace, while product cost and customer service are the means of gaining an advantage. IBM has created solutions that function with SAP to optimize these methods.

IBM's process industry matches SAP goals, so that the process industry SAP team can offer specific solutions, technology, services, and products that are specifically needed by each industry segment to provide you with a competitive advantage through the implementation of your SAP systems. These solutions include CIMView/CIMWork Integration to SAP PP-PI, integration of production operations with SAP, MetalView (high-level manufacturing execution system created for the metals industry), Mill Scheduling, and the integration of paper mill scheduling and optimization with R/3.

In addition to these industry-specific offerings that supplement SAP, IBM has made certain that all functions necessary for providing these solutions are integrated with key IBM resources.

Petroleum Industry

IBM's petroleum industry solutions unit offers a global team of more than 300 people working closely with oil and gas companies to satisfy these IS requirements. In addition to client teams and their petroleum consulting organization, IBM's solutions team concentrates on creating industry-specific solutions and strategic business partners to meet your needs.

IBM stresses its open architecture data management solutions and services for the efficient creation and examination of hydrocarbon reserves. Petrobank provides an important field data management tool that is crucial in this industry. IBM's partnership with Fintech allows them to jointly offer an SAP solution that provides this field with information and land administration and industry-specific accounting. It provides superior performance with respect to industry standards to optimize performance.

Refineries must struggle against increasing competition, reduced margins, and strict product and environmental specifications. IBM and SAP offer solutions that help optimize refinery processes online and integrate processes for planning, production, and controlling operations. The primary objective is to integrate important process control and optimization products into SAP for your requirements.

The natural gas segment incorporates restructuring, mergers, acquisitions, centralization of organizational structures, modifications in the regulatory environment, and increased international focus by the large corporate entities. IBM created a partnership with Altra Technologies to offer a gas trading system for several customers through the IBM Global Network. This offers global communications support for these clients. This high-growth area for SAP projects is integrated with IBM's total natural gas solution.

Meeting Your Needs

You will find that you are in a growing environment that requires a highly integrated and complete package to satisfy your process reengineering needs. IBM offers a Lotus connection for R/3 that offers a high level of integration with SAP. This combination of products offers a collaboration of Lotus in an SAP environment together with established Intranet and Internet capabilities.

In terms of supply and transportation, IBM's data management systems are crucial to the petroleum industry. IBM's dedication to object technology is very active in supply and transportation. These functions can be integrated into SAP for optimal solutions.

When dealing with gas stations, it is important to note that oil companies who want to automate customer services and increase back-office efficiency do so in order to get customers to purchase both gas and groceries. IBM's work with SAP assists in the creation of SAP retail and linkages to the storeplace product that is important to petroleum industry organizations.

The petroleum SAP team at IBM works with all of these segments to expedite the use of SAP and the linking of complementary functionalities.

Refining Implementation

IBM refines the SAP implementation process for the chemical industry by introducing new processes that translate into new opportunities. The chemical industry is a rapidly changing market experiencing stringent regulatory conditions that create new requirements. When you consider the extensive diversity of products and raw materials (for example, polymers of paints, agricultural chemicals, and consumer products), then you realize that the chemical industry is one of the most rapidly changing industries.

SAP Retail Solutions

IBM offers a retail interchange that promotes the SAP retail connectivity solution. IBM's SAP retail solutions offer the integration of SAP retail with the IBM suite of in-store systems to offer a comprehensive integrated enterprise solution for store-to-headquarters applications. This integration will offer the framework to link other IBM and non-IBM applications to SAP as a complementary software provider.

There are several advantages to IBM's R/3 retail solutions. IBM provides an SAP-certified point-of-sale (POS) interface that works toward integrating IBM and non-IBM store systems with the SAP retail solution. IBM has strong ties to the retail sector, and is the North American market share leader in POS devices. IBM offers a dedicated retail industry consulting practice that offers BPR, best practices, and in-depth retail knowledge to several global retailers. In addition, they are the second largest SAP consulting practice in the world and offer a suite of retail-based applications in merchandising, inventory forecasting, and replenishment and warehouse management that supplement SAP's retail solution.

IBM operates jointly with SAP to make SAP retail viable for the IBM SP platform. IBM has a Retail Distribution Industry Competency Center whose primary responsibility it is to work directly with SAP retail development to provide retail resource and skills, and create a consulting practice, link our applications, and benchmark their hardware.

IBM distribution solution industry applications include:

- INFOREM which is used for inventory forecasting and replenishment.
- CRP (continuous replenishment product) connects firms in the consumer package goods industry with both customers and suppliers.
- Worldwide chain stores (WCSS) is the IBM warehouse management and distribution solution that links to SAP retail.
- Makaro which is used for merchandise planning.

IBM application linkages include:

- Product Manager
- Lotus Notes
- Information Warehouse
- ADSTAR ADSM
- DB2
- MQ Series
- Print Services Facility
- Advanced Function Printing
- IBM Global Services Outsourcing

IBM Global Services provides an SAP practice that concentrates on both retail and distribution customers.

Retail Interchange

IBM's retail interchange offers an adaptable, transportable, scalable, and simple solution for SAP retail connectivity for any size retail chain. The retail interchange package permits data to flow across endless paths between different point-of sale terminals (IBM and non-IBM), store controllers, in-store processors, SAP retail application servers, and legacy applications.

Retail interchange is used as an R/3 interface for any third-party software that can be connected to R/3 through the IDOC interface. Retail interchange combines current polling packages and benefits from the most recent data mapping technology.

The retail interchanges data-routing capabilities ensure data delivery via IBM MQSeries, logical grouping of files, configurable prioritization, time-independent delivery, workload, and speed balancing.

The retail interchange core is a reusable class library compiled in Java. It provides platform independence and the ability to add specialized functionality. This pure Java API offers rapid application development, focuses on business logic, and maximizes transportability.

The retail interchange offers a simple graphical user interface (GUI) that facilitates easy configuration viewing status and statistics, task manager, error and event viewer, and easy Web browser. The retail interchange has been certified by SAP for retail, while the data-mapping component has been certified by SAP for data conversion.

It benefits from having SAP-certified data conversion, data routing, ensured data delivery via the IBM MQSeries, logical grouping of files, configurable prioritization,, time-independent delivery, workload and speed balancing, scalability for any size chain, operates in heterogeneous POS environments, offers a pure Java API for rapid application development and maximized portability, is extendable to other types of application environments, and offers an easy GUI.

Utilities Industry

Electric and gas utility companies, both domestically and globally, depend on IBM's ability to deliver the types of solutions that utility companies need: reliable, robust, and cost effective. IBM assists each organization with their constantly changing regulations and marketplace structure. In addition, IBM gives you the ability to exploit these changes by providing inventive information technology solutions.

IBM's utilities and energy services industry organization (UESI) benefits most from the team of client executives and managers who represent IBM in their assigned utility industries. These client managers comprehend the utilities industry, information technology, and the practical decision-making processes that occur with their customers. They have a great deal of knowledge to offer their clients and can offer solutions that make the best business sense regardless of what product brands are involved. In addition, they have access to a wealth of IBM's resources that concentrate on solving any customer problem.

UESI client managers are primarily responsible for customer satisfaction with respect to doing business with IBM. UESI understands that, in order to achieve success, the utility companies must work with the entire value chain of processes necessary in offering services to their customers.

Your goal is the primary motivating factor for your enterprise executives. UESI's business transformation services (BTS) can assist you in navigating through incoherent issues so you can end up with a strategy that is advantageous and makes your implementation effort more efficient. The goal is to apply expertise to decision making to provide a structured framework that allows you to analyze and resolve any business issues.

When you deal with utilities, execution is the most important factor because you need a simple method for measuring the delivery of core services. You need to know how much gas is flowing through your lines at all times. In addition, you must have a very high level of performance that allows you to use both technology and services that offer viable solutions. UESI satisfies this need by offering a portfolio of solutions created by IBM and its business partners that work to support the functional requirements of utility companies. These customer offerings deal explicitly with transmission, distribution, and corporate management.

The cornerstone of these solutions is SAP's suite of software that permits utilities to operate their businesses in an efficient and integrated method. UESI, in combination with its global partners in the United States, Europe, and Japan, is connected directly into IBM's large SAP resource centers. UESI can pilot a utility through the steps needed to determine the advantages of implementing SAP, as well as the specific modules that must be deployed in the proper order in order to gain the highest return on your investment.

IBM and SAP professionals can architect an implementation plan for the client. You gain an experienced staff of professional SAP consultants in an effort to provide the systems platform to support development, testing, training, and production. The goal is to utilize methods that can compress the analysis and decision-making process, as well as accelerate the implementation of SAP modules. This results in increased availability of an organization so that you have one unified source for the development of an SAP-based real-time enterprise.

ProductManager

ProductManager is an integrated suite of object-oriented applications created to control product and process data in any size manufacturing organization. It offers a centralized, secure storehouse of data that supports business processes involved in new product introduction, engineering modification management, and the release and distribution of data throughout a multiplant enterprise. Several systems and users may share this data across your entire organization.

IBM *ProductManager* software, in combination with SAP R/3 business management applications, functions well to refine the entire product production life cycle in your organization. When you implement an electronic file folder to group records into logical sets for serial or parallel distribution, *ProductManager* can specifically create work rules and routing procedures implemented in systems including R/3. In addition, it permits redlining crucial engineering documents, thus allowing reviewers to view the current version of documents and execute modifications made earlier in the review cycle, and to view the sources of those modifications.

ProductManager is created for global implementation. It is available with date, time, currency format, screen prompts, help messages, and online documentation in several languages, such as French, Canadian French, Spanish, Italian, German, Dutch, American English, and Japanese. There are several benefits from the integration of *Product-Manager* with R/3. It offers close engineering change and distribution control of product data across multiple SAP sites. It ties together bidirectional synchronous integration with SAP R/3. Any changes executed in a *ProductManager* record will automatically be available in R/3 applications. This integration makes certain that your data will always be recent, system-to-system, plant-to-plant, enterprisewide.

Benefits include a shortened time to market; quicker, more accurate information acquisition; replacement of paper-intensive processes; elimination of duplicate data input; elimination of inventory scrap and rework; multiplan support with multiple manufacturing views; and increased engineering responsiveness to changing market conditions. Support is also available for ISO/9000 certification through documented repeatable processes and audit trails; a more secure, centralized point of control for vital product data; total life-cycle support for your products; and user-level integration to attain the best ease of use possible.

Factory Operations Executive

In order to satisfy the needs of modern manufacturers, there is a new generation of line control systems designated as manufacturing execution systems or MES. IBM offers its own MES called Factory Ops, which is a manufacturing line control system for businesses. It employs discrete flow manufacturing methods. This product suite integrates shop floor control, operator guidance, quality management, and interfaces to other applications, including production planning, scheduling, and supervisory control. This solution offers several manufacturing environments such as build-to-order, repetitive, and batch. In addition, its functionality offers a powerful MES solution that provides manufacturers with real-time visibility into their manufacturing operations.

Factory Ops provides an interface for your SAP R/3 enterprise resource planning system in order to foster a higher level of connectivity. When you utilize standard SAP interface protocols (for example, RFC and ABAP/4), the interface between Factory Ops and SAP R/3's *Production Planning* module arranges for the download of production orders, routings, bill of materials, and part number information to the factory floor. In addition, production order status and production order completion data (for example, backflush) are transmitted from the factory floor to your SAP R/3 system. A complete transaction audit trail logs the information; reconciliation reports are also available. Its design for integration, database independence, and published APIs significantly reduces the implementation time by months as opposed to MES products.

There are several benefits in offering real-time information. You achieve superior order tracking, operations and products, and factory operation, all of which can help you reduce manufacturing cycle time; satisfy regulatory/compliance requirements; reduce production lead times; shorten work-in-process inventory; lessen data entry time; respond quickly to alterations in processes, products, and orders; and enhance control of production resources. All of these elements produce reduced production runs, increased quality/lower costs, greater on-time deliveries, and enhanced customer response.

Telecommunications Industry

IBM offers an integrated customer management system (ICMS) that provides an advanced customer care and billing solution. In order to compete in today's communications market, it is crucial to optimize the use of the enterprisewide business support systems. IBM's ICMS offers a highly integrated customer care and billing solution for telecommunications service providers. ICMS was developed through partnerships with several leading telecommunications and cable companies which allows them to compete in deregulated markets.

ICMS offers an enhanced customer care and billing solution for scalability, while providing complete customer service support that provides continuity and supports a centralized point of contact. It provides totally customizable menus and the power to customize billing information with exceptional performance and handles multiservice billing and provisioning on one central application. You gain a higher level of system flexibility through special layering architecture. It shortens time to market through rapid introduction of new services and decreases operating costs through increased productivity and reduced computing costs. You gain the capability for more efficient provisioning and simpler ordering of several services.

ICMS is flexible and user-oriented, and employs standardized table-driven software to reduce data entry and increase data integrity, so that any modifications made to the way the system functions are executed by altering the parameters as opposed to reprogramming. These changes can be illustrated quickly throughout your system or at a preestablished date. This flexibility permits a telecommunications company to respond rapidly to market-driven competitive circumstances via the system's capability to quickly inject new products and services.

ICMS meets telecommunications operator requirements for the following areas:

- Customer account management
- Customer care
- Billing and collections
- Provisioning
- Usage processing
- Inventory
- Location management

- System management
- Product management
- Planning

ICMS gives you the ability to select a multiservice indicative of a wireline, wireless, cable television, or a single line of business system. There are other services, including the Internet or data services that may also be configured. ICMS permits telecommunications and cable television organizations to provide single or multiple services. At the same time, they may also offer you a single invoice.

In terms of connectivity to SAP, ICMS offers you general ledger information that can be used to send information to R/3 for financial analysis. This information is based on financial transactions that pass through ICMS. This involves calls, such as tolls, USP, and other service and equipment items such as call plans, discounts (for example, MOA-corporate concessions), taxation, external transactions via external/generic feeds, journal adjustments, payments, and bad debt write-off. These transactions are developed at the same time as a billing run or through posting.

Golden Gate

The Golden Gate solution links standard R/3 functionality with extra extensions and enhancements to satisfy the requirements of organizations in the software industry. The existing extensions are mostly meant for sales and distribution systems that need to support a variety of product licensing, billing, maintenance, and service arrangements. These extensions and improvements are beyond the standard R/3 package and are presented as add-ons.

These standard solutions were created for the software industry, while the majority of functionality can be used to support hardware.

The Golden Gate functionality includes entitlements and software product structures that can designate software through a configurable material type. Golden Gate permits each user to choose parameters that influence prices or factor-based pricing.

Contract management has been improved for enterprise contracts (contract terms that deal with more than one customer), product list eligibility, price protection, multicurrency call-off, value contracts, and customization.

An installed base of support that has information on software licenses is also available, and it contains serial numbers (license numbers), customer business information, delivery information, license status, and information on configurations. There is also billing and revenue that supports billing processes for one-time, recurring, and mixed-charge products. It also supports deferred revenue recognition by employing both time-based and performance-based methods. It permits designation of the accrual period for each contract item and each billing plan item.

Royalty accounting is something that Golden Gate offers via samples of customized standard functions in R/3. It can support distinct royalty accounting and reporting processes. Service call management employs R/3 standard call management functionality; it offers extensions for telephone connectivity in the call logging process and business API to connect to knowledge-based systems during call handling, electronic integration throughout call closure, and resource-related billing specifically from notification.

SMOOTH

IBM decreases R/3 implementation time for both small and mid-sized businesses. IBM offers SMOOTH for R/3, which is a business management solution that offers small and mid-sized businesses several benefits of the R/3 enterprise resource planning (ERP) software with greatly accelerated implementation times. This permits users to attain business benefits more quickly and cost effectively.

IBM's SMOOTH for R/3 incorporates the IBM server preloaded with SAP's enterprise business application solutions, as well as SAP's rapid implementation methodology of AcceleratedSAP and IBM global services implementation services. IBM services and implementation techniques have been designed to reflect industry-specific best practices and to integrate a great deal of the customization work that is usually necessary to implement R/3. Therefore, your users can see an earlier return on their information investment which results in a total ERP solution that is implemented to satisfy the customer's cost and time expectations.

SAP and IBM: Creating an R/3 Database

SAP has certified the IBM System/390 platform to support the database server for the R/3 system. The connection between R/3 and S/390 can provide you with a powerful combination of performance and mainframe computer capabilities. CIM software is known for its structural flexibility and superior functionality. S/390 offers you industry scalability and system availability.

Both companies offer an R/3 database server for S/390. More than 150 IBM and SAP customers from a wide variety of regions and industry sectors will utilize the S/390 database server for R/3.

R/3 on S/390 offers you a flexible, cost-effective platform for medium- and high-end enterprise applications. R/3 uses the IBM high-performance DB2 for S/390 relational database systems to offer you an additional database option that satisfies several computing requirements in applications that deal with payroll, personnel, manufacturing, sales, distribution, and human resources.

These types of applications require a powerful solution that can withstand the demand of high transaction workloads in constant use. The combination of R/3, DB2, and the S/390 platform will offer a high-performance system that provides advanced functionality and scalability. It has the ability to adapt to future business requirements. IBM and SAP worked closely to refine this solution, and provided extensive functionality for increased R/3 performance.

The R/3 solution on the S/390 utilizes the three-tiered client-server architecture of R/3. It then has the ability to produce a great deal of system pliancy and functionality. In utilizing this level of reliability, availability, and scalability of IBM S/390, in addition to DB2 for OS/390 relational database, you have the power to deploy the solution to satisfy several application needs and transaction workloads. The R/3 database server for S/390 is also very beneficial for you if you are running an R/2 system and want to balance both hardware and data investments while you acquire advanced business-process functionality and three-tier client-server architecture of R/3.

R/3 tested on an S/390 solution resulted in exceptional performance and predictable scalability. Using both OS/390 and DB2's integrated capabilities configured in a common SAP sales and distribution (SD) application configuration has allowed IBM to gain support for more than 1000 simultaneous SD application users on an S/390 parallel enterprise server. Furthermore, three-way Parallel Sysplex configurations have gained support among more than 2000 SD users, resulting in the highest levels of performance and scalability that R/3 can deliver. IBM's S/390 parallel enterprise servers offer double the processing power in the latest version, therefore IBM and SAP will provide even higher performance.

S/390's high level of performance, in combination with its potential for substantial growth, provides you with the very best high-end platform possible for deploying R/3's business-process functionality. The S/390 offers an increased level of scalability and power designed to supplement R/3's functionality. It allows you to select a joint solution for very detailed, long-term business decisions.

The solution benefits you by using recent business trends, including Internet commerce, extended supply-chain management functionality, and the R/3 *Business Framework* architecture. You will have the ability to deploy R/3 on AIX-based RS/6000 as well as Windows NT systems from IBM as application servers. These machines work in combination with your installed S/390 platform and your DB2 database system. SAP and IBM also add support for R/3 application servers from other vendors as well.

The combination of both R/3 and S/390 allows you to scale your networked environments to meet your changing needs. You have the ability to scale from a pilot of 50 users to 500 users in the multinational level. In that way, you can transfer the information they need quickly and efficiently.

R/3 is a complete suite of client-server business applications that ties together all of the activities in your organization into a centralized, integrated software solution. The R/3 system handles enterprisewide financial control, sales, distribution, materials management, production planning, quality management, plant maintenance, and human resources functions.

IBM's S/390 makes certain you maintain data security, system availability, and integrity. It makes certain you have complete systems management for applications with large numbers of concurrent users. S/390 processors are used frequently to operate the most crucial business applications.

IBM is an SAP partner that provides SAP customers with a complete systems-integration solution, including all consulting services, complementary software, industry solutions, platforms, and technology. There are more than 3000 IBM consultants that offer global business reengineering support for industry solutions, education, training, and outsourcing. IBM SAP Competency Centers are located in major cities to offer technical expertise for successful SAP system implementations. In order to satisfy the mission-critical application requirements that R/3 needs, IBM provides high-performance, scalable servers, a database family, and powerful systems management.

SAP offers extensive client-server enterprise application software to give you comprehensive solutions for different size organizations in all industry sectors. SAP provides scalable solutions that allow its customers to perform continuous improvement for best business practices. Their products permit you to quickly meet changing market conditions, and help businesses maintain a competitive advantage.

Conclusion: IBM and SAP Affiliation

This chapter examines several SAP services to determine how they can add value to your R/3 investment. We then examines shorter implementation periods that permit customers to realize the benefits of business process engineering more quickly. In addition, you can save costs by creating R/3 expertise in-house, thereby reducing your dependence on consultants.

SAP is a leading alliance partner of IBM. IBM provides benefits as an SAP customer. You gain a comprehensive, enterprise solution that deals with consulting services, supplementary software, industry solutions, platforms, and technology. There are nearly 4000 IBM consultants globally that offer business reengineering, application implementation assistance, training, and outsourcing for R/3 solutions. IBM SAP Competency Centers are located in major cities around the world and offer technical expertise for successful R/3 implementations.

In order to satisfy the needs of mission-critical applications of SAP R/3, IBM provides a selection of high-performance, scalable servers with robust systems management in addition to network computing technology that enhances the scope of R/3 to more users.

CHAPTER 17

Preventative
Maintenance

Check and Monitoring Services

The *EarlyWatch* service marked the beginning of a very significant change in the IT industry. It allowed modification of the business prototype of the software service delivery. The specific service packages for R/3 are shown in Fig. 17-1.

These ideas are based on your needs in the very early stages of an R/3 implementation life cycle. The objective of the SAP concept review service, as shown in Fig. 17-2, is to determine potential problems that might occur early in your implementation efforts. This information allows you to take very specific steps to avoid them. Reports are then forwarded to SAP and analyzed by SAP specialists.

GoingLive Check

SAP professionals have the ability to remotely log into your computer system. These professionals can then analyze the communication between the hardware, database, and operating system. This occurs during the critical GoingLive stage of your implementation life cycle. The SAP *GoingLive* check is illustrated in Fig. 17-3.

Figure 17-1
R/3 Service Packages.

	R/3 Standard Service Package	R/3 Optimizing Service Package	R/3 GoingLive Service Package	R/3 Productive Operation Service Package	R/3 Concept Review Service Package
Check & Monitoring Services					
• SAP Concept Review	●				●
• SAP GoingLive Check	●	●	●		
• SAP EarlyWatch	●	●		●	
Training Services					
• Network	●				
• Online Service System	●				
• System administration	●				
• Implementation	●				
• IDES	●				
• GoingLive	●	●			
• R/3 Knowledge Products	●				
Consulting Services					
• Remote Consulting	●	●	●	●	●

Figure 17-2
Concept Review Service.

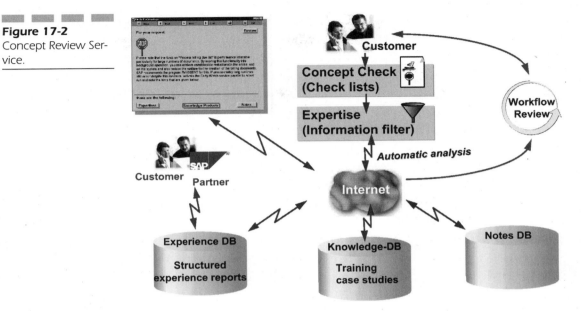

SAP *EarlyWatch*

This check is utilized to make certain you acquire smooth performance of your R/3 system. SAP *EarlyWatch* analyzes potential system bottlenecks before they become problematic. This preventative service has

Figure 17-3
SAP *GoingLive* Check.

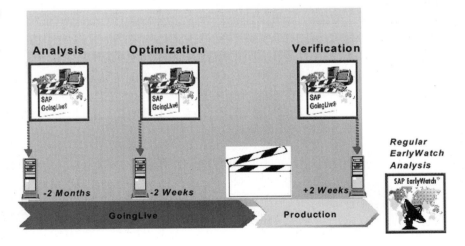

met with a great deal of success once it was used and tested in various implementations.

Creating Partnerships

Formidable partnerships are formed with leading companies in the information technology, while business consulting industries create the foundation of the SAP service and support network. R/3 logo partners, implementation partners, and value-added resellers offer services from strategic business consulting to implementation project support. Service and support form the foundation for your effort. SAP distinguishes between standard support and complementary services. SAP support deals with all levels of annual support, including online corrections, upgrades and enhancements, access to customer information sources, and the Online Service System (OSS).

SAP services complement regular support by offering valuable knowledge transfer and assistance through training, workshops, performance tools, and consulting. SAP R/3 service and support specifically meets all stages of your R/3 product life cycle, so you can satisfy the needs of your R/3 system implementation. These R/3 services are incorporated in the R/3 service packages, so you can acquire easy administration in your SAP R/3 service program.

Benefits

Regardless of whether you are implementing R/3 by yourself or with the assistance of consulting partners, SAP provides complimentary services throughout the entire R/3 implementation. Active knowledge transfer, information services, consulting, and check and monitoring services offer you crucial expertise that you need in order to successfully complete your R/3 project.

Faster implementation is achieved when you install a complete R/3 system or add an application. SAP services permit you to correctly complete your project and gain the necessary expertise to make the best technology and planning decisions. These decisions are based on the successful implementation of SAP services. All of the SAP R/3 service and support provisions are ISO 9001–certified to ensure that you receive the best possible quality. This certification represents a detailed process analysis of your service delivery. Regular internal and external quality is guaranteed throughout the delivery of your services. This may involve either information or on-site consulting, however, the result is that you can be certain you achieve the best possible services to speed your implementation to a successful completion.

SAP services provide you with the opportunity to provide input. There are customer feedback loops for workshops and training courses that permit these services to offer total customer satisfaction. All service personnel are very responsive to customer comments in terms of timeliness, responsiveness, and accuracy of service delivery.

In order to achieve better system performance benefits, you will find that SAP increases your system availability and performance to satisfy your corporate needs. They accomplish this task by offering preventative services and tools. In addition, SAP service lessens the chance of the occurrence of any unplanned events. Standard checks include *Early-Watch* sessions that diagnose the location of any bottlenecks and work to relieve them before they can become problematic.

Reducing Costs

SAP services add value to the information technology investment in your R/3 system. Shortened implementation time frames permit you to realize the extraordinary benefits of business process engineering much more quickly. When you utilize knowledge transfer, you can generate R/3 expertise in-house by reducing your dependence on consultants. When dealing with the Online Service System, you will find a repository of solutions that creates enhancements, updates, and modification to the R/3 system. This allows more efficient utilization of your time and resources. If you require addition expertise, then remote consulting offers useful information quickly. It allows you to avoid any unproductive costs of travel and expenses that you would experience with on-site consulting.

Data Bridge

Information Builders Inc., offers SNApack *Data Migrator* Builders Inc. and SNApack *Data Warehouse* meant for use with SAP's R/3 software. It was created to ease the transition to SAP decision-support systems. *Data Migrator* assists with DBMS extracting, cleaning, mapping DBMS utility, and migrating of legacy data. It combines Information Builders' existing Enterprise Data Access/SQL and *Enterprise Copy Manager* products. This package offers access to 65 data sources on 35 platforms, then stores it in a flat file, focus file, or relational database. Special methods are added, particularly for *Migrator*, while SAP logic assists in solving interface and data-conversion software problems. *Data Warehouse* is meant for organizations that have recently migrated to SAP and permits comparison of data across packages. SAP's 400,000 fields and 9000 tables offer individual English-language descriptions. However, this can pose a difficulty when you are migrating from other database architectures.

When dealing with SNApack, it is important to look at how *Data Migrator* ties together three pieces to assist you extract, clean, map, and migrate legacy data to an SAP system. The product links Enterprise Data Access/SQL (EDA/SQL) which yields access to 65 sources of data on 35 platforms. *Enterprise Copy Manager* takes data from EDA/SQL and records it in a flat file, focus file, or relational database. Information Builders then adds special methods required to load data into SAP by using SAP logic.

The resulting application assists SAP users in resolving data-conversion and interface problems. Converting data into SAP formats and continuous migrations are important issues because Information Builders believes that 25 to 70 percent of the cost of implementing SAP involves interface creation and migration.

Interface problems are most common when your organization implements various packaged applications for each department. For example, if accounting and sales are supported by two different packages, it is hard to update one when a change happens in the other. *Data Migrator* supports these interfaces to satisfy your changing business requirements.

Often, it may take an organization as many as 2 years to migrate from one system to another. During this period, both systems may be operating in parallel and allow you to establish another interface requirement. Even though *Data Migrator* employs a batch process to complete the updates, it incorporates a scheduler so these batch dumps can be scheduled at various intervals.

Information Builders also offers the SNApack *Data Warehouse*. The *Data Warehouse* ties together *Enterprise Copy Manager* with interfaces to SAP. The *Data Warehouse* offers comparison capabilities across packages for organizations that have migrated to SAP recently. You will find that, after you have migrated to a new business application, it is often difficult to perform historical comparisons of data from the previous and the current systems.

Information Builders concentrates on applications like *Data Migrator* and *Data Warehouse* because of the increasing popularity of packaged applications. The middleware market is changing with respect to people's desire to buy packaged applications. However, in order for you to offer a comprehensive decision support solution, *Data Warehouse* must also function with two other Information Builders products:

1. *Reporter*
2. *Fusion* (a multidimensional database server)

Data Warehouse is available for Windows NT and UNIX platforms. The acceptance of data warehousing in the marketplace has generally been quite slow with respect to the AS/400 platform. However, that package might be released for the AS/400 in the future.

Data Mart Tools

Information Builders Inc. offers a pair of data and data warehousing extraction software modules for report generation for corporations via SAP's R/3 enterprise planning software. CIM Software SNApack SmartMart offers an integrated data mart and *Data Warehouse* package for R/3. The package allows users to create, manage, and use a *Data Warehouse* based on R/3 source data. The pricing structure begins at $37,500.

SNApack Power *Reporter* for SAP R/3 permits users to establish reports and execute queries against those reports and graphs. The price is $795 per user.

SAP is creating a *Data Warehouse* for the R/3 suite. SAP demonstrates its information warehouse, *Data Warehouse,* which is an independent component of the data warehousing company's *Business Framework*. The *Business Information Warehouse* software product allows users to implement business development components as soon as the components become available. It does this without disrupting your current R/3 system. The product is composed of the *Business Information*

Warehouse server, the *Administrator Workbench,* and the *Business Explorer.*

The server is part of the OLAP engine and metadata repository that has already been configured. These features prevent you from having to establish a *Data Warehouse.* The explorer provides a graphical interface for Web access and displays data in Excel spreadsheets. The *Workbench* allows you to create, track, and manage the warehouse from one centralized point. You will find that this program is better than the *Open Information Warehouse* because data may be stored in a separate database.

Deploying Business Components

SAP builds on its *Business Framework* structure with its *Data Warehouse* which is used for deploying business components in R/3 environments.

SAP's *Data Warehouse* allows you to rapidly deploy business components as they become available, without interrupting your current R/3 system.

The *Business Information Warehouse* has three main components, including:

1. *Business Information Warehouse* server

2. *Business Explorer*

3. *Administrator Workbench*

The *Administrator Workbench* assists you in acquiring and analyzing information rapidly. The *Business Information Warehouse* server incorporates a preconfigured online analytical processing engine and metadata repository. This makes it unnecessary for you to create a *Data Warehouse* from the ground up. You will also find that the *Business Explorer* offers a graphical Web-access interface for customizing desktops and displaying data using Microsoft Excel spreadsheets.

The *Administrator Workbench* offers a centralized point of control for establishing, monitoring, and maintaining your entire *Data Warehouse* environment. The *Business Information Warehouse* is an improvement over SAP's *Open Information Warehouse.* It permits you to put the data in an individual database, however, you can still balance the knowledge of your SAP system. There is, however, a great deal of complexity with respect to the implementation.

Products

Bool & Babbage Inc. offers its Command software that is meant to manage end-to-end availability of R/3 systems. The software optimizes the performance of crucial R/3 system and application resources across multiplatform, distributed environments. The pricing structure begins at $15,000.

IntelliCorp Inc. offers two products, including:

1. *LiveModel*

2. *LiveAnalysts*

LiveModel is a business modeling tool that assists developers in predicting R/3 system behavior. *LiveAnalysts* imports the scenario process models of R/3's *Reference Model* directly from *LiveModel*. *LiveModel*'s pricing structure begins at $4995 per seat, while *LiveAnalyst's* price is $9995 per seat.

Business Information Warehouse

The *Business Information Warehouse* server offers the quick retrieval and interpretation of information saved in the *Data Warehouse*. This information includes a preconfigured, online analytical processing engine as well as the metadata repository.

Its *Business Explorer* component offers a graphical Web-access interface that allows you to customize desktops and display data by using Microsoft Excel.

The *Administrator Workbench* component offers a centralized point of control that allows you to establish, monitor, and easily maintain your entire *Data Warehouse* environment.

SAP User Recovery

SunGard Recovery Services Inc.–created SAP Services Inc. concentrates on the details of your disaster recovery needs. In addition to offering disaster recovery, consulting, and testing services, SunGard has created regional disaster recovery SAP user groups.

S-Link Fosters Real-Time Data Capture

Ernst & Young's S-Link is the first commercial solution for automated data collection. S-Link integrates with Par Microsystems' TPS/2 to offer you an interface between automated data collection systems and SAP R/3.

Samsung Semiconductor was one of the first to deploy S-Link. They found that it saved them a significant amount of time and made certain that they received the best quality data entry together with automated materials management.

When you use SAP, you realize benefits from S-Link. At any time when you are scanning, S-Link gathers data and transmits it directly to the SAP system.

Real-time communication offers the latest type of processes for your convenience. Errors are reduced by eliminating most of the manual data entry requirements. In addition, the data collection server validates your data for accuracy.

S-Link can be utilized in any area of your corporate operations where data needs to be captured. These areas are best depicted by receiving, inventory management, shipping, asset management, plant maintenance, work in process, and employee time and tracking.

In addition, S-Link can automatically track and update any item that carries a bar code in your R/3 environment. As an SAP user, you can acquire an automated data collection and shop floor control system. Ernst & Young can work closely with you to create a solution that quickens the pace of data entry, increases data integrity, and assists users in reducing inventory and labor costs.

SAP Success Stories

When you are looking for the best solution for your information investment dollar, you will find that significant value is added through your relationship with SAP and Ernst & Young, mostly due to the fact that Ernst & Young offers the right combination of resources when you need them at the proper stages of your implementation effort. The combination of teamwork and collaboration allows Ernst & Young to offer the best solution to your business practices. You can then contribute significantly to the implementation of the resulting business process reengineering effort.

Ernst & Young's SAP consulting practice offers value to your company. They tie together their understanding of your business and corporate needs along with SAP's innovative, advanced software solutions.

Examples of companies who have successfully implemented SAP R/3 include:

- *Hoechst Celanese* experienced efficient deployment of SAP R/3 through teamwork.
- *Oklahoma Gas & Electric* were able to compete, grow, and innovate with SAP and Ernst & Young.
- *Buckeye Cellulose* used an established SAP R/3 system that offers long-term flexibility by satisfying international growth.

Effort and Profit

Ernst & Young worked with the team at Hoechst Fibers to develop a future vision for procurement. This future needed to integrate people, process, and technology, and is defined by three levels that has SAP R/3 as the primary technology enabler:

1. Leverage purchasing power
2. Reducing non-value-added activity
3. Knowledge documentation and sharing

The future ties together a well-understood and well-executed SAP plan that leads to the first site going live with the new procurement support team in place inside of 1 year.

An elementary program implemented through R/3 involves the electronic procurement catalog that is available to all sites online. This program offers a centralized source for maintenance, repair, and operating materials. Users can access the catalog, making purchasing decisions and placing orders directly.

Another key component is significantly reduced transaction costs. This is executed solely within SAP's *Materials Management* and *Plant Maintenance* modules. A significant reduction in the number of suppliers cut down this amount from thousands to only a handful. This reduction has offered a great deal of savings. There are even greater savings achieved through refining processes and reducing nonvalue-added activities such as approvals and invoice matching.

The combination of Ernst & Young and Hoechst Fibers illustrates how working together can combine process improvement and automation to gain strategic objectives.

Working with Ernst & Young

Most of Ernst & Young's project success is due to the care they take in building relationships between team members. The future state definition and design work allows Ernst & Young to have a more detailed understanding of your organization and environment. This organizational structure provides the foundation for creating an accelerated implementation that leads to a successful working relationship. The overall SAP planning process is detailed enough to eliminate all of the major obstacles involved in the initial site's accelerated implementation.

The combination of Ernst & Young and Hoechst Fibers illustrated that a concentrated approach that emphasized commitment to knowledge transfer is an important step that allowed Hoechst Fibers to continue rolling out the future state design at the remaining Hoechst sites alone.

Ernst & Young also trained and transferred important knowledge to Hoechst Fibers' outsourcing firm for system maintenance. The most important step that was taken in this particular relationship is that Ernst & Young demonstrated their ability to quickly comprehend and adapt a business environment in the Procurement Reengineering Project. This permits you to gain a business environment that produces a highly integrated, effective team.

Working with Your Consultant

Oklahoma Gas & Electric (OG&E) selected Ernst & Young as its consultant because of the reputation held by Ernst & Young. Essentially, they have a well-established mix of people, processes, and technology. All of these components were strategically deployed to get the job completed in the shortest time possible. This philosophy agrees with the Accelerated-SAP environment that this text offers for specific organizations in order to make certain that your SAP implementation work develops the most efficient solutions possible. Therefore, the combined OG&E and Ernst & Young implementation team fostered a close working relationship that made certain the system rollout would be as smooth and comprehensive as possible for an accelerated implementation.

Developing Your Solution

OG&E had created an assertive SAP R/3 implementation across all of its business units. OG&E used the following SAP modules to achieve their tasks:

- FI/CO (financials and controlling)
- MM (materials management)
- HR (human resources)
- PM (plant maintenance)
- SM (service management)
- SD (sales and distribution)

Ernst & Young has worked extensively on system design, software configuration, testing, and training. All of this work was done in combination with the entire SAP system. This new enterprisewide system will deploy the SAP R/3 client-server solution as the cornerstone of new systems at OG&E and then move to progressively replace or improve on other mission-critical systems. The system employs IBM's SP2 hardware and DB2/6000 database architecture. In addition to the extensive level of application integration, this system provides the solution for OG&E's Year 2000 problem at the same time—an issue that plagues almost every IT shop across the board.

Ernst & Young and OG&E created a system that can easily satisfy additional applications required in the future. OG&E can utilize Ernst & Young's S-Link to integrate automated data collection with SAP R/3. OG&E gains the ability to enhance data accuracy and efficiency by using bar code technology and hand-held scanners. Utilizing S-Link, data is automatically updated in SAP from the storeroom floor by one tap of the scanner.

In addition, the SAP R/3 system offers a service management module that permits OG&E customer service representatives to establish field work orders for new electrical service, schedule the work, and rapidly inform customers about when the service technician has the power to execute the work. OG&E plans on enhancing this method to incorporate even more services by the end of the century.

OG&E's adoption of a unified IT environment, together with Ernst & Young's extensive experience in SAP and change management, created a complete solution that will help convey expanded growth and industry competition to OG&E's utilities edge.

Changes That Can Hurt You!

The most prolific corporate experience involved a major challenge that was the recent focus for a midwestern utility. Once they had realized that they were in a deregulated marketplace, this company was forced to learn an entirely new way of doing business.

In order to expedite recordkeeping, monitor inventories, and support customer relationships, they chose SAP as their software integration package to replace their current outdated legacy system.

Since they realized that wasted time could destroy their entire business operation, they chose to implement this change in less than 1 year. Since this was such a short time period, they chose Ernst & Young as their consultant to facilitate their AcceleratedSAP solution.

Their SAP R/3 package was developed specifically to integrate their financial, materials management, and plant maintenance operations. In addition, it was required to accommodate future functions in billing, general ledger, and human resources.

Conclusion

This chapter discusses SAP's concept review services with respect to your specific needs during the R/3 implementation process. This chapter also looks at how Ernst & Young's services can detect possible problems early in your implementation process, so you can take preventative measures, as seen in Fig. 17-4, to avoid problems.

Some of the resources that can help you achieve an effective, trouble-free implementation include SAP *GoingLive* Check, SAP *Help Desk,* and SAP consultants to help you analyze your problems and determine an effective and timely solution. Figure 17-5 shows how each of these resources provide critical factors that ensure the success of your accelerated implementation.

Figure 17-4
Preventative Measures.

Figure 17-5
Critical Success Factors.

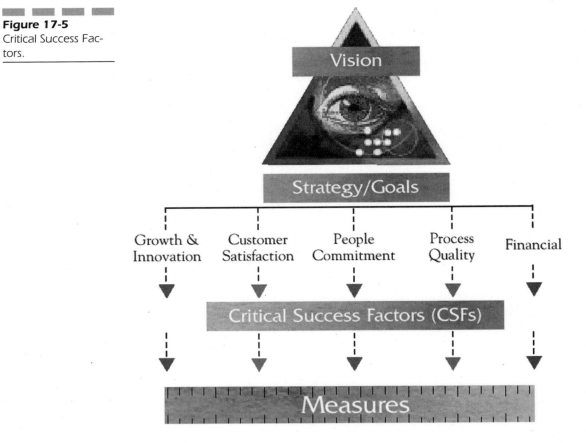

CHAPTER 18

R/3 Service Packages

Introduction

In spite of the method used to implement the R/3 system, R/3 service packages provide integrated SAP services that are created around your requirements during your R/3 implementation life cycle.

Service Packages

The SAP R/3 standard service package provides a total complementary range of services for your entire R/3 implementation life cycle. This package incorporates workshops, check and monitoring services, and remote consulting. It offers a very important level of knowledge for every project phase. The differences between online and remote consulting are illustrated in Fig. 18-1.

There is also an SAP R/3 optimizing service package that includes several services that make certain all your system components are working correctly during your GoingLive phase and is carried into your productive R/3 operation.

The SAP R/3 *GoingLive* service package guides you throughout the knowledge transfer aspect of your R/3 implementation project. The SAP R/3 productive operation service package is beneficial for you because it combines system check and monitoring services with consulting. It assists in enhancing your performance and ease of operation in your pro-

Figure 18-1
Online versus Remote Consulting.

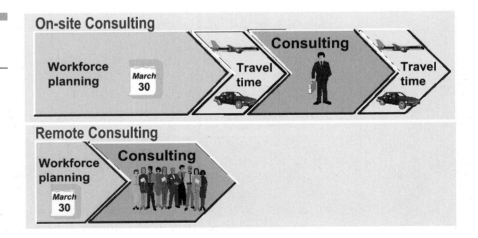

Figure 18-2
Performance Management.

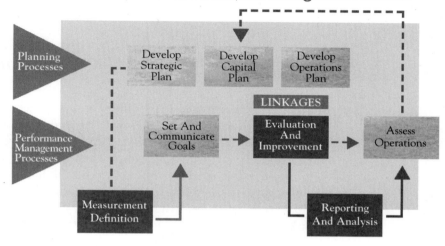

Evaluation And Improvement: The Key Links Between The Planning Processes And The Performance Management Processes

ductive R/3 system. Figure 18-2 demonstrates performance management executed throughout your organization and accelerated implementation.

The SAP R/3 IDES service package offers information regarding IDES utilization, which is the R/3 system for testing, demonstration, and education prospects. The R/3 service packages help you decide about the specific services that you need.

Upgrading Effectively

SAP has developed more efficient methods to migrate R/3 users to its most current release, version 4.0, without significant interruption to any business processes.

R/3 Release 4.0 yields a much easier accelerated upgrade process. You can deploy far easier and gain increased functionality for your information investment. AcceleratedSAP is a key factor in assuring that your upgrade proceeds quickly and efficiently. You have the power to upgrade to the latest version of R/3. You can benefit by utilizing crucial techniques from the best practices offered by the AcceleratedSAP program. ASAP will allow you to acquire an easier, faster upgrade process.

Benefits

You can benefit from R/3 upgrades by using technology that has been refined to reduce your overall downtime and make certain you have an easier upgrade process. It works by offering you a more detailed level of understanding for your upgrade process. The upgrade *Roadmap* guides you step-by-step so that you can accomplish critical milestones. You achieve your implementation and upgrade objectives by using SAP's estimation tools to gain the easiest upgrade process. You also have the ability to integrate all services from SAP and its partners in an easy-to-use upgrade technique. The process does not degrade the stability or security of your current R/3 installations.

Functionality

AcceleratedSAP is highly beneficial for your upgrade strategy as it offers you new tools, techniques, and services to make certain you have a very easy upgrade process.

R/3 Release 4.0 upgrades are scheduled on a refined time frame and *Roadmap* to make certain that your project remains on schedule. This time frame incorporates initial preparation time and time to test your upgrade before you Go Live.

There are also new substitution methods to reduce the overall downtime during your upgrade. Sections of your upgrade can be executed while your production system is up and running without experiencing any impact on stability or security. Automated procedures can also be utilized to alter your production system.

You can benefit from an enhanced planning tool. This tool was created as a Java-based graphical upgrade assistant that also has database measuring and data volume estimates that permit you to utilize remote upgrades.

The upgrade *Roadmap* and planning tools give you an accurate upgrade process that specifically meets your individual corporate needs.

The remote upgrade service offers you a cost-effective and resource-saving alternative to executing the upgrade process in-house. This service is offered by SAP all the time from the European Service and Support Center in Dublin, Ireland, as well as other global locations. There are also Advanced Technology Application and Design Centers in the United States to help you with the evaluation and optimization of your upgrade.

SAP R/3 Release 4.0 Specifics

R/3 Release 4.0 incorporates 300 business processes that can be used in various IT industry sectors. SAP has integrated a great deal of functionality for different industry sectors, including software product banking for its R/3 client-server development applications.

These 300 new business processes are offered for retail companies in addition to risk management and a transfer pricing tool for banks. The banking features in R/3 permit banks to compute profits from loans as well as other activities that deal with all aspects involved in risk management.

SAP's industry-specific enhancements don't end with the financial industry. They have also produced components specific to utilities and telecommunications companies that work on enhancing many business processes. In addition, R/3 is also integrated with Microsoft's Merchant System (integrated in R/3) so it can add electronic commerce functionality.

Many users are seriously examining SAP's Internet and Intranet offerings because this is an area of phenomenal growth that will, no doubt, play a significant role in any future business processes. Many suppliers are embracing the Internet in a variety of ways. Any ERP solution must take advantage of this trend in order to find success in any modern industry.

SAP is also integrating with Microsoft's Exchange messaging server. SAP will still support its competing products such as Netscape Communications Corp.'s World Wide Web servers and browsers.

SAP also has a reporting server with R/3 Release 4.0 that will function independently of R/3. It will create forms in HTML and permit users to access information that is produced by R/3.

Release 4.0 will foster SAP's migration toward object-oriented technology. In addition, it will segment *Human Resources* functions into their own applications area.

Client-Server

SAP's R/3 is a comprehensive CIM. R/3 is a client-server–enabled packaged application as opposed to a client-server development tool. R/3 utilizes standard databases so other client-server development tools can access it. In addition, R/3 has a three-tier architecture that is Web-enabled and composed of 70 software modules. The modules apply to CIM software business applications, and have the ability to automate functions, including sales, human resources, finance, and distribution. These modules may be customized to fit the users' business requirements. In addition, SAP offers an Advanced Business Application Programing (ABAP/4) *Development Workbench* to assist in the modification of some basic R/3 functions including reports, field size, screen layout, and business logic.

R/3 Experience

In terms of experience with R/3, it is important to note that it is not a client-server development tool but rather a client-server–enabled packaged application that is very robust. Large companies use it to track various types of information about their businesses.

SAP R/3 has grown significantly in terms of its acceptance in the marketplace. SAP R/3 is the client-server version of its host-based software. This product is the leading client-server package software which allows your company to get into the client-server architecture, without the difficulty of custom client-server development. In addition to the existing host-based SAP-installed base, R/3 can be implemented for organizations of any size. The advent of AcceleratedSAP has made this product more available for smaller organizations who needed to implement R/3 in a short time frame without going bankrupt in the process.

Client-server developers have a great deal invested in SAP R/3 because SAP does not necessarily meet the needs of most organizations right out of the box. Therefore, client-server developers need to be hired in order to customize some aspects of R/3 functionality. Then, R/3 utilizes standard database servers so that R/3 data is accessible by other third-party client-server development, OLAP, and reporting tools.

Since SAP R/3 is Web-enabled and incorporates object-oriented development, it is possible for both developers and tool vendors to update and customize R/3 for specific organizational requirements.

R/3 Modules

R/3 is a collection of 70 complex software modules for business applications that utilize the client-server model. Its modules automate most major business functions, such as manufacturing, finance, sales, human resources, and distribution. Each SAP module can access over 1000 business processes and utilize over 8000 tables to store data and business rules. Every module is composed of a set of subapplications. For example, the *Financial Accounting* module offers accounts receivable, general ledger, and accounts payable.

The *Financial Accounting* module offers the accounting functionality of R/3. There are three major subapplications that incorporate financial (FI), controlling (CO), and asset management (AM). FI includes accounts payable, accounts receivable, capital investment, and general ledger. The *Financial Accounting* module can generate reports for each user, execute document processes, and archive data.

The *Human Resources* module provides the majority of functionality that large organizations need to manage, pay, schedule, hire, and fire employees. The subsystems support payroll, benefits administration, applicant data administration, workforce planning, scheduling, and shift planning, travel expense reporting, and personnel development planning.

The *Manufacturing and Logistics* module is the largest and most complex of all of the modules listed. It is composed of five subapplications that incorporate materials management, quality management, plant maintenance, production planning and control, and project management.

The *Sales and Distribution* module allows you to locate customers, acquire support, and process sales orders. It provides functionality for product distribution, export controls, shipping, and transportation management. This module incorporates billing, invoicing, and rebate processing.

R/3 Structure

SAP R/3 has a thin-client, three-tier architecture that utilizes proprietary components. SAP clients operate on numerous operating system platforms, including UNIX (MotiF), Windows 3.11, Windows 95, OS/2, and Macintosh. The R/3 client doesn't offer a great deal more than an attractive interface to a transaction processor, but this is normal on many three-tier client-server models. The real processing occurs on the middle tier (application server). SAP R/3 employs a transaction model, however, it does not utilize a standard transaction-processing monitor. SAP's transaction application services are proprietary to R/3, and this proprietary structure functions well and can support heavy processing and user loads. This is a required feature because many of SAP's current customers ran SAP on mainframes (SAP R/2) prior to migrating to the client-server version. Therefore, R/3 had to exhibit high-performance, scalable expectations in order to satisfy your needs.

R/3 clients are essentially data collectors for the transaction-processing subsystem. The client transmits data to the application servers. This process invokes the required application services that support the business functions to the transaction. R/3's application server operates on several platforms that include most UNIX and Windows NT operating systems. SAP functions on hardware architectures, including AS/400, MVS, and the PowerPC.

The database may operate on the same machine as the application server. It is important to note that, on the majority of three-tier client-server architectures, the database engine usually operates on its own processor linked to the application server through the network. SAP can execute its own proprietary database or use true database server software (for example, Microsoft's SQL-Server).

The benefit of using a database out of the box gives you the ability to use standard reporting tools and application development environments outside of what R/3 offers. However, going around R/3 services could result in data integrity problems. The R/3 clients perform remote function calls (RFCs) to transfer information from the clients to the application servers. RFCs are functionally equivalent to RPCs (remote procedure calls), invoking services on the application server by performing procedure calls on the client. RFCs are platform independent and employ protocols, including TCP/IP, SNA, and IPX/SPX.

R/3 can benefit from its three-tier architecture to provide fail-safe capability. This function allows system managers to establish numerous application servers, where each one is capable of supporting the processing load of another if a server fails. This configuration offers load-balancing capabilities, because system managers can connect clients to underutilized application servers. In addition, application servers provide fundamental data caching, which lessens the load on the database server by allowing repeated requests to be served from the cache.

Developers

R/3 offers an integrated set of canned modules, as well as module customization. Not many companies deploy R/3 as a standard implementation without any customization whatsoever. They do, however, customize R/3 to satisfy their business requirements. This is the point where the R/3 client-server developer adds to the value of your product. However, this developmental effort can add a great deal of complexity and make modification efforts difficult for other developers if your changes are not well documented.

Prior to allowing developers to modify R/3, you need to learn a great deal about your application development structure. R/3 utilizes a Data Dictionary referred to as the R/3 *Repository*. This *Repository* contains information about screens, business rules, forms, modules, and locations of application servers. The R/3 *Repository* provides you with a tool that allows you to enter, appraise, and exploit company data. It is an active *Repository* that is encompassed within the R/3 *Development Workbench*. The *Repository* is made up of tables, domains, and fields. The rules for processing business data are stored in tables that are similar to relational tables. They work as a matrix of information, while domains depict a range for a specific field. Fields are attributes of the table that include items such as the customer number. In order to modify or enhance the functionality of R/3, SAP offers a fourth generation, designated as an Advanced Business Application Programming (ABAP/4) *Development Workbench*. ABAP/4 allows you to alter its fundamental R/3 application capabilities, such as altering business logic, screen layout, reports, and field size.

ABAP/4 *Development Workbench*

The ABAP/4 *Development Workbench* integrates a *Repository,* editor, dictionary, and tools for tuning, testing, and debugging R/3 applications. The *Development Workbench* is a component of R/3's middleware. It has the ability to communicate with both the application server and your R/3 clients. The *Development Workbench* is unlike modern development environments that employ features like a *Repository*-driven development, object dictionaries, and object-oriented development concepts. The *Development Workbench* is a basic development environment that employs traditional procedural development methods. When developers execute changes to your R/3 system, they move to a transport system. Once the quality check is complete, the changes are transferred to the live system.

The ABAP/4 *Development Workbench* offers a query feature that allows you to designate reports on the fly. The query feature does not require that you have knowledge of the *Development Workbench*'s 4GL.

The *Workbench* offers a subsystem called application link enabling (ALE), which permits your company to utilize numerous independent R/3 systems. This allows you to maintain common data and business functions across your entire system. This functionality will work well for your organization if you have many divisions that execute different tasks around the world.

Enhancing R/3

It is important to note that you are not restricted in terms of R/3 tools for R/3 application enhancement. *SApplication Builder* (from Cenmra Software Corp.) provides a connection between R/3's business application modules and Centura's SQLWindows or *Team Developer* tools. *SApplication Builder* allows you to develop front-end applications that can call up functions on your R/3 application server. However, it does not circumvent the application server to access the data, therefore, *SApplication Builder* can utilize the power of the R/3 system, such as the business processing, data integrity, and security features.

SApplication Builder offers a true object-oriented client-server front-end development environment that provides an alternative for enhancing R/3's capabilities above the capabilities of the *Development Workbench*.

Centura can benefit from this direction because R/3 developers require better methods of customizing R/3. Many other client-server development tools will follow this procedure in order to benefit from market trends. When dealing with query and reporting, Cognos Corp.'s (located in Burlington, Massachusetts) offers both *PowerPlay* and *Impromptu* OLAP tools.

Aside from third-party products, such as *SApplication Builder,* R/3 takes advantage of being Web-enabled. SAP R/3 incorporates SAP's Intranet transaction server for Windows NT. It links and controls R/3 electronic-commerce applications with the users operating common Web browsers. NeXT Software Inc. (located in Redwood City, California) offers a Web interface to R/3. NeXT Software utilizes its new WebObjects Web-enabled development software with integrated links to R/3.

SAP R/3 implementations are finding new acceptance with the AcceleratedSAP program. This growth illustrates that larger organizations exist well with packaged client-server applications for enterprise-level, business-critical requirements as opposed to creating applications from scratch. R/3 does not always meet the needs of most businesses without any customization. For that reason it is important that client-server developers realize an enormous amount of R/3 customization work.

R/3 is a good platform on which you can develop client-server applications. R/3 offers a complex variety of base functions, causing developers to learn how to offer proper functions to end users. New technology tools will help your R/3 implementation grow into a superior platform for your business process needs.

SAP's Future

Network managers often get caught up in product features for examining 3D topology, CIM Software views, or functionality used for printing full-color error as opposed to utilization reports. Problems can result from protocol discussion, difficulties with vendors regarding vaporware, or poor customer support.

SAP R/3 is an Enterprise Resource Planning (ERP) application, which is a highly integrated product. It gathers information about your business processes and goes across organizational lines such as human resources, financial management, inventory, and manufacturing. Many big organizations (i.e., Nestle and Chevron) have spent millions of dollars on just software. In addition, they have spent several times more than that with respect to hiring support staff for deploying and maintaining SAP R/3 projects.

Therefore, if your SAP R/3 application were to crash, it would be devastating to your overall productivity. Many SAP R/3 customers could only use the Computing Center Management System (CCMS) offered by SAP in this type of case. CCMS offers tools for starting up, shutting down, logging into, and configuring CCMS numerous servers. CCMS also offers job scheduling, workload balancing, and database backups.

CCMS does not offer windows or perspectives into the health, status, or configuration of the underlying servers or network infrastructure that supports R/3. Network managers are forced to search out third-party products to satisfy this need and get the solutions they need for their objectives. There are several third-party vendors who are working toward the goal of integrating SAP R/3 management into the network and systems management scheme.

Corporate Efforts

BMC offers a *Patrol Knowledge* module for SAP R/3 that supports central monitoring of several SAP R/3 implementations by acquiring both SNMP MIB data and SAP layer statistics from the CCMS. BMC has formed alliances with several vendors for transmitting information from its RPC-based patrol agents to other consoles (for example, Hewlett-Packard and Computer Associates).

Cabletron is reselling an SAP R/3 management facility created by another vendor. This product is unique because it is integrated with Cabletron Spectrum's modeling facility so it can be used for modeling business processes.

Hewlett-Packard provides an agent that can be used for managing SAP R/3 under IT/Operations (IT/O). IT/O supports consolidation of syslogd as well as other UNIX system messages. In this way, operators can view TCP/IP network topology, as well as the status through an embedded copy of HP OpenView Network Node Manager. IT/O agents are RPC-based and can report only up to the IT/O console.

IBM and Tivoli market a *TME* module for R/3 that supports software distribution through a customized version of Tivoli/Courier and fault-performance monitoring. This is achieved through a customized version of the Tivoli/Sentry intelligent agent.

Tivoli's product requires the purchase of the basic TME agent software. This software is RPC-based and isn't compatible with other vendors' consoles. The Tivoli AMS for R/3 is very detailed, however, its hardware requirements and price are very expensive. For example, its entry price is $200,000, which makes this a very expensive software product.

Pyramid and Siemens offer an SNMP-based SAP R/3 management application for their TransView management system. This system is based on HP OpenView which is available on platforms that include SunOS, HP-UX, Sinix, and Windows NT. TransView's *Live Network Integrator* (LNI) gathers information from R/3 instances and translates it into statistics, including global R/3 performance data that deals with averages and thresholds with respect to response time, throughput, and waiting times. Integrated trouble ticketing and software distribution are optional, while an enterprise console is offered. It is important to note that LNI can also operate independently as a plug-and-play SNMP application.

R/3 Modules

SAP has refined their modules for hospitals and utility companies. SAP has developed modules for their R/3 enterprises that support specific industries, including utility companies, hospitals, and CIM software retail. SAP has created a customer information system for utilities and telecommunications companies. They have also produced *IS-Oil* modules for accounting and inventory processing meant for the oil and gas industry.

SAP has 13 individual vertical business units in industries such as automotive and insurance. This effort is meant to provide modules to match each of their supported vertical industries, so they can meet each client's varied needs.

SAP's customer information system has the ability to control billing and service management. SAP's telecommunications business unit and utilities unit will offer this product. When dealing with oil and gas companies, SAP has created two modules:

1. *IS-Oil Upstream*

2. *IS-Oil Downstream*

IS-Oil Upstream was created for joint-venture accounting. It allows users to tabulate cost allocations between business partners.

IS-Oil Downstream takes care of detailed oil and gas manufacturing needs, including hydrocarbon inventories and bulk distribution requirements.

For dealing with hospitals, SAP has developed a patient management and accounting system that handles processes for areas that include in-patient and out-patient care. This module was released through the company's healthcare unit.

SAP has created the *IS-R* module for the retail and wholesale market. *IS-R* is a merchandise management system that combines purchasing, supply-chain management sales, and retail information into a single system. *IS-R* ships through SAP's retail unit. The exact pricing for this module will be a fraction of the total R/3 cost, but will depend on the configuration.

SAP has found success in the R/3 architecture development of BAPIs (business APIs) and creation of components for the R/3 client-server applications suite. BAPIs allow users to have the ability to integrate their R/3 systems with key applications from organizations that can take advantage of industry support centers for the different industries.

SAP Industries

SAP's individual business units are tailored specifically for automotive, banks, chemicals, consumer products, healthcare, high technology and electronics, insurance, oil and gas, pharmaceuticals, public sector, retail, telecommunications, and utilities.

Parts Procurement

SAP R/3 can support parts procurement within your organization. SAP is dedicated to refining the parts procurement process for engineering departments. To that end, SAP integrated its R/3 client-server applications with Aspect Development Inc.'s Agreement for CSM (Component and Supplier Product Management) system. The combination of Aspect and SAP CIM software will allow engineers to locate the parts they need from idea conception and order them through SAP's procurement modules. This type of service package will effectively accelerate engineering projects.

SAP is creating an important link between engineering systems and business systems. This is a very important method of permitting engineers and the business systems to communicate effectively. The relationship with Aspect's parts database can offer a great many resources with respect to both time and effort for manufacturing projects.

This is an ideal process if you are looking for a specific part that has a certain value. You could essentially access Aspect's software and find what you are looking for immediately. When you combine an ERP system, you can connect it to the procurement and manufacturing functions and increase your overall value significantly.

The initial step involves integration. This connects R/3's *Material Management* modules (for example, procurement and purchasing) into the CSM database and decision-support software. CSM's Very Important Parts database incorporates a list of more than several million electronic and mechanical parts from 700 vendors. Aspect adds up to 20,000 new parts every week, and then users obtain updates automatically on CD-ROM or through the Web via Aspect's online update engine.

Aspect markets its Explore decision-support application. This application was created specifically to help engineers locate the right parts in the database. It can be integrated into the majority of CAD tools and can function on UNIX servers with 32-bit clients. In addition, this application is now being ported into the Windows NT operating environment.

SAP R/3 Applets

In order for SAP to fully embrace Java, SAP is using Java on several of the following areas:

1. Desktop
2. Servers
3. Internet

In order to develop solid R/3 client-server software business applications, more flexible components are needed. Java has demonstrated itself to be a very powerful programming language that can be used in multiple online applications. It plays a critical role in any Web-enablement and will prove to be a very important part of R/3 Release 4.0.

There are many similarities between Java and ABAP/4. ABAP/4 is the proprietary language that R/3 applications are written in. As a result, it shouldn't be very hard to benefit from the basic similarities between Java and ABAP/4. Some of these similarities include:

- Processor neutrality
- Operating system neutrality
- Power to compile data in real time

SAP created its first component that was totally written with Java using a product configurator that permits your organization to access, make orders, view shipment dates, and view the availability of parts via an Intranet or the Internet.

SAP created a user interface to R/3 with Java which allows the object *Repository* of the component-based R/3 Release 4.0 to store Java applets. SAP developers are developing Java applets to complement R/3, however, it is not a language that will subsume SAP's other programming efforts.

The future direction of SAP will focus on how the common object model, distributed common object model, and common object request broker architecture (CORBA) will adapt in the R/3 environment. SAP is concentrating on a way to integrate both Java and *ActiveX* into its applications. Microsoft's BackOffice server applications and Microsoft Exchange are critical to achieving a more distributed R/3 system. In addition, business APIs, business objects, and several Internet components are tools that illustrate how SAP will extend R/3 to embrace the Internet.

SAP R/3 Release 4.0 introduced prepackaged sets of components for vertical markets. One such example is a process manufacturing set that centers around each corporate plant. Figure 18-3 demonstrates process manufacturing for your organization. This includes components brought together from departmental areas including human resources, plant maintenance, quality assurance, and environmental health and safety.

It is becoming more apparent that SAP is embracing a more object-oriented model to meet your individual corporate needs. The idea is to meet both development and business needs.

Figure 18-3
Process Manufacturing.

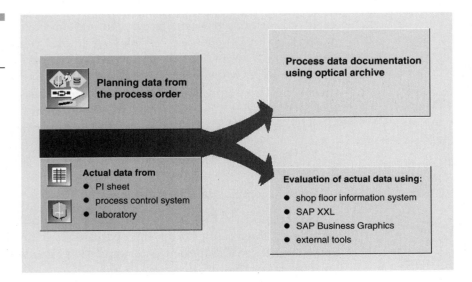

Simplifying SAP's R/3

SAP is working toward the goal of making SAP R/3 Version 4.0 enterprise software simpler to use for corporations by offering prepackaged sets of components that reflect SAP's *Business Framework* plan.

These prepackaged sets will have the ability to interface with products of other vendors via standard interfaces with the assistance of configurable software modules. The *Business Framework* modules in R/3 Version 4.0 incorporate both business and integration technologies, Internet and Intranet applications, product data management, *Human Resources, Treasury,* and *Business Engineer* for R/3.

SAP is teaming up with third-party partnerships (for example, Cognos, Compuware, and Intellicorp) to enhance its plans for creating components. SAP's objective is to have a large number of products, including electronic commerce, financials, and sales force automation.

Prepackaged Modules

Prepackaged modules are being constructed for specific industries to meet their specific goals. SAP is trying to simplify its solid R/3 enterprise software in order to make it easier to integrate in various organizations.

R/3 Release 4.0 offers the core of SAP's *Business Framework* plan with respect to prepackaged sets of components for various markets. These prepackaged sets are composed of configurable software modules that work together through standard interfaces and interface with other vendors' products.

SAP's goal is to provide you with an open component-based architecture that allows you to develop systems that have *only* the functionality you need to achieve your business objectives.

SAP's third-party partnerships work to further its R/3 componentization plans. You will have the ability to choose from a large set of products from tool vendors and best-of-breed applications, including financials, sales force automation, and electronic commerce.

SAP initiated its *Business Framework* strategy so they could offer their R/3 software systems as components. They could offer 150 business APIs and 35 new Internet and Intranet applications that function with the planned business components.

SAP made its BAPIs available to the open application group so they could be considered as a standard for interoperability between back-end business applications.

The *Business Framework* component software modules involve Internet and Intranet applications, business and integration technologies, open integration interfaces, *Human Resources, Product Data Management, Treasury, Available to Promise Server, Business Information Warehouse, R/3 Business Engineer, Logistics,* and *Financials.* However, users are split on the benefits of the *Business Framework* strategy.

There is no significant learning curve, and there are not many demands made on your hardware. There is a great deal of potential for midsized organizations to purchase the integrated suite of products. These products offer you a great deal of efficiency, so you need not link into a great deal of other software or require a large number of patches.

SAP's Component Strategy

The most significant number of elements involved in this component strategy includes over 35 Internet and Intranet applications and 150 business APIs. However, there are also several more software modules that have been introduced for business, *Human Resources, Product Data Management, Treasury, R/3 Business Engineer,* and integration technologies.

Other software modules for *Financials* and *Logistics* that will significantly benefit your organization include:

- SAP GUI in Java
- Available to Promise Server
- *Business Information Warehouse*
- More powerful and diverse BAPIs

Service and Support

When it becomes necessary to modify your mission-critical applications, it is important to avoid any delay that could cause service interruptions. Increasing competition is emerging from both domestic and international sources making quality a *must.*

SAP service is paramount to the success of your accelerated implementation. You must, at all times, receive the highest level of customer service and support, so you can add value to your information technology investment regardless of the size of your company or the revenue you earn. The SAP service and support network ties together the expertise from over 3000 SAP consultants and support professionals in a tightly integrated network of more than 20,000 certified partner consultants. This combination of professional expertise assists you throughout your implementation process by reducing costs and providing you with a valuable end product.

SAP R/3 service and support results from the combination of the collective experience of SAP professionals that work to offer your business expert software solutions to multinational corporations globally. SAP R/3 service and support satisfies your country-specific requirements and maintains a standard quality throughout your industry-specific functions. An extensive level of effort is required in order for you to enhance your service delivery and establish valuable new services.

Conclusion

This chapter discusses integrated services for R/3. This section has examined how R/3 service packages offer integrated SAP services created around customer needs during your R/3 implementation. Some of the packages include the SAP R/3 standard service package which offers supplementary services for your complete R/3 implementation. This chapter also discusses other services, including the SAP R/3 Optimizing Service Package, SAP R/3 Going Live Service Package, SAP R/3 Productive Operation Service Package, and the SAP R/3 IDES Service Package. These R/3 service packages allow you to make decisions about which service is needed and when.

Accelerators

What Is SAP?

SAP is a market and technology leader in client-server enterprise application software. It offers comprehensive solutions for any size company in all IT industry sectors. It produces innovative technologies based on a firm foundation of business experience. SAP provides scalable solutions that permit its customers to provide ongoing improvement based on best business practices. SAP products permit your personnel to respond quickly and decisively to dynamic market conditions. This helps your business acquire and maintain a competitive advantage.

SAP was founded in 1972. It is based in Walldorf, Germany, and employs more than 12,000 people at offices in more than 40 countries. They are all dedicated to offering the highest level of support and service for more than 12,000 installations of R/3 worldwide.

Introduction

The AcceleratedSAP program reduces both the time and cost of a standard R/3 implementation. This accelerated program is made possible with certified AcceleratedSAP partners who have gained a great deal of success with the AcceleratedSAP program. ASAP has made it possible for more than 100 companies to reduce the time and cost of their R/3 implementations by as much as 30 to 50 percent.

New Features

There are several new program features that will make deploying release changes and upgrades much simpler. There is also an enhanced knowledge-based, interactive version of R/3 *Business Engineer* which significantly simplifies configuration. In addition, SAP has enhanced the R/3 *Business Engineer* for Release 4.0 making this release a very detailed, knowledge-based configuration tool for quicker, more efficient R/3 implementation and continuous business process improvement. The R/3 *Business Engineer* is the cornerstone of this program. It acts as an enabling tool of AcceleratedSAP that makes rapid R/3 implementations possible.

AcceleratedSAP Partner Certification

ASAP partner certification programs offer a unifying industry standard for accelerated R/3 implementations. This is accomplished through TeamSAP, which offers two distinct programs.

1. AcceleratedSAP Partner
2. Powered By AcceleratedSAP

Both of these programs offer a high level of quality assurance and acceleration of R/3 implementations for numerous industry sectors.

SAP America provides these AcceleratedSAP partner certification programs to give you an industry standard with high-quality R/3 rapid implementations. The AcceleratedSAP Partner and Powered By AcceleratedSAP are components of SAP's TeamSAP program and are created to certify both National and Logo consulting firms that have conquered SAP's AcceleratedSAP implementation technique. SAP has more than 35 certified AcceleratedSAP partners and has the ability to identify certified partners to assist you in gaining quicker and more cost-effective implementations and a more rapid return on information.

TeamSAP

TeamSAP is the environment that embodies SAP, its partners, and customers. This harmony makes certain you achieve success throughout your relationship with SAP. These benefits extend to everything beginning with planning, implementation, continuous change, and innovation. Partners are extended members of TeamSAP if they are certified in any of SAP's partner certification programs.

TeamSAP was created with the purpose of establishing an optimal project team that meets each client's individual needs. Partners have already produced a great deal of interest for the TeamSAP certification programs. This interest is indicative of the fact that partners provide written proof as to the value of the AcceleratedSAP techniques and integrate it as one of their industry standards for accelerated implementation methods.

AcceleratedSAP ties together experienced consultants, accelerators, tools, templates, and best practices. All of these elements combine to clarify and refine your implementation. ASAP was created for your long-term success by offering a proven, flexible platform for your organization to grow and change.

AcceleratedSAP Partners

AcceleratedSAP partner certification permits partners to achieve instant credibility in the market. Regardless of your size, you can have the utmost confidence in your certified partners and faith that they will leverage the techniques in AcceleratedSAP. This allows you to gain a consistent and rapid R/3 implementation solution to help make certain you have a successful relationship.

When you select an implementation partner, it is comforting to you to know that companies, such as Hewlett-Packard, have been certified by SAP as a consulting firm who has successfully satisfied the conditions for accelerated and cost-effective R/3 installations.

SAP has a growing number of partner organizations certified as AcceleratedSAP partners (now more than 50), and are working to satisfy the increasing demand for more certification classes.

In SAP's first AcceleratedSAP partner certification, as shown in Fig. 19-1, efforts concentrated on current members of SAP's National and Logo partner programs. This certification process incorporated the AcceleratedSAP implementation training classes, management courses, and continuous quality control programs.

Figure 19-1
SAP Partner Program.

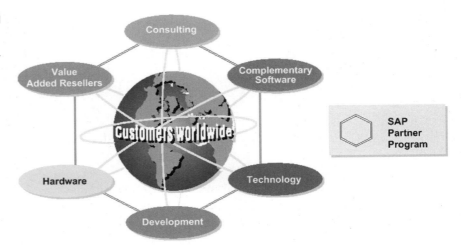

SAP's AcceleratedSAP program offers you an important implementation foundation to constantly and successfully satisfy your implementation needs as soon as possible.

Powered By AcceleratedSAP

Partners certified as Powered By AcceleratedSAP utilize sections of the AcceleratedSAP methodology together with their own implementation practices. This program offers partners more opportunities to accelerate enterprisewide efforts and supplement continuous efforts. These efforts are especially useful when there is a need for an accelerated deployment within a specific geographic location, business unit, or pilot project. This program is especially useful for partners who work with a shortened implementation time frame needed for a crucial year 2000 conversion effort.

Early Consultancies

SAP selected three early adopter consulting firms to initiate its Powered By AcceleratedSAP certification efforts. These organizations include Ernst & Young, Deloitte & Touche Consulting Group/ICS, and Price Waterhouse LLP. There are now more than 10 consulting firms dedicated to the Powered By AcceleratedSAP certification process.

This level of certification necessitates that specific AcceleratedSAP methodology ideas be added to the partners' implementation practices. Additional ASAP techniques are optional with respect to each partner's experience and implementation objectives.

As a whole, many organizations enjoy being part of TeamSAP by being certified as a Powered By AcceleratedSAP partner. Employing the AcceleratedSAP methodology in combination with SAP's Fast Track for SAP methodology gives you best practices and principles for a successful R/3 implementation completed in a timely and cost-effective manner.

Certification Process

The certification process is a very crucial step in the enterprise application market that was not present until this program was developed.

Both the AcceleratedSAP and Powered By AcceleratedSAP certification programs are very important levels in the enterprise application industry's move toward establishing successful implementations that are more predictable, timely, and cost effective. SAP continues to demonstrate its commitment to your long-term success.

It is often advisable to look at some of the AcceleratedSAP partners to learn more about the program itself. Some of these partners include:

- Affiliated Computer Services Inc.
- Applied Integration Services Inc. (AIS)
- Arthur Anderson LLP
- Axis Consulting International Inc.
- Bureau Van Dijk Computer Services Inc.
- CAI Advanced Solutions CaRD America Inc.
- CIScorp Inc.
- Clarkston Potomac Group
- Comsys Technical Services Inc.
- Conley, Canitano & Associates Inc. (CCAi)
- DA Consulting Group Decision Consultants Inc.
- EMAX Solution Partners Inc.
- Global Core Strategies Inc.
- GROM Associates Inc.
- HJM Consulting Inc.
- Holland Technology Group
- IDS Scheer Inc.
- IMI Systems Inc.
- Intelligroup Inc.
- Kurt Salmon Associates
- MultiVision Consulting Inc.
- Osprey Systems Inc.
- Plaut Consulting Inc.
- RCG Information Technology Inc.
- RSA Co.
- SCS America LLC
- Siemens Nixdorf Information Systems Inc.

- Softline Inc.
- Software Consulting Partners Inc.
- Spearhead System Consultants (US) Ltd.
- SPO America Inc.
- Technology Solutions Co.
- Waypointe Information Technologies
- Whittman-Hart Inc.

Reducing Deployment Time

ASAP has shown that it reduces time and costs for any given R/3 implementation. AcceleratedSAP has caught on significantly. This is illustrated by the fact that the number of certified AcceleratedSAP partners has increased twofold and there is additional support for global rollouts, upgrades, and accelerated industry templates.

The AcceleratedSAP program has reduced deployment time and cost dramatically in a period of 1 year for R/3 enterprise business solutions. When you use ASAP, you can realize benefits with respect to reductions in both time and cost in your R/3 implementation.

The majority of R/3 implementations have been completed in only a few months, however, the average implementation time for AcceleratedSAP projects is from 6 to 9 months. This proves that AcceleratedSAP is quickly becoming the gold standard for quick and cost-effective R/3 implementations.

In order to support this increasing demand for AcceleratedSAP implementations, SAP has doubled the number of certified AcceleratedSAP partners in its TeamSAP network. This means that, in a period of 6 months, they have added more than 2800 consultants who are trained to support accelerated implementations of R/3.

Accelerators

SAP is producing new accelerators to satisfy a more diverse range of corporate needs. AcceleratedSAP incorporates a global *Roadmap* that can handle the clear definition of the enterprise strategy, global rollout, and an upgrade *Roadmap* for release changes and upgrade projects. Furthermore, SAP's *Business Engineer* has created industry templates that depict preconfigured R/3 processes for several industries.

AcceleratedSAP had its beginnings in the middle of 1996 and was deployed worldwide in June 1997. ASAP ties together an established set of techniques that include the AcceleratedSAP *Roadmap,* accelerators, tools, templates, and services that refine and simplify your implementations.

AcceleratedSAP allows small companies to take advantage of their collective best implementation practices from many thousands of SAP customers. This program offers multinational organizations with a centralized approach for implementing R/3 across global operations.

SAP has distinguished itself as a leading ERP supplier that offers solutions to both small and midsized organizations that are exhibiting rapid growth patterns. AcceleratedSAP allows these organizations to implement R/3 in a timely manner and accomplish their tasks under budget using only a part-time team. Your company team members can maintain their operational responsibilities while implementing SAP, and receive a distinct increase in your business operations realized early after your Go Live phase. AcceleratedSAP techniques for your global or geographically dispersed operations connect your users around the world and remain close to your real-life operational needs.

Sterling Diagnostics Imaging was one of the first global Accelerated-SAP implementations to Go Live. This organization chose R/3 from among six competing ERP solutions. When dealing with a global comprehensive integration concept, most organizations will select SAP to shorten SDI supply-chain cycle time from order to delivery. In addition, it also serves to shorten global inventory and order-fulfillment costs, which allows both users and customers to benefit.

AcceleratedSAP has tools and techniques that make R/3 faster, simpler, and more cost effective to implement. This makes it the best possible business solution for any size organization.

TeamSAP gives all of SAP's partners the ability to use an established R/3 implementation methodology. This program assures you that you are receiving a standard R/3 deployment approach that will be successful in your specific industry sector.

Tools, Templates, and Speed

The addition of new tools and enhanced R/3 templates in *Business Engineer* allows you to realize quicker, simpler implementations in your business processes.

The most important enabling tool for AcceleratedSAP is the R/3 *Business Engineer,* a comprehensive configuration tool initially released globally with R/3 Release 3.0. The R/3 *Business Engineer* simplifies initial and continuous configuration of R/3 with new business scenarios that collect R/3 functionality into simply managed views.

SAP R/3 Release 4.0 is an interactive *Business Configurator* in combination with an HTML-based interface. This makes installation as simple as browsing a Web page. The knowledge-based, question-and-answer–driven configuration process makes your business processes easier. There are also integrated validation checks that make certain you maintain your design integrity and confidence. In addition, this effectively avoids the trial and error of enterprise application configuration. The flexibility needed for ongoing business engineering facilitates adaptation of the majority of configuration settings to business modifications in a business environment that is continuously being improved in R/3 Release 4.0.

New Templates

There are new vertical industry templates that are preconfigured in R/3 systems, including a preconfigured industry model that provides you with a lead in implementing R/3. The preselected business scenarios and processes are linked with system settings and sample master data, so that you don't have to configure key business processes. Your implementation team concentrates on the key differentiators of your enterprise's business. The next step is for the team to tailor your preconfigured system for your enterprise's individual needs.

For example, in the steel and metals industry, the preconfigured R/3 system has been deployed successfully by several key steel manufacturers. The preconfigured R/3 systems for the chemical and consumer products industries is offered for R/3 customers and implementation partners as well as for other industries.

TeamSAP and AcceleratedSAP

Due to the success of AcceleratedSAP, SAP has enhanced its dedication to customers and partners with TeamSAP (a program that was originally launched at SAPPHIRE Conference Orlando '97.) TeamSAP makes

SAP responsible for integration, coordination, and certification of SAP, its partners, and third parties. This offers you a centralized and integrated environment for continuous success.

SAP has integrated TeamSAP at every level of their organization. This integration ranges from product development and industry solutions to sales, marketing, professional services, and customer support.

The basis of TeamSAP involves the role of the SAP leader and the AcceleratedSAP programs that contain the expertise achieved from more than 12,000 prior R/3 installations (best practices). TeamSAP is highly illustrative of the dedication that SAP has made to its customers and partners.

TeamSAP is made up of several distinct and very important elements that include:

1. People
2. Processes
3. Products

The people aspect includes SAP professionals; consulting partners; and complementary software, technology, and hardware providers. These people provide solutions' expertise to meet your corporate needs. TeamSAP makes certain that the right combination of vendor skills are integrated in the right combination at the right time. TeamSAP has more than 15,000 consulting professionals besides the expertise of SAP hardware partners, technology partners, and complementary software providers (CSPs).

In terms of processes, the AcceleratedSAP programs are the key to TeamSAP processes. They offer a systematic approach, resources, and tools that include the R/3 *Business Engineer*. The *Business Engineer* is very helpful because it offers both accelerated and predictable implementations in combination with a platform for ongoing modifications.

In addition, SAP provides accelerated services, education, and knowledge-sharing programs to assist in the accelerated deployment of your R/3 product.

As far as products, the SAP *Business Framework* incorporates R/3 business components, integration technologies, and open interfaces that permit customers to enhance their R/3 solutions with independent products from SAP or third parties.

TeamSAP's objective is to achieve the successful integration and interoperability of designated components in your R/3 solution.

SAP IQ

The SAP IQ solution was recently introduced for educational institutions and is based on best business practices. SAP R/3 enhanced the information management functionality from the business world in an effort to give the academic world the ability to focus on the business of education.

SAP IQ is a solution meant for educational institutions that builds on the powerful functionality of the R/3 system. It has the ability to support educational processes and resource allocation for schools, universities, institutes, and businesses that work with education, training, and extended learning.

SAP IQ permits educational institutions to benefit from business practices of SAP. It can integrate your business operations and enhance your ability to succeed in the growing competitive education marketplace environment.

SAP created three unique software components inside the SAP IQ solution that were individualized for public and private educational organizations:

1. *IQ-CAMPUS* addresses the distinct needs of higher-education institutions.

2. *IQ-TRAINING* addresses the needs of commercial training organizations.

3. *IQ-CONGRESS* is meant to reflect the needs of conference organizations.

The SAP solution for higher education called *IQ-CAMPUS* is meant, specifically, for use with R/3 Release 4.0 along with the additional software components *IQ-TRAINING* and *IQ-CONGRESS*.

SAP IQ enhances the R/3 enterprisewide solution in an effort to provide educational institutions with best business practices and specific functionality to satisfy their various requirements.

The mainstay of the R/3 capabilities satisfies enterprise requirements for administrative processes that include financial accounting, funds management, human resources management, materials management, facilities scheduling, and maintenance management. SAP IQ offers this essential functionality and enhances them so that educational institutions can manage their operations better and have the flexibility to grow.

IQ-CAMPUS

In order to comprehend educational organizations' individualized needs, SAP held workshops and user-group sessions along with global educational institutions. This joint development effort utilized the standard R/3 functionality as a cornerstone of the *IQ-CAMPUS* solution.

IQ-CAMPUS was created specifically to enhance the power of the R/3 system to satisfy the specific needs of higher-education institutions to efficiently handle their human, financial, and material resources.

In dealing with an increasingly competitive higher-education environment, the *IQ-CAMPUS* solution provides a distinct advantage by offering institutions a total level of education decision support and additional management processes, including student information management, alumni information management, financial aid management, research and grant management, space utilization, and space optimization.

The fiscal environment in which many organizations function is changing constantly. The trend is for governments and companies in the private sector to find new ways of distributing shrinking resources, stimulating universities to introduce and rapidly embrace cost-effective methods. There is an increasing number of universities and other educational institutions that are refining their administrative processes by using R/3. This type of integrated enterprisewide support for campus operations is offered by the *IQ-CAMPUS* solution. *IQ-CAMPUS* permits institutions to concentrate on their core education business processes.

IQ-CAMPUS **Technology**

There is more power to the *IQ-CAMPUS* functionality. The R/3 platform-independent three-tier client-server architecture provides the foundation for maintaining both existing and future institutional requirements. Whenever new technologies are developed, the importance of selecting a market-leading software provider becomes extremely crucial to the long-term success of your mission-critical systems.

IQ-CAMPUS is based on R/3 system technology. The particular technical capabilities that *IQ-CAMPUS* uses includes Internet-enabled applications that handle manual paper-based processes and support of Intranets to relieve administrative staff of mundane duties.

In addition, it also employs the SAP *Business Information Warehouse* to create an abstract of the enormous amount of information within a decision support system. It also uses smart cards for identification purposes, access control, and as a payment method. Most importantly, it integrated the SAP *Business Framework,* which permits the integration of third-party solutions. Furthermore, SAP *Business Workflow* is used for purposes of automation of business and administrative processes.

Implementing these technologies allows any institution to take advantage of their existing resources and significantly enhance the service delivery across campus.

Back-Office Functionality

The SAP financial services solution builds on the core R/3 enterprise application suite to provide the most powerful financial solution possible for financial services firms.

Core R/3 functionality provides financial organizations with unique integration throughout the enterprise and across all back-office functions. It easily links business process into a logical flow. This logical flow includes financial accounting, corporate services, management reporting, treasury management, and human resources. This integration, in combination with the openness of R/3, allows financial services organizations to extract information from front-end systems and then gain access to the transaction level for significant financial reporting, enterprisewide risk management, and strategic decision making.

The SAP financial services solution provides several important levels of functionality, including:

- *Business Management.* This level includes financial accounting and management that deals with the general ledger, accounts payable and consolidation, procurement, fixed assets, human resources, activity-based costing, real estate, project systems, executive information systems, global integration, multijurisdiction, multicurrency, multilingual support, and electronic commerce support.

- *Profitability.* This level includes profitability by organization, customer, product, and channel.

- *Risk management.* This level includes market and credit risk and asset and liability management.

- *Supplementary functionality.* This extra level includes Internet and Intranet integration, year 2000 compliance, and eurocompliance.

Financial companies can take advantage of an accelerated implementation. In addition, there are also several benefits achieved from both industry expertise and the support from TeamSAP's methodology.

People and Processes

TeamSAP combines people and processes to make certain you attain a successful SAP solution. Two key factors of TeamSAP include the AcceleratedSAP implementation program and implementation partners.

AcceleratedSAP programs offer a combination of methodology, resources, and tools to offer accelerated and predictable implementations. In addition, you gain a platform for ongoing change. Implementation partners offer you a great number of solutions intertwined with business and industry expertise for TeamSAP clients.

The combination of AcceleratedSAP and your implementation partner gives you the ability to complete your implementation in 6 to 9 months on average. You will also find that your implementation will proceed very easily and your system will be ready to go online in a timely manner within your budget.

SAP Solution Demand

There is an increasing market demand for SAP's solutions. When dealing with the midsized market, AcceleratedSAP and TeamSAP have nearly eliminated all implementation worries. It has distinctly illustrated the meaningful returns on the information investments that can be realized by midsized companies with an accelerated R/3 implementation. SAP has seen a great influx of new, large customers from the public sector, aerospace/defense, as well as other new industries. SAP has achieved a notable expansion in both their industry focus and coverage. This success will improve as new industry sector ambitions are developed.

The Future of SAP

SAP will ship its new version of the R/3 system, Release 4.0, on a general basis at the end of the second quarter of 1998. Release 4.0 enhances the R/3 system a great deal by adding functionality for industries such as accounting, logistics, human resources applications, as well as other complete and mature industry solutions. These solutions involve packages for the public sector, utilities, and retail industries.

SAP was the first to provide a comprehensive retail solution that deals effectively with the whole value chain that extends from product development to the final consumer. R/3 4.0 also offers additional functionality that was previously stated in early development of this product.

SAP's future is very bright; they will be listed on the U.S. stock exchange in the latter part of 1998. The preparations have progressed much more quickly than expected. SAP expects that the German Parliament will pass the appropriate legislation that will permit SAP to report a set of consolidated financial statements in U.S. GAAP (generally accepted accounting principles). They also wish to buy back shares of their stock.

SAP AG preference and common shares are listed on the Frankfurt Stock Exchange and several other exchanges too. SAP is a component of the DAX, which is the index of 30 German blue chip companies. In the United States, SAP's unrestricted ADR (where each one is equivalent to one-third of an SAP preference share) trades on the Over the Counter exchange with the symbol "SAPHY."

Information on the SAP AG preference shares is available from the following information services:

- *Bloomberg.* Symbol SAG3 GR.
- *Reuters.* Symbol SAPG_p.F or IB.
- *Quotron.* Symbol SAGVD.EU.

SAP Internet Solutions

SAP Internet solutions allow you to deploy a cost-effective R/3 Internet solution. The goal is to simplify your implementation process, increase sales, and enhance the supply chain.

SAP America Inc., has formed several multinational customers who have deployed Internet solutions with SAP R/3 enterprise client-server business applications that permit various organizations to execute Web commerce, leverage the Internet to extend their supply chains, and create company Intranets.

These customer solutions illustrate how businesses are leveraging their existing investments in R/3 to benefit from the Internet to perform electronic commerce, establish virtual corporations, and develop extended supply-chain solutions.

TeamSAP allows you to rapidly deploy and extend these solutions. Some examples of organizations integrating R/3-based Internet and Intranet functionality into their systems include:

- Mott's North America
- Simon & Schuster
- National Semiconductor Corp.

These organizations are illustrative of the types of companies that have chosen R/3 Internet and Intranet functionality. The goal is for Internet application components to enhance business operations and offer a continuous, inexpensive service to customers, employees, and brokers to allow them to access Web-enabled purchasing systems at any time of the day. Customers also gain the ability to leverage R/3 best business processes in combination with Internet capabilities to develop internetworked virtual corporations.

SAP provides additional Internet functionality as well as the most detailed extended supply-chain functionality possible on the market. Furthermore, the SAP *Business Framework* and the Internet-related products and technologies created by third parties are now simpler to integrate into R/3-based business systems.

R/3 offers powerful and accurate information necessary to perform the best decisions about your business. In addition, it provides Internet capabilities that play an important role in your growing business processes.

R/3 and the Internet together will be a powerful combination that allows you to extend the reach of information available through R/3. This information allows you to increase and expand your business operations significantly and excel in a highly competitive marketplace.

Profile: Mott's North America

For example, Mott's North America is a $700 million supplier of fruit juices, applesauce, and cocktail mixes. They implemented R/3 to assist them in reducing operating costs, increase efficiency, and improve customer service.

Once they had gone live, the company chose to upgrade to R/3 Release 3.1 so that its brokered sales force had the ability to utilize the Internet to access data used from R/3. A test group of brokers was responsible for selling the complete line of Mott's North America products. The goal was to gain the ability to instantly retrieve a wide range of order and delivery data through the Internet. This information is available 24 hours per day, 7 days per week without the need for brokers to call customer service or install extra expensive hardware or software.

Mott's North America initial program was very successful, therefore, they executed a framework to make their R/3 Internet solution available to all its brokers. They are now looking into expanding the system's capabilities to incorporate Internet ordering. Figure 19-2 shows both planned and process orders. This is a very crucial functionality that will provide Mott's smaller brokers with an inexpensive method of submitting orders electronically. Mott's is working on leveraging their R/3 Internet components to enhance its supply chain through Internet as well as purchasing directly through the Web browser.

Figure 19-2

Dispatching, Deallocation, and Rescheduling of Planned/Process Orders.

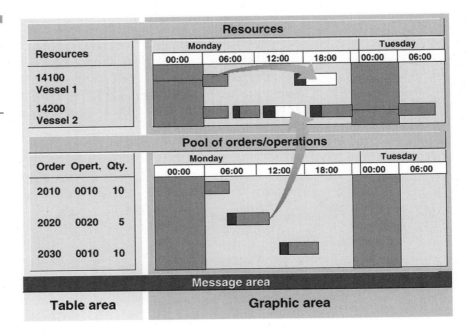

Profile: Simon & Schuster

Simon & Schuster is a global English-language book publisher. They initially chose R/3 to enhance and integrate their core financial, sales, and distribution functionality. Then they chose to integrate R/3 with an existing Intranet to establish a Web-enabled purchase requisition system that could be accessed through normal Web browsers. The goal was to enable several hundred Simon & Schuster employees to use the company Intranet to make purchases electronically. This proved to be a very cost-efficient, cost-effective process as opposed to their previous paper-based requisition system.

When they implemented R/3 and Intranet applications, they gained a refined purchasing process that allowed them to reduce paper costs, turnaround time, and response time in the requisition process. Figure 19-3 shows the types of gains you can expect on your customer order turnaround times—both before and after your R/3 implementation. The requisition information is very reliable due to the fact that it is validated directly against R/3, while the proper data is imported directly into their financial systems.

Simon & Schuster formulated a plan for linking browser technology and R/3. Their objective is to use the Internet to enable purchases directly with the company's suppliers as well as for placement of customer orders.

Figure 19-3
Before and After Implementing R/3 Gains Improved Customer Order Turnaround.

Before R/3	After R/3
● **Batch transfer of orders to plants, overnight**	● **Orders immediately available at plants**
● **Standalone scheduling system**	● **Integrated production scheduling**
● **Manual capacity planning**	● **Immediate visibility of capacity problems**
● **Incomplete inventory status for raw materials**	● **Full raw material availability information**
● **Manual shipment planning**	● **Automated shipment planning**
● **Advance Ship Notices sent in batch, overnight**	● **Automatic sending of ASNs throughout the day**

Profile: National Semiconductor

National Semiconductor's employees have gained the ability to leverage their company's Intranet in combination with a set of R/3-based human resources applications. They have the ability to execute modifications to their benefits, register for training classes, and maintain personal information, including address and emergency contact. Employees can access several levels of personnel information and execute relevant adjustments online right from their workstations.

Prior to implementing R/3, employees performed human resources tasks using a cumbersome paper system. They searched for specific paper forms, completed them, and then waited for someone else to enter the data into the system. The employee self-service applications now reside within R/3, which allows National Semiconductor employees to input their own personnel information. This is an important step that makes certain personal records are accurate. It also avoids the inefficiencies of several points of data entry. In addition, all employee information is accessible from one centralized source. This centralization refines the dissemination and updating of information to personnel.

Their objective was to transfer the R/3 information to a point closer to the employees and their managers. They wanted to provide personnel with the power to support their own records, and make certain that those records are reliable, accessible, and up to date.

In order to enhance the efficiency of human resources processes, National Semiconductor is also implementing an Extranet that links to third-party medical insurance and retirement providers. Just by accessing the Extranet, personnel will have the ability to select doctors and services, as well as modify investment elections in a 401(k) plan directly from their own workstations. The result is a definite savings in time for personnel and a cost-effective plan for the organization itself.

SAP's *Business Framework*

Business Framework stresses open, stable access to R/3 business processes. SAP *Business Framework* has gained a great deal of support from several third-party vendors. The main objective of the SAP *Business Framework* is to make certain that, as an R/3 customer, you can select from a variety of certified, compatible, packaged applications, and development tools. A few of these products are based on SAP *Business Framework* as well as BAPIs that were introduced at the Technical Education Conference.

Delphi/Connect for SAP

Borland's Delphi/Connect for SAP is a comprehensive collection of tools that allows your company to rapidly and simply interface with SAP R/3. Delphi/Connect for SAP utilizes the SAP *Business Framework* and permits your current systems to grow efficiently when new technology is implemented. This allows developers to use both the simplicity and robustness of Borland's Delphi product set to benefit from accessing R/3 by employing SAP *Business Framework* and BAPIs. Delphi can establish stand-alone applications that can access R/3 or extra COM/DCOM interfaces to R/3.

Inspector

Envive Corp., offers service-level reports, automated diagnosis, and preventative management for mission-critical client-server applications. Envive's *Inspector* software concentrates *only* on R/3. Envive utilizes SAP *Business Framework* to access R/3's inner workings. This makes certain that there is greater system stability and performance in offering a global view of R/3 to the CIO. *Inspector* benefits from Java by establishing a cross-platform user interface that can be accessed from any workstation with a Java-enabled browser. The result is instantaneous on-site diagnosis.

VisualAge for Java

IBM's *VisualAge* for Java is an integrated development environment that can be used to create completely pure Java applications that function together with R/3 through BAPIs. Developers need not leave the *VisualAge* environment to access R/3 application functionality. This allows them to benefit from the growing pool of developers who are knowledgeable about Java as well as the productivity offered by *VisualAge*.

Figure 19-4
Industry-Specific Reference Model.

LiveModel

IntelliCorp's *LiveModel* product connects to the SAP *Business Engineer* Release 4.0 through open BAPIs. This allows you to benefit from AcceleratedSAP consultants and implementation partners to enhance the R/3 *Reference Model* to depict the business processes for your individual corporate installation. The SAP industry-specific *Reference Model* is shown in Fig. 19-4.

SAP Utilities

The utilities division is enabled by the SAP *Business Framework* architecture. SAP utilities offer industry-specific functionality that provides enterprisewide business process and information management tools for a successful SAP R/3 system. SAP utilities offer a strong infrastructure and functionality to better manage your businesses operations, so that you have the flexibility to grow and succeed in a future of global change.

SAP utilities do more than provide you with standard R/3 functionality; they also include industry-specific components that satisfy your utility company's needs.

IS-U/Customer Care and Service (IS-U/CCS) is an industry-specific component that responds to client-server customer care and your information system. It is integrated with standard enterprise business applications software. The IS-U/FERC regulatory reporting system incorporates specifications for the U.S. Federal Energy Regulatory Commission. It refines the complicated regulatory reporting process to make certain you achieve compliance with interstate regulations.

SAP Retail

SAP retail is the first enterprise solution with extensive retail and wholesale functionality. It offers a crucial element necessary to motivate the entire value chain, including the supplier, manufacturer, wholesaler, retailer, and consumer. SAP retail utilizes SAP's *Business Framework* architecture and benefits from SAP's comprehensive R/3 solution. It links a retail-specific configuration of multiindustry best practices together with a complete set of retail business processes to make certain that both intercompany and supply chain are fully optimized.

SAP retail offers more than 300 new business processes created specifically for the retail industry. These processes incorporate:

- Merchandise planning
- Promotions management
- Purchasing and replenishment
- Sales
- Retail information system (RIS)

SAP has also preconfigured core R/3 enterprise business processes for the retail industry. Preconfiguration of the core R/3 solution facilitates rapid implementation and deployment of SAP retail. There were initially 30 pilot customers globally, but that number has risen significantly. This rise is illustrative of the growth of the following market segments that have embraced SAP retail:

1. Apparel and department stores
2. General merchandise
3. Grocery (food and drug)

SAP retail permits you to execute a total supply-chain methodology for satisfying the difficult requirements of your suppliers. It also allows you to make certain you achieve an efficient delivery of goods to your retail outlets.

Many organizations are standardizing their business on SAP retail. The trend has been very productive with SAP's R/3 financial applications with respect to:

- Implementing merchandise
- Planning
- Purchasing

- Replenishment
- Sales
- Promotions
- Projects
- Workflow
- Human resources
- Asset management
- Business planning
- RIS

The SAP retail solution can easily handle several thousand employees across several geographically dispersed distribution centers and retail stores.

SAP Retail *GoingLive*

Lidl & Schwarz Stiftung & Co. KG, which is the seventh largest retail group in Germany, went live after an 8-week period. They are using the SAP retail solution at their new distribution center for replenishment and assortment planning of fruits and vegetables distributed to nearly 40 Kaufland supermarkets. By using the integration of SAP retail, this organization has gained instant information access from its point-of-sale systems. However, because fruits and vegetables have an extremely limited shelf life, this information is the difference between success and failure. SAP retail allows them to monitor local demand and respond rapidly to changes in consumer buying trends.

Meeting Your Business Needs

BBC Hardware is Australia's largest hardware retail chain. They found that, in order to keep on track with its rapid growth, they needed to cope with two primary problems:

1. Poor inventory control
2. Inability to share stock between stores

SAP retail assisted them in managing their hardware division's customer accounts, integrating their complete organization, managing its rapid growth, and enhancing the deployment of new products. SAP retail was able to offer BBC Hardware a real-time description of what was available store by store. They were also able to integrate new point-of-sale systems within its individual stores and provide a wider range of other retail-specific levels of functionality.

The SAP retail solution was perfect for BBC's retail environment since it offers:

1. High level of functionality, including refined stock control

2. Improved push and pull marketing capabilities

3. Electronic commerce

4. Tighter control over pricing mechanisms

5. Increased access to customer information

This type of functionality allowed them to expect faster service at the counter and reduce stock shortages for their customers.

SAP's global experience with more than 200 R/3 customers in the retail and wholesale industry was the prerequisite to the development of SAP retail. This solution started with only 30 companies as part of a unique first-customer-ship program.

Today, SAP retail can offer the retail industry an innovative, industry-specific technology and business solution to compete efficiently in today's very competitive marketplace.

When you count year 2000 compliance, electronic commerce capabilities, and third-party solutions, then SAP retail can offer you a very comprehensive solution that can optimize your value chain from consumption to production.

SAP Retail Functions

SAP retail was created specifically to support retail and wholesale organizations in a consumer-focused marketplace. It yields functionality for sourcing, planning, and tracking merchandise movement throughout your retail supply chain. It ties together retail management functionality, including assortment planning, price and promotion management, distribution, and store management. There is also a high level of integration that enables SAP retail to be integrated with other applications.

SAP retail functions include:

- Internet functionality to manage consumer-to-business and business-to-business commerce
- Electronic data interchange (EDI) interface for data interchange with business partners, vendors, and customers
- Comprehensive services to implement a distributed application architecture as required for distributed merchandise management
- RIS, which is an integrated data warehouse that supports decision makers with precise and recent information
- Complete merchandise management such as purchasing, supply-chain management, and sales
- Interfaces for point-of-sale systems
- Promotion support
- Range management
- Listing procedures
- Retail-specific stock planning
- Price calculation
- Article maintenance (for example, color, size matrix, and sets)
- Retail reference model specifically for SAP retail business processes.
- *Business Workflow* for accelerating the flow to make certain there is a high level of information consistency
- Third-party systems support

SAP retail is based on the *Business Framework* architecture that expedited integration of leading industry-specific applications such as EDI, labor optimization, layout planning, warehouse automation, POS systems, and store merchandise management systems.

SAP's standard business APIs (BAPIs) offer established and long-term interfaces into SAP data. This permits information access throughout geographically disparate systems across your entire extended supply chain. Unlike any traditional client-server architectures, *Business Framework* permits SAP to offer new capabilities, components, and technology (including SAP retail) to you on a continuing basis. This is accomplished regardless of conventional upgrade release cycles.

SAP's partner organization has allowed them to create the most extensive partner alliances throughout the enterprise application software industry.

In terms of availability, SAP retail allows you to start your efforts immediately. You can initiate your implementation for the purpose of accelerating savings from operational efficiency. The result is that you will gain a much faster return on information. SAP retail is integrated into SAP R/3 Release 4.0 which incorporates extra enhancements as well as extra retail-specific business processes.

Conclusion

This chapter discusses the accelerators for all types of implementations that can be used together or separately. The objective of this section focuses on how these factors play key roles in your ASAP implementation. These crucial elements include faster implementation, delivery of business results, quality, efficient use of resources, synergy of results for future implementation, and reduced implementation costs. This chapter also looks at how ASAP works to achieve the best possible implementation and business practices. This chapter concludes by discussing why accelerators provide partner consultants with a standard approach for rapid implementation and configuration support in R/3.

The Future of AcceleratedSAP

Introduction

SAP has established a high level of marketing with respect to adapting its R/3 CIM software to the various enterprise network computing needs. SAP initially built its business and maintained a 70 percent growth rate just by working with corporations that had over $500 million in annual revenues.

AcceleratedSAP

The AcceleratedSAP program has done an excellent job of homing in on companies with less than $200 million per year in revenues. SAP is marketing its software in a far more modular fashion, which provides you with increased flexibility and the ability to customize applications to meet your individual corporate needs. SAP is entering Internet technology and getting ready for the assault of electronic commerce. A joint venture company between SAP and Intel, called Pandesic, has been established, and it is working to provide a turnkey version of R/3 powered by Intel processors and operated on the Windows NT platform.

Old Philosophy

SAP was often thought of as being far too big to stay current with the Internet. Although some people believe SAP is too big, it can now be implemented more quickly.

The most recent and upcoming versions of R/3 are illustrative of SAP's dedication to providing richer functionality in current and future releases of their product. Figure 20-1 demonstrates how R/3 functionality has evolved in the recent past. This is further exemplified by the fact that AcceleratedSAP is finding ways to implement their core product far more quickly and effectively in industry segments of varying size.

The majority of SAP implementors in the United States are large companies who have revenues greater than $500 million per year. In order to maintain a high growth rate, SAP is achieving success by selling to all market segments. That route has led them to selling to smaller organizations who generate less than $200 million per year.

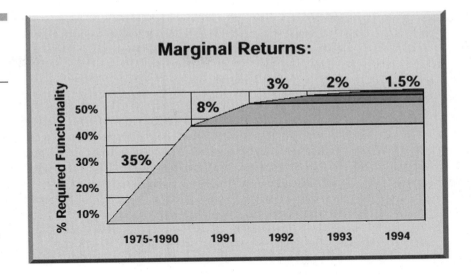

Figure 20-1
Functionality Evolution. (*Courtesy of SAP*)

SAP has concentrated on the lower end of the market. Accelerated-SAP has reached new pinnacles of success for creating a SAP following in midsized organizations.

Future Directions

SAP is developing a flexible framework by offering individual parts or modules called components. Companies can implement or upgrade these modules which include human resources and supply-chain management, individually without sacrificing core R/3 services.

Pandesic

SAP is rapidly embracing E-commerce. SAP realizes that your resources need to be used appropriately to make certain that your business runs as efficiently as possible. The majority of this efficiency stems from R/3 and ASAP. Pandesic, a joint venture between Intel and SAP, offers turnkey R/3 installations to the many businesses.

Pandesic is a great idea because it has evaluators that realize the need to be careful about its pricing scheme. Pandesic will charge between 1 and 6 percent per transaction. This technique is good because it allows organizations to factor infrastructure costs into their resource planning, however, the total from this surcharge adds up like an unwanted tax.

The Pandesic solution is based on Intel servers operating Windows NT. The motivating force behind R/3 is that nearly half of all SAP installations are based on Intel servers operating Windows NT. Microsoft and Intel want to collaborate on this enterprise.

SAP's corporate goals point to acquisitions that could only hurt the R/3 product line. SAP still needs to improve weak or untested areas, including supply-chain management and E-commerce. Most organizations need to get acquired because they can benefit from SAP's effort.

Building a Solution

It may often seem as though reengineering business processes are relatively simple. Replacing or retooling a legacy system with a new generation of computers often appears far easier than it really is. As much as AcceleratedSAP speeds SAP R/3 implementations, your organization may benefit more from reengineering your entire organization. However, that effort takes a great deal of time and money. This is why it is important to find an experienced consultant who can look at your organization and know where to start.

This chapter focuses on Ernst & Young because they provide an accelerated and systematic way of approaching systems reengineering with SAP that offers a total solution to the satisfaction of its clients.

There are several important steps to follow when expediting your implementation, including:

1. Value proposition is useful when creating your business case for an SAP solution.

2. Reality check is an important step when assessing your corporate readiness for change.

However, your ultimate solution should include some very necessary indicators to help you determine what factors need to be in place:

- Aligned approach
- Setting expectations
- Providing short- and long-term value

- Correct people, skills, methods, and management
- Delivering value
- Measuring results
- Acquiring success

The value proposition is an important element in any process. It starts by making certain that any endeavor you entertain makes business sense.

In order to make certain your business decisions are appropriate, you need to ask yourself the following questions:

1. Is your technology investment necessary and justifiable?
2. Does your investment meet with your organization's objectives?
3. Does your upper management comprehend what "change" means?
4. Do your proposed changes have full support?
5. What is the framework for making decisions?
6. What milestones will determine your implementation's progress?
7. Is value being delivered throughout the process?

These crucial questions determine your value proposition.

The reality check determines when your project is ready to be executed. Experience has shown that hardly anyone openly opposes change, but it is often far easier to stay with the business processes you already have. However, change is at the heart of the growing IT industry and must be achieved to stay competitive in a constantly changing environment.

Prior to determining the implementation method, you need to execute a reality check and determine the following factors before your implementation goes any further:

1. Is your organization ready for change?
2. Are there any undetermined factors?
3. How are these factors managed?
4. Are all parties within your organization in agreement on the scope and pace of change?
5. What are management's expectations?

The way you answer these questions will significantly affect your implementation methodology. Once you determine the answers to these questions, you can avoid a one-size-fits-all approach that may look good but doesn't satisfy your evolving business requirements.

The aligned approach provides both short- and long-term benefits that are crucial to the success of your implementation. Although change may be difficult, it is often easier to embrace if you gain significant progress in your corporation's endeavors. The aligned approach is often best for any implementation project.

In order to succeed in this methodology, you need to carefully examine your alternatives to a complete reengineering project, and then develop an approach that can best permit your implementation to function in well-defined modules. Then you must communicate your anticipated results to upper management and continue communicating throughout your entire project, so that you are comfortable with all aspects of your implementation. This method allows you to make certain that your entire project remains on time, on budget, and part of upper management's recipe for success.

In order to achieve success, you need to combine the right people, skills, methods, and management so that you can work with your consultants in process management, change management, knowledge management, and industry skills.

Ernst & Young

The Ernst & Young team works with you to provide high levels of integration with people and skills in process management, change management, knowledge management, and industry skills. In addition, they work with your project team to transfer knowledge and skills so that you can assume ownership for the project as it is being implemented and, most especially, when it is completed.

In order to provide you with exceptional levels of teamwork, they deliver value. If a project doesn't demonstrate significant results, it can result in a loss of confidence by your personnel in the way that the business runs and may hurt your overall productivity.

Ernst & Young works with you at every project phase to provide you with implementation value and reduce the overall risk in changing your business processes. Each success they bring to your organization results in a greater profit potential for your organization. They can take a comprehensive approach to your SAP implementation, and then give you a way to utilize the AcceleratedSAP environment and customize it to meet your individual corporate needs.

Management Consulting

Ernst & Young offers six sets of management consulting services. Each set can be purchased individually or grouped with others. These services include process transformation, systems integration, business change implementation, knowledge management, performance measurement, and industry best practices.

Process transformation allows Ernst & Young to analyze and consult with you about how your SAP R/3 solution will impact functions and personnel throughout the entire organization.

Systems integration, development, and outsourcing allow you to determine systems within your organization that can be best integrated by SAP R/3. In addition, you can identify specific systems that must be created and outsourced.

Business change implementation determines how SAP R/3 will impact your organization's culture. You can isolate the specific areas where change may make personnel uneasy and offer strategies for assisting management and staff in embracing new methods as a result of SAP R/3.

Knowledge management allows you to create both systems and practices that make it simple to share knowledge and experiences across your organization. It assists you in accelerating SAP R/3 acceptance and implementation.

Performance measurement allows you to create parameters for measuring personnel and systems success during and after implementation.

Industry best practices allow you to determine and utilize SAP R/3 practices within your industry. You can then employ benchmarks throughout project development and implementation.

Tools

There are specific tools that give your organization far more power in business. These tools offer specialized and unique software solutions that are both systematic and powerful. They work to improve the quality and efficiency of your SAP R/3 implementation.

Director is a central part of Ernst & Young's project planning, impact analysis, and available resources. It is especially useful for geographically dispersed teams.

Mentor is an object-based, process-driven tool, and is unlike any other support tool in the marketplace.

Advisor has the ability to answer your questions since it provides Internet access to experienced global Ernst & Young SAP consultants. Figure 20-2 illustrates the SAP interface *Advisor* for your organizational needs.

S-Link offers specialized solutions by linking automated data collection technologies with software developed by Ernst & Young. It uses bar coding and radio frequency technologies to allow you to execute real-time data capture and analysis.

Director is an integrated program management tool that centralizes project planning, impact analysis, risk, issue management, and available resources. It is very useful for geographically dispersed teams to use this tool to facilitate implementation.

Project managers who use *Director* have the ability to review status, solve problems, and utilize their resources efficiently. Information is provided in a journal format and supplements in other project-status reporting software (for example, Microsoft Project).

Mentor is an SAP R/3 support tool that is both object based and process driven. It is unique from other support tools in the marketplace because it is completely integrated with SAP's *Implementation Guide* (IMG). *Mentor* complements and improves on the IMG's capabilities by capturing the following information:

- Issues tracking

- Gap management

- Configuration decisions

Mentor then sends that data to a cross-relational knowledge base that illustrates one of this tool's several features.

Advisor illustrates the SAP critical number that allows you to use the Internet and access global SAP professionals. In addition, it also maintains a list of frequently asked questions. Its goal is to utilize Ernst & Young's knowledge and experience to avoid the delay and expense of developing an implementation practice or business process from scratch.

S-Link is the first commercial, automated data-collection solution for SAP, and it provides a crucial connection in real time between R/3 software and data-collection technologies. These technologies are illustrated by bar code scanners and handheld terminals that are very valuable for transaction volumes such as in warehouses. Shipping and receiving, production, inventory management, time, and attendance are all functions that can be captured, relayed, and analyzed as they occur.

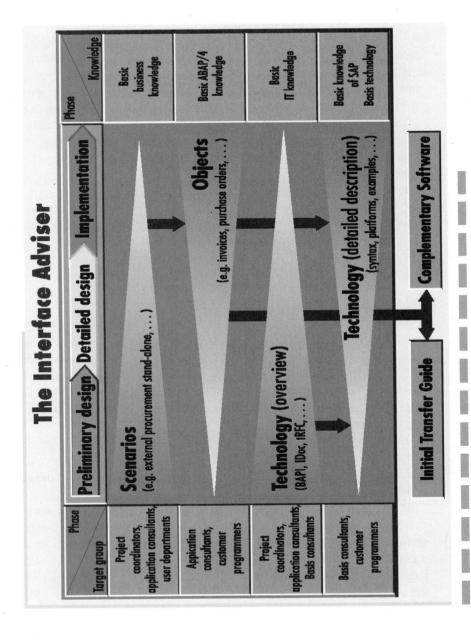

Figure 20-2 SAP Interface Advisor. (Courtesy of SAP)

Achieving a Successful R/3 Implementation

Your SAP R/3 implementation can be very beneficial to the entire organization. It is important to note that the effort and commitment on your part must originate from all levels, especially upper management.

The modifications SAP can offer deal with cultural, organizational, and operational aspects of your company. Since these modifications may be problematic for some of your personnel, the benefits from your implementation of SAP should occur quickly, so that you will have long-term benefits.

If you are thinking about the SAP solution for your company, remember to make specific suggestions regarding your R/3 implementation. Your input will help the implementation proceed smoothly and reflect your business operations more effectively.

Management Issues

You already know that it is very important for you to have very strong leadership skills within your organization. However, these skills must be very supportive of your implementation efforts in order for your efforts to reach completion quickly and effectively. Support for your implementation project is essential, especially if you plan on accelerating your implementation.

Your first step should be to designate a core team for your SAP project. Your team members should be part of your immediate organization and key resources should be assigned to them so they can complete the project quickly.

If you don't already have someone who fits the bill, how do you find the right people to hire for this type of implementation project? You should look for prospective employees who have an established track record in managing diverse aspects of a corporate implementation project. Since this is such an expansive project, every member in your organization is responsible for the correct implementation of R/3. When everyone is responsible, a serious and dedicated effort will be made to succeed.

It is important to concentrate on specific SAP-enabled process improvement. You must be very specific so you can gain instantaneous feedback at any stage of your implementation. You need to create a specific pace for your implementation project. Since you are focusing on AcceleratedSAP, it is best to choose a relatively fast pace, but one that doesn't burn out your employees.

Then you must develop a plan whereby you can test all of your systems for validity in your new operating environment. You need to look for specific alternatives that can quicken the pace of your business operations. You are charged with being an "efficiency expert" and so finding the best alternative for your organization is critical to your overall success.

Bullpen Environment

You must create an environment where sharing of information is easy. One of the ways that Ernst & Young achieves this is to foster a type of "bullpen" environment. In your organization, try to set up a room without any individual offices or cubicles. When each member of your team checks in, they must leave their rank at the door. Everyone must have an equal opportunity to communicate in an open room so that sharing of ideas becomes easy. This type of environment is often the most productive and least claustrophobic. An open space allows information to flow freely, much more efficiently than any groupware solution such as Lotus Notes or e-mail.

In order to foster this type of open business environment, you need to make certain that individual and group relationships are encouraged, so that communication is easy and simple among your personnel. You may find that it is often simpler to have all of your resources, consultants, and personnel work together to develop their bullpen environment to the point where it is a friendly working environment for everyone on the implementation team. You may find that the bullpen environment is so productive for your R/3 implementation that you will want to institute this across many sectors within your organization.

The bullpen environment provides your project team with an avenue of growth that can be used as a springboard to promotion. Any environment that is productive is often stimulated by the fact that there is room for growth. You want your employees to give their "life's blood" to fostering your corporate growth. Motivation is one of the best accelerators for you R/3 implementation.

Employing these types of incentives is often a good motivation for your personnel to archive excellent progress in their career growth within your company. A bonus infrastructure allows employees to achieve to their potential because they know they will be rewarded for their accomplishments in your organization. You can then expect to see your workers dedicated to a higher level of well-being and a more proficient team spirit.

The utilization of incentives is an effective way of motivating people to progress in their careers. Making these types of achievements goals, followed by a bonus reward structure, are methods to use for a more productive working environment for your corporate needs.

An actual implementation necessitates significant thought and analysis, however, utilizing these analyses allows you to reap benefits for your entire organization. You can then understand, utilize, and benefit from the efficiencies and enhanced communications that SAP offers.

Ernst & Young is recognized for their strength in AcceleratedSAP R/3 implementations. ASAP has been a breakthrough for many small to medium-sized organizations, but once you implement SAP R/3, you need to ask yourself: Where do I go from here? Having a consultant on your side is a cost-effective, prudent move that will ultimately pay for itself in success and improved business processes.

Ernst & Young Services

Information systems and assurance advisory services (ISAAS) was developed to provide an audit-ready SAP implementation. Ernst & Young created this type of an approach so that when you use ISAAS, you can increase the predictability and quality of your project. ISAAS also foster documentation throughout all phases of a project to make certain that you achieve an early and continuous transfer of knowledge throughout all phases of your implementation effort.

Tax-enabled implementation is important to your business processes. When these business processes are optimized through your SAP implementation, tax consequences are often an oversight. Tax-enabled implementation avoids those problems and offers you a great deal of savings through items that include the optimal utilization of foreign sales corporations (FSC). This deals with state and local tax minimization, reorganization of global tax minimization, reorganization, fixed asset depreciation, tax credit optimization, and implementation of policies and procedures that meet regulatory record retention requirements.

Ernst & Young Wins SAP Award of Excellence

Ernst & Young is recognized as a leading SAP consulting and implementation firm. This has been proven numerous times; they were awarded the SAP Award of Excellence for 3 years in a row. SAP chose Ernst & Young based on their annual customer satisfaction survey.

Ernst & Young created strong capabilities for delivering business systems solutions to meet their client's specific needs. Winning SAP's Award of Excellence illustrates that, overall, they can provide you with the highest level of customer satisfaction available.

Ernst & Young offers global R/3 implementation services to more than 200 clients, including industry leaders such as Eli Lilly, Phillips Petroleum, Oklahoma Gas & Electric, and Farmland Industries, Inc. More than one-half of Ernst & Young's SAP clients utilize this software in a live production environment. Globally, there are more than 2000 consultants within Ernst & Young member firms dedicated to global SAP integration services.

Ernst & Young expands its SAP services through the investment and development of creative tools and techniques to accelerate R/3 implementations. They have more than 400 knowledge bases, so you can retrieve leading practices and solution objects empowered by SAP. Their service capabilities are increased through alliance partnerships with leading software and hardware vendors that concentrate on collaborative development of Web-based solutions and Internet services.

Ernst & Young has consistently had a successful track record in integrating enterprise applications that rely on using leading-edge technology. The combination of SAP and Ernst & Young professionals is a significant benefit that provides you with a quick, reliable, and high-performance solution.

Mentor for SAP Users

Ernst & Young introduced *Mentor* in August 1996. *Mentor* is a very powerful tool that accelerates your entire SAP implementation process. *Mentor* is a desktop application that functions as a crucial link between SAP's R/3 software and Visio. This link permits you to more effectively decide the most optimal SAP configuration, and, as a result, effectively reduce the time needed for configuring software.

As an R/3 user, you have the ability to capture and share critical information on business procedures, processes, and objects pertaining to R/3 implementation. In addition, looking for objects by industry, business core area, or business transaction is simpler and more effective.

Mentor provides complete integration with *Business Engineering Workshop* (BEW) as well as the Visio *Business Modeler.* This combination allows you to visualize your R/3 processes so long as you use high-quality graphics. You then have the power to configure R/3 software and share project implementations.

Teamwork: Deploying R/3 Efficiently and Quickly

One real-life example is the Hoechst Group, a company that is one of the world's largest supplier of industrial, chemical, pharmaceutical, and agricultural products. This corporation is organized into business units that function in close proximity to their customers. Hoechst Celanese is the North American counterpart of The Hoechst Group, and is the fifth largest chemical company in the United States. Hoechst bases its customer relations in terms of endurable development that concentrates on improving processes together with strategic objectives.

Hoechst Fibers executives in the United States ordered an intensive review of the division's business strategies. This review indicated the need for step-level changes for several key process areas in order to satisfy financial goals and to satisfy expansion plans.

One area that required change included the procurement process. Ernst & Young was hired by Hoechst Fibers because the procurement activity at Hoechst Fibers was spread across eight geographically dispersed sites. These sites functioned relatively autonomously and were employing several computer systems at each site that were not integrated. These systems were also significantly customized at each site.

Gaining an Edge over the Competition

The utilities industry is becoming significantly more competitive as the trend toward government deregulation has increased. One company,

OG&E Electric Services, is in a good position to remain more flexible, reduce costs, and offer a higher level of customer service. This allows them to provide greater enterprisewide information in the most effective manner possible.

Oklahoma Gas and Electric has nearly 3000 employees and nearly 700,000 customers. Therefore, a great deal of importance is attached to shuttling the right information to the right employee at the right time. It is critical to have improved data about the costs of providing electric service, marketing information, and performance. Working with this data is seen as a primary challenge in the utility industry. In addition, deploying timely and reliable information assists OG&E to effectively support its inevitable growth beyond its nearly $2 billion annual revenue.

This endeavor is still very difficult because, like most large organizations, OG&E has many different departments, and each department works with different types of information systems—a nightmare for accurate and timely information management. Also, a combination of various individual computers with a distinct mix of mainframe, computers, and PC applications ran the business.

OG&E examined the business processes necessary to comply with the industry's deregulation. They then decided they needed a complete new information infrastructure. The result was the introduction of a completely integrated enterprise software that offered the best economic choice to substantiate OG&E's endeavor.

Coping with Growth

Buckeye Cellulose is a leading manufacturer and global marketer of high-quality, value-added specialty cellulose pulps. This company meets several market needs and customer demands. Most consumers use fiber from specialty cellulose pulps every day in applications ranging from camera film and diapers to paper and ice cream. This diversity of fibers, processes, and end products requires complicated, but flexible, business system processes.

Buckeye currently has six corporate, manufacturing, and freight-handling locations in the United States and Europe. The company, which recently went public, has more than $500 million in annual revenue, as well as an aggressive growth and acquisition strategy focused on maintaining leadership and expansion into greater international markets.

The most difficult period occurred when Buckeye Cellulose spun off from Procter & Gamble in 1993. At that time, they had to overcome the problem of developing their own infrastructure for the entire organization while providing excellent customer support.

Buckeye needed new systems for sales, order processing, finance, inventory management, and finished products that functioned together perfectly. Buckeye also needed to make certain that they had the ability to expand into new countries and markets and that their information systems could rapidly adapt without compromising their business solutions.

Buckeye depended on Ernst & Young to understand their business and integrate all elements of a comprehensive, enduring solution. Ernst & Young started the endeavor by trying to align Buckeye's business objectives together with their information system needs. They accomplished this by identifying the factors that motivated their IT implementation. As a result, Ernst & Young was able to rapidly set up the best technical solution.

Buckeye's objective was to develop long-term direction and growth. They were one of the original SAP R/3 users. At the present time, Ernst & Young still assists Buckeye to improve on its SAP infrastructure by developing new facilities and placing effective business processes in place to enable transparent corporate acquisitions with respect to inventory, sales, financial, and order-processing departments across the entire organization.

Ernst & Young created an effective solution by working closely with Buckeye to assist in implementing a powerful SAP R/3 system across four locations and multiple departments in a time period of only 8 months.

SAP offered an optimal solution to satisfy Buckeye's requirements for long-term strategic direction and global implementation. Buckeye also selected SAP for its advanced interface and compatibility with Hewlett-Packard systems.

Buckeye relies on SAP to support real-time data in its sales, order processing, inventory, finished products management, and financial departments. SAP R/3 permits Buckeye's globally geographically dispersed systems to maintain consistent part numbers, update inventory, and export statistics, and to more accurately forecast sales. The result is an increased level of integration and timely corporate data that permits executives throughout this organization to execute business decisions quickly.

Even after Buckeye had used SAP R/3 for 3 years, they continued to realize benefits from the enterprisewide integrated systems. They also gained the power to integrate new acquisitions simply while reducing costs. The SAP R/3 system makes certain that both training and technology updates in new locations are quick but transparent to the remainder of the company. When you use one centralized tool in several countries, then supply-chain management is also perfect.

The result has been high speed, flexibility, and cost control, which allows Buckeye to be competitive in any market it enters.

Client Experiences

If you are like most companies, you are struggling with the idea of finding the lowest cost and quickest solution. You don't have unlimited time or monies to implement an effective ERP solution. Whether you are a small, medium, or large organization, you need to find the most value for your information investment. By examining the experiences of the clients listed here, you can find your own niche in this rapidly evolving, highly competitive environment.

You will note that the utility companies scheduled for deregulation so change is an imminent part of this evolving IT industry. Regardless of your industry sector, you face change. Whether that change comes from the impending year 2000 crisis or changing market conditions, you are at risk if you stay with the status quo in the majority of cases. That is why implementing an effective ERP solution can integrate your business environment into a more manageable condition.

In terms of the utility example, the biggest problem you may experience occurs when software is written for a regulated industry, but then the rules in that industry change. This leaves you in a very precarious situation without a definable course of action. This is the primary reason for choosing an effective consultant. You want to direct your efforts toward your business practices not technological side issues that take your attention away from your primary business objectives.

Summary: SAP and Ernst & Young

An accelerated solution can make or break your company, literally! Even though SAP R/3 is a superior reengineering package, it also is known as a complicated solution.

You may choose Ernst & Young because you need a consultant who can reduce your risk in developing accelerated solutions. Ernst & Young has established techniques, experienced staff, client teamwork, and project management to provide a completed project in under a year.

Consider a semiconductor manufacturer with $4 billion in sales and over 30,000 employees and 650 divisions globally. If this company needed to do something to stay competitive with global demands from both its customers and its competitors, they would require a highly centralized management structure. This solution would have to be very comprehensive and highly flexible. Information would have to flow quickly and easily vertically and horizontally throughout the entire organization.

The biggest problem often involves adapting quickly and effectively to change. You choose SAP because of its strength in global integration solutions. SAP often recommends Ernst & Young to assist in their solutions because they offer a very productive phased approach to implementing R/3 solutions.

The most important problems involve the size and speed of your implementation solution. Most people and organizations can only accept a certain amount of change at any given time. A relief factor is very important. Each member of your team needs to feel at ease with your business solution so that you can be certain you will obtain a high level of success in your endeavors.

In order to achieve success, you need to develop a standard form of global design that can be modified to satisfy your specific needs. Then you need to be able to perform an analysis and design of your process transformation to incorporate factors that include inventory management, order management, and financials (that is, electronic commerce). Your next step is to effectively integrate change management to assist management and staff to comprehend, accept, and benefit from your new information system. Finally, you must achieve an effective system configuration that incorporates the ability to test with limited data, and then replicate that information across your entire company.

In order to support your entire implementation, it is important to look at business units with similar functions. You should be able to implement a model for one type of unit, make it work, then replicate and alter it for other units within your organization.

This minimized enterprisewide disruption permits each stage of your project to build on its previous successes. This stage is a critical component to change management.

Teamwork is the last and most important step to any accelerated implementation project. Project success is the most important factor to your business. Ernst & Young has proven that they understand this need and it is reflected in their services to satisfy your corporate needs.

An integrated software management system that can be completed in 2 years as opposed to 4 or 5 years is an effective solution. You can utilize best practices from previous implementation experience to guide your implementation to a beneficial success.

You choose SAP because of its product and ability to give your company a competitive edge. In order to reduce risk, Ernst & Young is a leading consultant that can satisfy your needs and bring your organization into a new level of productivity for the next century.

Conclusion

This chapter pieces together all of the elements described in this book to examine ASAP's past and their plan for the future. This section looks at how SAP continues to enhance AcceleratedSAP and adapt it to match new R/3 releases's functionality. The future of SAP is in their consulting partners and the evolution of R/3, and how both affect your implementation and in the future.

Appendixes

APPENDIX A

IMPLEMENTATION OVERVIEW

Enterprise Resource Planning has become quite prominent in successful management strategies. SAP has always offered a competitive product that enabled organizations to manage the diverse functions of their enterprise in an efficient manner. The only problem that an organization had was that it simply took too long to implement an effective solution. In addition, by the time a standard SAP R/3 implementation was complete, the budget had exceeded original estimates. The type of multilayer client/server environment that R/3 functions within is shown in Fig. A-1.

Until recently R/3 was useful to only very large organizations with the resources for an exceptionally high budget. SAP R/3 really did not concentrate on small to medium-sized businesses. In order to capture that market segment, it was necessary to redefine the implementation scheme for smaller-scale businesses; time and cost factors had to be

Figure A-1
Multilayer Client/Server Concept.

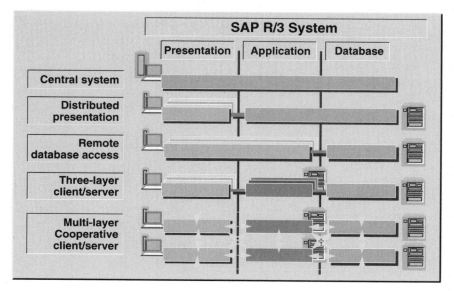

improved in order to place the program in reach of these smaller organizations. The R/3 system environment is shown in Fig. A-2.

Since there was a definite need for SAP R/3 in smaller businesses, ASAP (AcceleratedSAP) was formulated to address the primary factors that made it difficult for this implementation to proceed. ASAP was able to decrease time to implement by as much as one-half. A standard implementation that had previously required as long as 4 years now could be accomplished in 18 months to 2 years.

The reason for this reduction in time and cost resulted primarily from ASAP's use of preconfigured templates that utilize the "best practices" observed from prior implementations. These practices define how to quickly implement each aspect of your SAP R/3 solution. Instead of "reinventing the wheel" every time an implementation takes place, you can rely on the strategies that have worked for other companies to assist your efforts.

The idea is to use solutions that are readily available. If a company can effectively implement a solution by following a specific procedure, then why should it be necessary to institute an entirely new method to accomplish the same thing? This is the strength of the ASAP program. ASAP takes the best method of implementing a solution and applies it for your corporate implementation.

Following a Plan

The ASAP program follows a specific plan called a *Roadmap*. This *Roadmap* defines specific procedures that allow the user to develop a five-stage plan. ASAP realizes that in order to obtain the fastest possible speed you need to plan your project very carefully so you can foresee any problems that might arise once you have begun.

The next step is to create your *Business Blueprint*. Just like any other blueprint, a *Business Blueprint* allows you to outline your entire implementation effort. When you look at your R/3 implementation effort, you know that your project is going to be one of the most complex installations you have ever started. Realizing the complexities is a crucial step in implementing your R/3 solution.

Although no two implementations are the same, utilizing the best business practices (used by those who have succeeded) can help you to refine your project steps so as to provide you with the success you are looking for in your project.

When you have taken all the project steps into account, you can then develop the final preparation for your R/3 project. You need to save as much time as possible in your project effort, so by developing a definite project plan you can be certain that your efforts meet with success.

Success is defined by the time required to Go Live in your project. Going Live is always a very crucial time in any organization. It is the culmination of your efforts over the past several months of work. Your steps taken in very careful preparation will help you achieve your goals in achieving a successful ERP solution.

Once the Go Live stage has been achieved, most organizations make the mistake of thinking that their effort is complete. However, maintaining support is perhaps just as crucial to your success as is your entire implementation effort. As with any new system, you always have to work the bugs out. Therefore, you will need to rely on the support of both your consultant and SAP to ensure that your R/3 solution will continue to work as efficiently as you have expected.

The Right Tool for the Right Job

In order to achieve an effective implementation, you will need to rely on several SAP tools to help your effort move in the right direction. The most prominent tool is the *implementation assistant*, which works efficiently as a director looking over your shoulder. The implementation assistant gives you the power to work your way through your project planning phases and move along SAP's *Roadmap* to effectively reach your implementation goals.

What are some of the things you must be looking at to gain success throughout your implementation effort? It is exceedingly important to focus on modeling your business to take advantage of your ERP platform. Your software should work for your needs to provide you with an added level of productivity. Your implementation should increase your business to the point where you can rely on your software to increase your market share in selected segments. This endeavor is all about efficiency and gaining the most benefit from your investment.

Your implementation is a critical aspect to the success of your ERP solution. Without adequate planning you cannot expect your software solution to perform. Your entire effort is dictated by the fact that you can gain an added level of productivity to make certain that your business will be able to gain a competitive edge in an increasingly difficult information technology marketplace. The entire philosophy behind ASAP is that you can accelerate your effort, but only through planning and pre-configured business practices or templates that will automate a great deal of the effort involved in your specific business.

All these aspects boil down to continuous improvement for your business activities. At one point, businesses dealt with paper and forms to dictate everything from supply to demand. This system was very cumbersome and often experienced problems in speed. The days when a paper office could excel in an information-dominated society are all but over. Today, products change constantly, and the need for updated information from your supply chain is crucial to your ability to stay in business.

The computer industry, for example, cannot possibly survive without taking chances on the market. Hardware companies need to determine the quantity of electronic parts to buy, build, and sell before they become obsolete. The computer industry experiences constant change, but in order to achieve continuous improvement there must be a tight level of integration throughout every aspect of the organization. Your organization also must act as one entity to prepare for the constant changes experienced by the market.

Once you take your business model and combine it with SAP's templates, you will experience an accelerated implementation over your larger competitors. In fact, the ASAP program has met with such success that many larger organizations are looking into ASAP for their projects. ASAP not only produces much quicker results but also achieves completion at a lower cost.

Project Team Training

Technology is useless without the expertise and knowledge of a company's personnel. The dream of the completely automated office will never occur, because as technology grows more complex more people are needed to maintain and work it. Automation is highly dependent on the expertise of your project team.

SAP offers a three-level methodology that integrates and accelerates your project team training process so that you can benefit from faster learning activities for each member within your organization. It is important to train team members and end users alike in the operation of your ERP solution, because you never know when you may need to reallocate your workers when your systems need attention.

The project teams are introduced to standard classes that offer training courses as well as site training. Your end users can learn from the project team members so that they too can gain sufficient and necessary expertise to operate and understand the basic concepts behind your system operations.

Support Services

Going Live is only the first aspect of your R/3 implementation effort. Once you Go Live you will need to access those SAP resources that will help you fine-tune your systems when they are functional. One of the benefits of SAP that has proven particularly helpful is that organizations can acquire information as needed to uncover problems that may degrade or impair system functionality. You can see the R/3 service and support structure in Fig. A-3; its offerings are illustrated in Fig. A-4.

Since R/3 has been widely implemented over the past several years, there have often been cases where the systems were not functioning properly. You can take advantage of the support infrastructure that SAP has created to assist your efforts and allow you to gain knowledge through the experience of other SAP customers who have dealt with the very same problems.

Figure A-3
SAP R/3 Service and
Support in the Product Life Cycle.

Consultants offer you the greatest resource for resolving many of the issues you may have with your R/3 implementation. Your three resources are the application, remote, and technical consultants. Each of these very distinct groups can assist your R/3 implementation so that you can gain help when and where you need it.

In addition to these three levels of consultants, it is important to look at companies such as Ernst & Young. Ernst & Young has made it a point to work with organizations and their SAP implementations so as to provide a crucial element that is lacking from many institutions today, namely, personal assistance.

Figure A-4
R/3 Service and Support Offering.

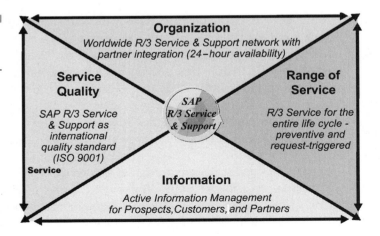

I have seen many implementations where much of the entire organization is on autopilot. Some consultants come in and try to offer a completely automated solution that simply guides the organization to completion without affording the personnel the feeling that someone is personally trying to assist their efforts.

Whenever you implement a global solution such as R/3, you need to feel that your consultant is showing a personal interest in the way you do business. You do business as an individual entity don't you? Don't you want to be treated as an individual company instead of just another number in a very long list of clients that get the least amount of attention? You should feel as though your consultant understands that your way of doing business is different from your competition's. Isn't that what sets you apart? Isn't that what makes you a success when all your competitors have failed?

TeamSAP

The personal touch provided by consultants is also offered by a team of dedicated SAP professionals called "TeamSAP." When you combine products, processes, and people you gain a significant resource that not only assists your implementation efforts but also gives you an incredible power to maintain your systems with expert help. While automated help is essential, nothing can truly replace a knowledgeable person who can answer your questions one on one.

The method by which solutions expertise is achieved is accomplished by the way in which TeamSAP builds on ASAP and SAP's *Business Framework* to expedite your implementation effort. You can also consider three very important factors when you think of TeamSAP: time, cost, and people.

ASAP is all about time and how you can accelerate your implementation so as to Go Live faster than any customer who used SAP in the past. That time is gained by using processes and preconfigured templates that allow you to benefit from prior expertise gained by customers who already know the benefits and pitfalls of this implementation method.

Cost is essential because there was once a time when an implementation took upward of 4 years. Organizations used to have to pour so much money into an ERP solution that they would literally go bankrupt trying to implement an efficient solution within their organization. The ASAP program answers this problem by making certain you can Go Live sooner and in a far more efficient manner. The entire concept of ASAP allows you to save both time and money by installing a solution on the best-practices principle. You can benefit from these ideas by making certain your implementation follows these concepts by the most expedient means possible.

People are an important factor. You want your solution to reflect your specific business practices. It is imperative that your R/3 solution reflect what you want out of your ERP environment. Therefore, you need people who are going to realize your needs and tailor your installation to meet your goals and desires. When you can gain that level of personal attention from your TeamSAP member, you can be assured that your chances for a successful implementation becomes a reality that fosters enhanced business productivity.

Preparing for Your Project

How do you save time and foster your ASAP program? The more preparation you devote to your project, the faster you will be able to implement your solution. You don't want to spend your time making crucial decisions about your migration effort. Instead, that time should be devoted to actual implementation. Your goal is to make certain that you spend the least amount of money in the shortest amount of time possible.

Your project is further accelerated when you plan sufficiently ahead to test all of your interfaces so that you can be certain your entire system functions up to your specifications.

You may also use this preparatory time to verify that all of your end users have completed their training and have collected sufficient resources to make certain your system will function adequately. You must be prepared to know every detail of your business architecture so that you can implement your solution wisely. Remember that ASAP works in conjunction with your system, not against it. You do not want to develop a situation in which your system is always having problems. I'm sure if you are like most organizations, you may have had a system that caused you significant problems and delays in filling orders or supplying sufficient inventory. Your ASAP solution should assist your development and growth, not hinder it.

Finally, you can migrate all of your business data to your new R/3 system. One of the nicest aspects of your R/3 solution is that you gain the power to import your data into a year 2000–compliant system. However, this is contingent on the fact that your users must have the knowledge to be able to convert all of your existing data into year 2000–compliant status.

Year 2000

One of the main points that this section must express is that the year 2000 is coming and will cause you significant problems if you are not prepared for it. You can rest comfortably knowing that R/3 is year 2000 compliant, but are your systems? This is the time to check all of your systems.

If you are not year 2000 compliant, you may wish to hire a solution provider to assist you during your implementation to migrate all of your current systems into year 2000 compliance. It is imperative that you have the ability to work in year 2000 dates. In addition, you must make certain that all of your personnel are trained sufficiently in using *only* year 2000 dates. This process also means going over all of your archives to make certain that your previous data has been converted.

When anyone in your organization is responsible for data entry, make certain he or she is well-versed in entering year 2000 data. If not, you will find significant problems in sorts, calculations, or charts that represent any information based on dates.

Don't ever listen to people who tell you that the year 2000 can wait until it becomes a problem. I highly recommend a definitive course of action that allows you to address this difficulty right away. Since the year 2000 is nearly here, you may have to devote multiple personnel shifts or hire a solution provider full-time until your systems have been upgraded.

In addition, don't try to fool your machine by using only two-digit years and believing you can sort the data later. SAP R/3 is truly year 2000 compliant and such alternative calculations will end up haunting you in the future.

Architecting Your *Business Blueprint*

Your *Business Blueprint* is the representation of the future of your computing environment once your R/3 accelerated implementation is complete. As you proceed through your implementation, you can see your business structure beginning to form. It is at this point that you want to check to ensure that your business is moving in the direction that you prepared for in the early stages of your preparatory phase.

All of this information allows your project team to concentrate on implementing all of the R/3 processes that are necessary to make certain your business will run effectively and efficiently.

It is important to develop your organization to follow the specific plan you have outlined for its future. One of the nice features of R/3 is that you can benefit from technology at a much faster rate. Although this speed requires far more up-front planning on your part, you realize that all of that effort pays off in the long run.

The speed of technology has grown exponentially in the last 20 years, and experiences continuous improvement on what seems to be a daily basis. The entire concept of this book revolves around the idea that the speed of business is quite fast and that you don't have the time or money to wait. You need a worthwhile solution today without the wait. AcceleratedSAP fosters the idea of being able to get results in a realizable time frame. It is absolutely crucial that you take every step possible to make certain you meet your implementation time frame so that you can Go Live and start running your new ERP solution quickly in order to be able to see a return on your investment in the short term.

Go Live

Sounds great doesn't it? However, the whole point in the first few weeks and months of your Go Live process is to keep a careful watch over your system for any problems that have not been foreseen in the preparatory or implementation processes.

SAP's support and services program can be an invaluable tool during your "first steps" as SAP can ensure that your system works correctly. It can provide you with special support that will help you stay live during these crucial first few weeks so that you can realize your implementation investment with as little aggravation as possible.

This is also the best time for fine-tuning your system so that it can reflect the individuality of your company and its specific business processes. It is important to reflect your specific preferences in your business processes so that your R/3 accelerated implementation can act as a time-saver and make your investment work for your need to increase your productivity.

Quality

Some people, at first glance, equate the speed of ASAP with reduced amount of quality in the final product, but that simply isn't true. Just because the product installs quicker doesn't mean that the product is any less effective. When you upgrade your computer to a faster computer processor, does the quality of your application functionality decrease? Of course not, and the same is true with ASAP. This program is an essential tool that allows you to gain increased business process functionality without the excessive wait that companies had to previously endure when implementing this type of solution.

You can execute a cost-versus-time study to determine what types of resources your typical implementation will require. You can then compare that information with a standard SAP R/3 implementation of the past. You will note that by comparing your efforts to a real-life example you will achieve increased productivity and find that you can obtain real results without sacrificing functionality.

ASAP is essentially the same as R/3 for larger clients. The difference is that your implementation will build on the knowledge achieved from prior implementations so that you can realize your results months or years earlier than what had been considered the standard time to implement an effective ERP solution.

Benefits

AcceleratedSAP provides realizable benefits by offering a standard implementation scheme to your R/3 installation. This accelerated approach eliminates a great deal of risk once associated with ERP solutions because you are working from a standards-based solution that provides you with the ability to tailor your installation in several predefined ways.

You can efficiently use your in-house and external resources to gain the fastest implementation time possible. Thus you will be able to allocate work so that you can implement R/3 and still effectively concentrate on your business activities.

Maintaining a uniform approach to your implementation allows you to reduce costs and gain a faster return on your investment. However, the most important benefit of all is that you can realize the power of R/3 for your business processes right away and gain an effective strategy for making your business activities flow more smoothly.

SAP's *Business Engineer* can also greatly benefit your implementation scheme. *Business Engineer* can foster a model-driver configuration for your business that allows your organization to gain increased functionality and alter the parameters of its business models to gain significantly better benefits from its core reengineering strategies in its ERP solution.

Performance and Speed

One of the factors you can achieve in your implementation is the ability to diagnose bottlenecks that might impair your system performance. One of the benefits of having consultants diagnose your computing environment is the ability to use their talents to refine your computing environment so that your business processes are lean and efficient.

The goal of your effort is to develop methods so that these system bottlenecks do not impair your system performance or cause any system failures. You are in business to succeed, and the last thing you need to have is a system failure that would cause your systems to become unavailable for any amount of time, no matter how short. Therefore, it is important to gauge your system performance against a predesignated benchmark determined by your consultant. In this way, you can see exactly how efficiently your system is running. If you feel there may be a problem with the ability of your system to process information, a simple utility can be executed so that you can determine if there is truly a problem within your computing environment.

Preventative Maintenance

In many ways, diagnosing your system performance is an important preventative maintenance measure that assists you in creating an efficient solution for protecting your computing investment.

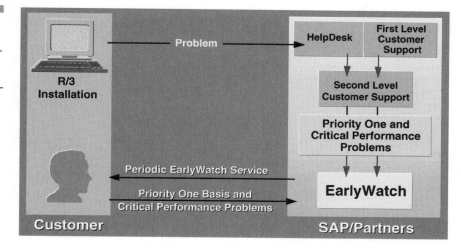

Figure A-5
Direct Assistance for Priority One and Critical Performance Problems.

When you detect problems early in your implementation phase, you can save yourself a great deal of problems in the future. You can often achieve a trouble-free implementation by using SAP's *GoingLive* check, calling the SAP *Help Desk* or simply importing SAP consultants into your on-site location to diagnose problems one on one. You can see how the *Help Desk* helps with a customer problem in Fig. A-5.

This last option often takes the guesswork out of trying to determine what your problems are. It gives you a chance to take steps that will ensure that your computing environment is secure. In addition, users can also benefit from the SAP *EarlyWatch* service illustrated in Fig. A-6, while a typical response time graphic for this service is shown in Fig. A-7.

Accelerating the Future

One of the major themes within this text is that there are several accelerators that have made it possible for you to achieve a realizable result in a short period of time.

Consultants can work by a standardized approach that can accelerate their consulting efforts to produce a solution that has proven itself to work time and time again. This is a very important step in making certain that R/3 can work in a variety of organizations and reflect the most efficient means of your ERP processes. Some SAP consulting activities

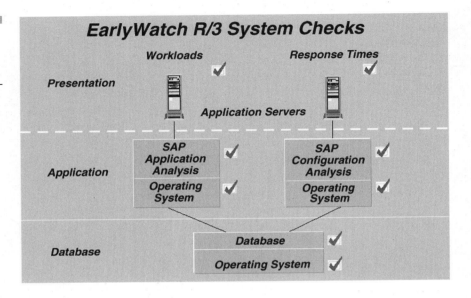

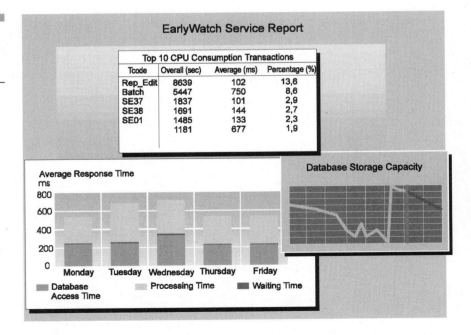

Figure A-8
Activities of SAP Consulting.

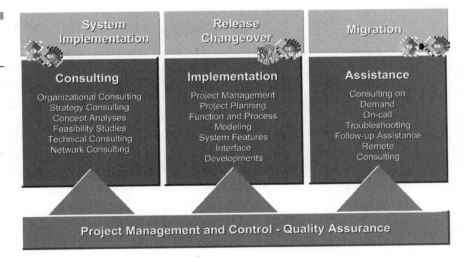

Figure A-8
Activities of SAP Consulting.

are shown in Fig. A-8. You can see the difference between on-site and remote consulting in Fig. A-9.

The ASAP program has become so popular that many larger organizations want to adopt this methodology for their larger programs. ASAP was really designed for smaller organizations. However, its success has made it the future standard of ERP solutions because it can offer speed and a quicker return on investment.

SAP R/3 was once seen to be valid only for larger organizations, but as the corporate infrastructure is no longer limited to big companies,

Figure A-9
On-site versus Remote Consulting.

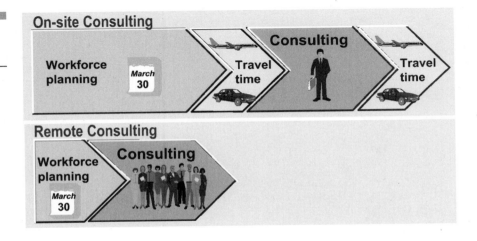

mid-sized organizations wanted to take advantage of this technology for their own business processes.

SAP has now expanded into a market tier that was once never considered to be a real market share. Mid-sized companies can now benefit from the ERP capabilities of R/3 without going broke in the process. This is an essential step in the future of developing installation paths that organizations can use to their benefit.

You will find that AcceleratedSAP is now placing R/3 in a very important position with respect to a large section of the market. Regardless of market segment or IT industry focus, AcceleratedSAP concentrates on individual business processes and implements a quality solution with less cost, shorter time, and more efficiency throughout the business infrastructure.

APPENDIX B

POINTS OF
CONTACT

What Is SAP?

SAP stands for Systems, Applications, and Products in Data Processing. SAP is a collection of software for nearly all business applications in mid- and large-sized companies. SAP AG Corporation was founded in 1972 and is today one of the most important software companies in the world.

SAP on Internet

SAP has the domain sap-ag.de and sap.com. Their Web site is found at http://www.sap.com/

SAP Contact Information

InfoLine is a common information service provided by SAP AG on the Internet.

For further information call 800-777-8SAP in the United States or + 49 6227 342362 in Europe. This service is only for SAP customers and partners.

SAP Deutschland

SAP Aktiengesellschaft
Postfach 1461, D-69185 Walldorf
Neurottstrasse 16, D-69190 Walldorf
Tel. (0 62 27) 34-0
Telex: 466 004 sap d
Fax (0 62 27) 34-12 82

SAP Oesterreich

SAP Ges.m.b.H.
Postfach 25, Stadlauer Str. 54
A 1221 Wien
Tel. (02 22) 2 20 55 11
Fax (02 22) 2 20 55 11-222

SAP Schweiz

SAP (Schweiz) AG
Leugenestrasse 6
Postfach 130
CH-2500 Biel 6
Tel. (0 32) 42 / 1 11
Fax (0 32) 42 72 11

SAP America Inc.

U.S. Corporate Headquarters
Chesterbrook Corporate Center
701 Lee Road, Suite 200
Wayne, PA 19087
USA
Tel. (610) 725 4500
Fax (610) 725 4555

SAP Asia

Bangkok Representative Office
23d Floor CP Tower
313 Silom Road
T-Bangkok 10500
Tel. (2) 2 31 06 13
Fax (2) 2 31 04 48

SAP Canada

SAP Canada, Inc.
4120 Yonge Street, Suite 600
CDN-North York
Ontario M2P 2B8
Tel. (416) 229-0574
Fax (416) 229-0575

SAP Japan

SAP Japan Co. Ltd.
Loop-x 17th Floor
9-15 Kaigan, 3-chome, Minato-Ku,
J-Tokyo 108
Tel. (03) 5440-2001
Fax (03) 5440-2021

SAP South Africa

Switchboard: 011 880 6775
Fax: 011 880 6535
Hotline: 0800 112 575
Train Centre 1: 011 269 4800
Train Centre 2: 011 269 4877
Train Centre Fax 011 447 6743

SAP Support

OSS (Online Service System)

SAP provides OSS, a system where you can ask your questions online, receive answers, and read answers to common problems. There is an R/3-based service system for R/3 customers, called R/3 Online Service System (OSS) and an R/2-based service system for R/2 customers called R/2 OSS.

SAP Product Group Distribution

- R/2
- R/3

What Is SAP R/2?

SAP R/2 was the first compact software package for the whole spectrum of business applications from the SAP Corporation.

What Platforms Run SAP R/2?

SAP R/2 runs on mainframes, especially IBM, BS2000 (Siemens machines) or Amdahl.

What are the modules of SAP R/2?

- RF
- RA
- RK
- RK-P
- RP
- RM-INST
- RM-QSS
- RM-MAT
- RM-PPS
- RV Financial Accounting (Finanzbuchhaltung)
- Assets Accounting (Anlagenbuchhaltung)
- Cost Accounting (Kostenrechnung)
- Projects (Projekte)
- Human Resources (Personal)
- Plant Maintenance (Instandhaltung)
- Quality Assurance (Qualitaetssicherung)
- Materials Management (Materialwirtschaft)
- Production Planning and Control (Produktion)
- Sales and Distribution (Vertrieb, Fakturierung, Versand)

What Is SAP R/3?

SAP R/3 is the continuation of R/2 on client/server and distributed open systems.

What Platforms Run SAP R/3?

SAP R/3 was designed for open systems such as UNIX. SAP R/3 is now based on various hardware and software architectures. It runs on most versions of UNIX, on Windows NT, and on OS/400. Experimental versions on mainframes (open MVS) exist. SAP R/3 runs on uniprocessors; it scales very well on SMP systems and also on MPP architectures. R/3 runs on a variety of databases: Oracle, Informix Online, ADABAS-D, DB2 for UNIX, DB2/400, and Microsoft SQL Server, and on an experimental version on DB2 for MVS.

All databases have their features, and it is easy to find a database that fits your corporate IS infrastructure. Ask the database vendor for the details.

What Are the Modules of SAP R/3?

- AM
- CO
- FI
- HR
- IM
- IS
- PM
- PP
- PS
- QM
- SD
- MM
- WF Asset Management (Anlagenwirtschaft)
- Controlling (Controlling)
- Financial Accounting (Finanzwesen)
- Human Resources (Personalwesen)
- Investment Management
- Industry Specific Solutions (Industriespezifische Loesungen)
- Plant Maintenance (Instandhaltung)
- Production Planning (Produktionsplanung)
- Project System (Projektsystem)
- Quality Management (Qualitaetssicherung)
- Sales and Distribution (Verkauf/Versand/Fakturierung)

- Materials Management (Materialwirtschaft)
- Business WorkFlow

Central to all these modules is BC-Basis.

Contacts

AK-Hochschulen, aka SAP-Arbeitskreis Hochschulen, is a working group of universities and the SAP Corporation.
Its official address is:

SAP-Arbeitskreis Hochschulen e.V.-Vorstand
D-69190 Walldorf
Germany

SAP-Arbeitskreis Hochschulen e.V.
c/o Prof. Dr. Oetinger
Goebenstrasse 40
D-66117 Saarbruecken
Germany
Tel. 0681-53410
Fax 0681-585733

ASUG (America's SAP Users' Group)

Within ASUG, there are about a dozen focus groups organized by function: SD, MM, Basis, EDI, etc. There are also some industry groups: Chemicals, Consumer Goods, etc. Some of the groups are more active then others. Some lean toward R/2; others toward R/3. The makeup of the focus groups is constantly changing. To participate, your company must be an SAP customer and must join ASUG. Corporate membership costs $600 per year. Once your company is an ASUG member, any of your employees are welcome to participate in any of the focus groups that interest them.

The CompuServe ASUG Forum is a private forum run by ASIG and SAP. You must be an ASUG member and be authorized by both SAP and CompuServe to get access to the Forum. You cannot use an existing CompuServe account. You must order the start-up kits from ASUG. Kits ordered from CompuServe will not work! The start-up kits cost about $40 each. CompuServe accounts cost a minimum of $10 per month. You can order as many ASUG kits as you want. This procedure is a bit restrictive and limits discussion on the forum, but SAP and CompuServe insist on it. To get information about joining ASUG or to order CompuServe start-up kits, call the network resources.

Network Resources

There are several network resources (on the Internet) you may use to get information or participate in discussions.
For SAP AG Corporation itself refer to the SAP section of this FAQ.

WWW (HTTP)

There are several WWW sites around the SAP topic.

SAP AG

http://www.sap-ag.de/

SAP America

http://www.sap.com/

SAP South Africa

http://www.sap.co.za

Australia

http://www.ozemail.com.au/~adbell/sap-faq.html

Austria

http://www.ifi.uni-klu.ac.at/Mirror/Sap-faq/sap-faq.html

Institute of Information Systems

Research Group "Information Engineering,"
University of Bern, Switzerland

SAP R/3 Project

http://www.mcs.net/~garth/SAP/
http://pflaume.informatik.uni-oldenburg.de/sap/sap.html
http://umawihp0.wifo.uni-mannheim.de:4000/~geyer/saplinks.html
http://www.rz.uni-duesseldorf.de/WWW/SAP-AK

SAP Arbeitskreis Hochschulen

(SAP working group universities)
http://www.netWeb.com/sap4

Information on the Annual Software Symposium

http://shaysnet.com/~dvelco/sapfaq.html
http://www.neosfot.com/~triplei
http://cn530.CNB.CompuNet.DE/sap-r3/sapr3.html
CompuNet SAP R/3
http://www.ozemail.com.au/~adbell/saprectr.html
SAP Resource Center

UseNet Newsgroup

To learn more about SAP, join discussions, ask questions, and so on, you may examine the following newsgroups:

- news:de.alt.comp.sap-r3
- news:comp.client-server

For job-related postings use

1. news:de.markt.arbeit.angebote (German)
2. news:misc.jobs.offered (English)
3. news:biz.jobs.offered (English)

FTP

There is an ftp site for information on SAP topics:

ftp://ftp.Informatik.Uni-Oldenburg.DE/pub/sap/

CompuServe

CompuServe has a private forum sponsored by ASUG (America's SAP Users' Group). You need to be an employee of a company that is using SAP, and you need to be a member of the above group. Beside ASUG topics there are technical discussions, mostly about installation and upgrade issues.

How Do I Get Trained?

Courses

SAP
The AK-Hochschulen provides some courses.

HP-Hewlett-Packard
Siemens
BOG Buero-Organisation GmbH
Siemensstr. 57-59
D-48153 Muenster
Germany
Tel. 0251/7604-612
Fax 0251/7604-399

Jobs

For job-related topics see the SAP Web page for Employment Opportunities:

http://www.sap-ag.de/discsap/career/career.htm

Resources

MAXIT
SAP R/3 CD-ROM training
MAXIT (Maximum Information Technologies)
Tel. 904-998-9520
Fax 904-998-0221
WWW: *http://www.maxit.com/training/*
E-Mail: maxit@jaxnet.com

LOGO-Partner
EFP Consulting
Wien/Graz-Oesterreich
WWW: *http://www.efp.co.at/*

Fisons Instruments
Laboratory Information Management Systems
(Product SampleManager)
Fisons Instruments
Phone: 919-380-7539
WWW: *http://www.labsystems.fisons.co.uk/*
E-Mail: pat.tormey@fisons-ls.com
Learning Tree International

SAP Hands-On Workshops
Learning Tree International
Tel. (USA) 1-808-843-8733
WWW: *http://www.lrntree.com/*
BIW Beratung und Informationssysteme GmbH
SAP Systemhaus Partner
BIW GmbH
Werkstrasse 24
71384 Weinstadt
Germany
Tel. + 49 (7151) 602-240
Fax + 49 (7151) 602-101
E-Mail: polzerj@biw-ag.de
WWW: *http://www.biw-ag.de/*

Insite Objects, Inc.
Houston, TX
USA
E-Mail: insite@insiteobjects.com
WWW: *http://www.insiteobjects.com/*

Job Search

Allen Davis & Associates
WWW: *http://clever.net/swjobs/*

Pro-Connect Worldwide
E-Mail: connect@net-link.net

ECLECTIC: International Executive Search
WWW: *http://www.cyber.nl/eclectic/*

Implementations Partner
Seitz GmbH, Pforzheim
WWW: *http://www.seitz.de/*

Live AG

Live AG is a sample SAP application implementation from AK Vulcan in cooperation with SNI (Siemens-Nixdorf).

Author Contact

Stewart S. Miller
President/CEO
Executive Information Services
Tel. 1-800-IT-Maven
Fax 1-888-IT-Maven
www: http://www.ITMaven.com
E-mail: Miller@ITMaven.com

INDEX

V

W

Y

ABOUT THE AUTHOR

Stewart S. Miller is one of the country's leading IT efficiency experts. The president of his own firm, Executive Information Services, he has consulted for a number of major businesses, including IBM and Ernst & Young, as well as software vendors such as SAP and PeopleSoft. He has written hundreds of feature articles for technical publications and is the author of three books: *IPv6: The Next Generation Internet Protocol* (Digital Press); *Protecting Your Data Goldmine* (Artech House); and *Windows NT Security Guide* (Digital Press). Mr. Miller can be reached by phone at 1-800-IT-MAVEN and by email at Miller@ITMaven.com.

CD-ROM Information

Introduction

It has always been my experience that a picture is worth a thousand words, but that an animated presentation can leave you speechless. It is for this reason that I have made every effort to include several multimedia presentations on the enclosed CD-ROM for your benefit.

AcceleratedSAP is much more than a faster method of implementing SAP R/3. It is important to show you the various facets of SAP R/3 so that you can understand exactly what is going on. In this CD you will find various multimedia files created by SAP, IBM, and Ernst & Young to illustrate through detailed animated presentations each respective facet. As you watch each file, you will feel as though you are peering over the shoulder of someone intimately familiar with the product. You will see exactly how each respective program works, and how specific tasks are accomplished.

The ScreenCam files created by SAP illustrate several key issues:

Rapid Project Setup

You can understand the usage of *Business Engineer* through a real demonstration that illustrates how a sample company is created. The steps involved in company creation for implementation reflect R/3 functionality necessary in rapidly building your project.

Graphical Tool

This tool allows you to define the relationship of corporate structures such as Distribution Channel, Division, and Plant and Company which are important parts of your configuration. The sample company illustrated in this presentation uses an enterprise tool to create a new distribution channel for Internet orders. This new organizational structure allows for detailed reporting by distribution channel and is available immediately to the users.

405

Configuration of Business Processes

The *Business Engineer* possesses the business blueprint of the processes within the R/3 system. The open interface of the R/3 business repository permits the user to work with third-party business modeling tools. The sample company in this illustration gains the ability to quickly determine relevant sales processes, as well as their functionality and interrelationships in other areas

Company and User Specific Customizing

This illustration shows how you can define user menus based on the intuitive profile generator. The profile generator offers a traffic-light graphical environment that permits users to determine the business processes for access, associated workflow tasks, and the allowed values. The user-defined authorities and business processes access are available instantly to the user.

Continuous Business Change

This illustrates the need for your organization to implement a new business process for Web orders that is a type of rush order using pro forma invoicing. The R/3 system allows for dynamic, real-time configuration allowing the quick integration of new business processes. The new sales order is immediately available to users.

Release Management

As technology and the marketplace changes so does your company. The ability to move quickly to new releases through automated release management allows you to remain ahead of your competitors by focusing on business.

Multimedia Presentations

In order to more fully illustrate how SAP functions, you will find two full-length multimedia SAP presentations that discuss SAP's Business Framework and Supply Chain Management in detail.

The first presentation is on Supply Chain Optimization, Planning, and Execution (SCOPE) given in Brisbane in November 1997 by Dr. Peter Zencke (Executive Board Member, SAP AG). This presentation deals with supply chain management. It then discusses the four main elements of SCOPE that involve extending the enterprise, process integration and execution, integrated planning and execution, and real-time decision support. It concludes with a discussion of the configuration of supply chain solutions.

The second presentation is of Dr. Hasso Plattner's speech given on IBM/SAP Partnership Day in Chicago, December 3, 1997. His speech discussed SAP R/3 Release 4.0, SCOPE, advanced planner and optimizer (APO), business information warehouse, sales configuration engine, personalization, optimization of the upgrade process, and technologies that are pertinent to your continued industry success.

Charting a Consultant

Ernst & Young is one of the most critical consultants working with SAP customers. Inasmuch as it is helpful to list its accomplishments, it is perhaps more important to list specific clients who have benefited from Ernst & Young's guidance.

For that reason, you will find several PDF files on the enclosed CD that deal explicitly with different companies in diverse industries. Ernst & Young and each organization have collaborated to produce these documents that detail specifically those accomplishments that have been made with respect to R/3 and those areas where this consulting effort will aid them now and in the future.

Conclusion

As you examine the content in this CD-ROM you should gain a deeper understanding not only of the AcceleratedSAP program itself but of the components that make this program possible. You will see what each program entails, what SAP offers, and how the consultant fits into your picture. The information contained in the enclosed CD should illuminate your understanding of this text and provide you with a clearer insight into what Accelerating your SAP R/3 implementation means by working at the speed of business.